FROM SURVIVAL
TO FULFILLMENT

D1594451

SERIES IN TRAUMA AND LOSS

CONSULTING EDITORS

Charles R. Figley and Therese A. Rando

Figley, Bride, and Mazza—*Death and Trauma: The Traumatology of Grief*
Valent—*From Survival to Fulfillment: A Framework for the Life–Trauma Dialectic*

FROM SURVIVAL TO FULFILLMENT
A Framework for the Life–Trauma Dialectic

By

Paul Valent

BRUNNER/MAZEL

Taylor & Francis Group

USA	Publishing Office:	BRUNNER/MAZEL
		A member of the Taylor & Francis Group
		325 Chestnut Street
		Philadelphia, PA 19106
		Tel: (215) 625-8900
		Fax: (215) 625-2940
	Distribution Center:	BRUNNER/MAZEL
		A member of the Taylor & Francis Group
		1900 Frost Road, Suite 101
		Bristol, PA 19007-1598
		Tel: (215) 785-5800
		Fax: (215) 785-5515
UK		Taylor & Francis Ltd.
		4 John Street
		London WC1N 2ET
		Tel: 071 405 2237
		Fax: 071 831 2035

FROM SURVIVAL TO FULFILLMENT: A Framework for the Life–Trauma Dialectic

1 2 3 4 5 6 7 8 9 0

Printed by Braun-Brumfield, Ann Arbor, MI, 1998.

A CIP catalog record for this book is available from the British Library.

♾The paper in this publication meets the requirements of the ANSI Standard Z39.48-1984 (Permanence of Paper)

Library of Congress Cataloging-in-Publication Data

Valent, Paul.
   From survival to fulfillment: a framework for the life-trauma dialectic/by Paul Valent.
      p.   cm.—(Series in trauma and loss)
   Includes bibliographical references (p.   ).

      1. Traumatology—Philosophy.   I. Title.   II. Series.
RD93.V34   1998
617.1'001—dc21   97–48882
                                                                    CIP
ISBN 0-87630-921-X (cloth)
ISBN 0-87630-922-8 (paper)

Contents

Preface

Threats to life have been a pervasive preoccupation throughout human history, as have desires for a safe environment in which humans could fulfill their unique selves. It is a basic contention of this book that the purpose of life is to survive and to fulfill one's life and to help others important to oneself to do the same.

Trauma, at least to some extent, inalterably compromises life's purpose. In the past, life and death were thought to form the basic human dialectic. Yet people may surrender their survival, feeling this to be purposeful to life, and they may also consider that an unfulfilling life is not worth living. Thus, it is suggested that fulfillment and trauma form the central human dialectic, and the purpose of this book is to explore and to help provide a framework for it.

Only philosophers have dared to explore something as large as life or happiness. Yet lately traumatology has been an expanding discipline spanning what can be damaged, from physiology to the soul.

The term *traumatology* was first used by Donovan (1991) to reflect an overarching field waiting to be recognized, organized, and developed. He defined traumatology as the study of the social and psychobiological effects of trauma and its predictive, preventive, and interventionist pragmatics. To not overlap with the term *biomedical trauma*, some have used the term *psychotraumatology* (e.g., Everly, 1995), but Donovan (1991, 1993) insisted that traumatology included biological, psychological, and social trauma and that it needed to use knowledge from disparate fields such as medicine, psychology, and sociology. The view in this book leans toward the broader definition. It defines traumatology as the study of serious threats to the survival and fulfillment of life.

Traumatology here includes but also expands on the field of traumatic stress studies (Figley, 1988, chapter 3). For instance, it examines systematically the following: fulfillment as well as maladaptive and traumatic responses; biological as well as psychosocial responses; and all levels of human function from physiological to spiritual levels. This inclusive view is developed throughout the book and is called the *wholist* view or perspective.

It is suggested that wholist or unified views are consistent with trends in modern science and that traumatology may well benefit from the nonlinear paradigms that they use. Two new concepts are developed in the wholist nonlinear view of traumatology: the triaxial framework and survival strategies. The latter in the main present already known concepts, but in a new way. It is suggested that the wholist framework helps to explain the variety of trauma and fulfillment phenomena in a logical, meaningful manner.

Because trauma and fulfillment phenomena cover more than clinical practice, of necessity traumatology touches on wider biological and human disciplines. For instance, for perhaps the first time traumatology can offer contributions to meaningful categorizations for emotions, morals, values, ideologies, and spiritual strivings. Though naturally in a book like this such topics cannot be covered in any breadth, what is offered may be of interest to those interested in a wide range of human sciences.

Although philosophers often approach the same questions from the fulfillment side as their starting point, traumatology has a bias to approach it from distortions to fulfillment. This does not mean that trauma or the pathological is considered of primary importance. Certainly fulfillment is an equal partner with battles to survive in the purpose of life. It is hoped that this will be apparent in the book and that readers will gain as much nonclinical as clinical satisfaction from what follows.

Because traumatology is so vast, most texts on it are edited. This allows many experts to cover many areas thoroughly and to provide up-to-date knowledge in them. The disadvantage of such an approach is the potential lack of a theme that gives deep meaning to the area as a whole. Individual authors who cover the whole field may provide a theme but do, however, have the potential to err and be incomplete in particular areas. I apologize to authors whose important contributions may have been omitted.

To try to give an overview of traumatology and to try to contribute to it may seem too vast a task for one person, and I have often stumbled in the mammoth task. If the attempt seems presumptuous, at least I can assure the reader that it was not born of arrogance, but of my particular traumas.

The need to know arose in a small, alone child who knew so little of so much that went on around him. My parents and I pretended to be Aryans, living 200 meters from Gestapo headquarters in Budapest. Another few hundred meters on, thousands of Jews were shot into the Danube. A little further away in the ghetto, Jews were sent to Auschwitz. Being bombed was clear. But unclear apprehensions of the other facts, or why I was left by my parents (who were apprehended by police while I was left in the street), have haunted me all my life. Luckily, my parents and I survived the Holocaust. Since the age of 9, I have wanted to write a book to explain my experiences and to make sure that other children would not need to undergo them.

This book is divided into four sections. The first section provides the situations and dilemmas that traumatologists confront. Chapter 1 poses the problem of the very varied, often contradictory responses in varied situations in traumatic stress. This is demonstrated by three cases. The first is the Ash Wednesday bush fires in Victoria, Australia; the second a case of angina in the emergency department; and the third the psychotherapy of a sexually abused child survivor of the Holocaust. A hypothetical case of fulfillment is also presented. The second chapter provides an overview of information gathered from different traumatic situations such as war, disasters, sexually abused children, and dying people.

The second section describes concepts and their interactions, which have been abstracted from different traumatic situations and apply to them all. The concepts are described in the next three chapters (3–5) along three axes.

Chapter 3 describes the process axis, so named because it involves the process from stressors to illnesses. It includes concepts such as stress, stress responses, trauma, defenses, and memories. Chapter 4 describes concepts on the parameter axis, so called because it describes the circumstances in which stresses and traumas occur. They include the nature of the stressor, phase of the disaster, developmental phase of the person, and social system under consideration. Chapter 5 describes concepts on the depth axis, so called because it describes evolutionary development from the physiological to the spiritual. The life–trauma dialectic is defined more closely here.

Chapter 6 looks at illnesses and the linear scientific paradigm that has influenced current classifications, including the *Diagnostic and Statistical Manual of Mental Disorders* (the 3rd ed., revised, or *DSM–III–R,* and the 4th ed., or *DSM–IV;* American Psychiatric Association, 1980, 1994) and in it posttraumatic stress disorder. Nonlinear paradigms are introduced, and their potential applications to traumatology are suggested. A nonlinear triaxial view of trauma illnesses is suggested that subsumes both linear and nonlinear paradigms.

Section Three examines the second major new concept, survival strategies. Although the triaxial framework provides orientation for traumatic stress responses, survival strategies define what they are and why they are. Chapter 7 introduces the concept and suggests that in addition to the two well-known strategies of fight and flight, there are six others. Chapters 8–15 look at each survival strategy in detail. The survival strategies are rescue–caretaking, attachment, assertiveness, adaptation, fight, flight, competition, and cooperation. Each survival strategy is described along the components of the triaxial framework.

Section Four draws together the triaxial framework and survival strategies in a wholist perspective. Chapter 16 suggests some applications of this perspective work. For instance, it allows meaningful orientation and explanation for the great variety of and often contradictory traumatic stress responses, and enhances clinical usefulness and refinement of research questions. It also facilitates categorization, perhaps for the first time, of contents of concepts such as emotions, guilts, shames, justice, meanings, ideologies, and the sacred. In each case, the framework provides equal opportunity to understand and classify the adaptive and fulfilling as well as the maladaptive and traumatic manifestations. Chapter 17 provides a brief summary and overview of the implications of the wholist framework.

Many workers have called for a model to draw together known phenomena in traumatology and to provide models for a second generation of ideas and conceptualizations. It is hoped that this book helps somewhat toward this goal. The book is also used as a basis for clinical applications to healing of stress and trauma effects, described in a further volume.

Acknowledgments

This book's journey has been very long. It is a fulfillment born of early trauma requiring much struggle. I had to learn much on the way, and there are many people, institutions, and disciplines of knowledge that helped me on the journey. My first and foremost gratitude is to my father, whose love of life, family, and me in particular helped us to survive. He also taught me that physical survival, and survival of truth, which he also loved passionately, may require separateness and independence from powerful majorities. Even if sometimes I longed to belong to groups who seemed to know everything, I did learn the advantages of independent thinking. My father emphasized the importance of a profession as a means of independent survival. I am grateful that medicine and psychiatry also facilitated independent fulfillment. I am grateful to my mother for her love and for bearing the brunt of our hardships. She taught me that stresses affected the body, mind, and soul. She also taught me how children may misinterpret events for decades, such as acts of sacrifice being perceived as abandonment. In retrospect, my experiences have alerted me to how much children may suffer quietly without awareness. They can hide their childhood traumas throughout their lives even when those traumas pervade their whole beings. My experience has allowed me to appreciate the high prevalence of personal holocausts even in supposedly normal communities.

I thank Australia and its people for offering sanctuary and a wholesome life where security and truth can flourish. Medicine gave me knowledge of how the body suffers in life's turmoil. It gave me respect for science, but also showed me how "scientifism" could be a result of stultified paradigms and politics and could dehumanize people. Similarly, psychiatry gave me a respect for the scientific study of the mind but also showed me how its own brand of "scientifism" could dehumanize.

Psychotherapy has taught me about early childhood thinking and recapitulation of early events in later life. It has given me a healthy respect for emotions and their power of communication. It has taught me its wonderful healing matrix in the therapeutic relationship. However, I have also learned how even the deepest explorations of the mind can carefully ignore major trauma, how much needs to be known at times about the minutiae of trauma to be effective, and how therapists need to deal with their own traumas to be effective with those of others.

I am grateful to Judith Kestenberg and Sarah Moskovitz, who not only discovered child survivors of the Holocaust but me as a specific child survivor. I learned how important it was to be recognized, to testify, and to have groups whose members understand each other.

My work as liaison psychiatrist, especially in the emergency rooms of major hospitals, has shown me the intimate interweaving of biological, psychological, and social stresses and illnesses, the advantages of this recognition, but the sparsity of and resistance to such recognition.

My work on the effects of the Six Day War in 1967 and my role in the Victorian bush fires of 1983 and other subsequent disasters made me aware of the vast range of human responses and a need to try to conceptualize them.

All this experience was of course mutual with that of patients and victims. I am extremely grateful for their trust in sharing with me their innermost pain. Together we learned much about the language that conveys the unformed questions and search for meaning of traumatized people. May our mutual efforts and learning be useful in the future, especially through this book. I am especially grateful to "Anne" for allowing me to use her material extensively.

At this stage, I would like to acknowledge specific people who worked with me in the development of the ideas that served as precursors of this book. Some of us formed an exciting nucleus at Prince Henry's Hospital during some of the formative years of traumatology in Australia. Out of this nucleus was formed the Australasian Society of Traumatic Stress Studies. Some of my colleagues at that time were Graeme Smith, Ellen Berah, Julie Jones, and Allen Yuen, and we were joined by Ruth Wraith and Rob Gordon from the Children's Hospital. I am grateful for continued collegial and friendship bonds with them.

I am grateful to Beverley Raphael for reading my material and for her encouragement that it was important to publish it. I am grateful to Bessel van der Kolk for his encouraging comments, too. I thank Jaak Panksepp for his helpful correspondence.

I thank personal friends not only for their tolerance of my distance from them at times, but for their forbearance, encouragement, listening, and critical appraisal of my work. I also thank them for their faith. These friends include the late Ludwig Engel, Ian Thomas, Di Clifton, Leon Gettler, and David Hines. I especially thank Tim Blashki. My mother-in-law Jo Bremner gave support over many cups of coffee. She also taught me that the victors and their families were also deeply and lastingly affected by war.

Without recognition, it is difficult to exist. The recognition that brought this book into existence came from Charles Figley. I am most grateful not only for his recognition of my ideas, but also for his initial encouragement of me to write this book. From then on, his continual and unwavering support, advice, good cheer, forbearance, reading and correcting of chapters, and ideas continued to encourage me and spur me on during hard times. It is true to say that without him this book would not have been written. It has been gratifying to come to know his generous spirit over the years and to have become personal friends with him.

I am also grateful to my publishers, Taylor & Francis, who have shown faith and patience during the publishing process. Although it is so helpful clinically to be able to put traumas into words, my editors have helped me to put those experiences into words understandable to the public. I especially thank Elaine Pirrone, Bernadette Capelle, and Alison Howson for their involvement in this difficult process.

I acknowledge Brunner/Mazel for allowing me to reprint Figures 4 and 5 and Table 2 and Heinemann and the *Medical Journal of Australia* for allowing me to use material from my previous publications. I thank my colleague Tony Catanese for allowing me to cite his case and for the many discussions we held during our work together. I thank my secretary, Juliette Zeelander, for her help with the manuscript and her personal support. I also give thanks to my very helpful librarians from Prince Henry's Hospital and Monash Medical Center, Sue Wind and Andrew Rooke.

Facing trauma is bearable only if beyond it one sees the worthwhileness of life. This is where my family has sustained me. I am especially grateful to my wife, Julie, who has recognized the life part of me and nurtured it. Her constancy, faith, loyalty, good cheer, generosity, creativity, and unwavering faith in my efforts has made her a sturdy ally. I also appreciate her good sense and practical help in reading my chapters. I am grateful for her patience, tolerance, and filling in on my duties where I was remiss. Above all, I appreciate her normality and love. My children, Dani, Ariel, and Amy, have shown me that love can survive, grow, and flourish in spite of trauma. Their bright eyes looking confidently to the future have been an antidote to the vision of the past. I thank them for their forbearance, unequivocal support, and love. I thank Dani for her help with the references in this book, Ariel for helping in designing figures and in printing, and Amy for her good will and good cheer. In different ways, my family and I have shared my memories and the creation of this book. Its completion is a sign of gratitude to them, and I hope that in my own way it may compensate for some nurturance and wisdom that I have missed providing earlier.

Part One

An Introduction to the Field
of Traumatology

This section introduces the magnitude and complexity of the field of traumatology. The magnitude involves the two major suggested streams in the dialectic of life—fulfillment and trauma. Trauma, it is suggested, threatens everything from the satisfactions of the body to the fulfillment of the soul.

The field's complexity includes a very wide range of varied, fluctuating, and often opposite biological, psychological, and social responses that at times lead to happiness and at other times to the worst human miseries.

This section includes two chapters. The first chapter, Introduction to the Magnitude and Complexity of the Field of Traumatology, uses three clinical cases to demonstrate the magnitude and complexity of the issues in traumatology. Two other vignettes illustrate the fabric of purpose and fulfillment which trauma disrupts. The life–trauma dialectic is introduced, though it is more fully described in chapter 5.

A new wholist perspective is introduced, which in Sections 2–4 is expanded under its components: a triaxial framework and survival strategies. It is suggested that the wholist perspective contributes to a theoretical grip on both the magnitude and the complexity within traumatology.

The second chapter parallels the first, but major traumatic situations replace individual cases to demonstrate the field's magnitude and complexity. Eight major traumatic situations, such as war, natural disasters, dying, and sexual abuse are reviewed. Children are given special consideration. As with the clinical cases, most traumatic situations have been treated within different disciplines both clinically and in research. This has led to emphasis on features that such situations highlighted. Although such features are very instructive, they can be integrated into a body of knowledge applicable across traumatic situations. Indeed, the varied situations can be shown to share common characteristics and concepts. The latter are developed in Section 2, together with the triaxial framework.

Chapter 1

Introduction to the Magnitude and Complexity of the Field of Traumatology

From time immemorial, people have tried to integrate two opposing experiential streams in their lives. One stream includes happiness, life itself, and creativity; the other destruction, sorrow, and disintegration. The protagonists have been variably labeled the forces of light and dark, good and evil, God and devil, life and death. Becker (1973) referred to death as the "worm at the core" (p. 15) of human happiness, "the skull at the banquet" (p. 16), or "the rumble of panic below everything" (p. 284).

Traumatology sees trauma as panic below everything, the worm at the core of human happiness. But it also has to understand the first stream within the dialectic, the one leading to fulfillment. In other words, even if it concentrates on the worm and its destruction, it also has to understand the apple.

Unlike religion, traumatology does not offer consolation that catastrophes are divine games, punishments for prior sins, or trials that will be recompensed in a future life. Indeed, it acknowledges that an essential feature of trauma is its lack of meaning and purpose. Nor does traumatology accept death as the opposite of happiness in life. Death at the right time, as Plato's Timaeus said, is a "debt of nature . . . the easiest of deaths . . . accompanied with pleasure rather than with pain." And if death has meaning, it may be embraced ahead of living even among the not so old. As Socrates spurned life if it meant sacrificing truth, so may soldiers willingly sacrifice themselves for a higher purpose. Traumatology deals with the threat of death when it is unwanted, without completion with self or nature, without honor, morality, ideology, or rounding out. Then it is pointless, meaningless, purposeless, absurd (Lifton, 1980). At such times, its imminence evokes instinctive resistance and survival fears (Becker, 1973; Brown, 1968).

As trauma is not only an attack on the body's survival, but on the whole fabric of fulfillment of highly prized singularly human qualities—morality, justice, values, principles, the sacred, and connection to the universe (the soul)— trauma threatens to make both body and soul absurd. Thus, it is trauma that is the destructive part of the dialectic with fulfillment of life. The following case seen by our emergency department team illustrates this.

> A widow whose husband had been executed by gangsters in front of her eyes 4 years previously cried, "Every night I have nightmares, every noise I think I will be executed. But what is more important is that I want my life back! I know I am alive, but I may as well be dead. The killing must make some sense. Without some purpose to it I am not alive and I may as well die!"

Traumatology as a science involves the study of responses to threats of physical and existential survival, the context and process in which stress and trauma occur, and the complex aftermath of the trauma process. Its challenge is to integrate understanding of the great range of aftermath responses and their connection to the torn fabric of human meaning and to help people redress the balance in their lives toward fulfillment.

Because trauma tears into the whole fabric of human life, its understanding inevitably extends beyond traumatology into other disciplines such as medicine, psychology, sociology, jurisprudence, linguistics, and philosophy.

In this chapter, two current conceptual approaches within traumatology are noted. Then a need to expand on them is shown through complexities demonstrated in three clinical vignettes. Last, some new concepts are introduced that promise to enhance understanding of the demonstrated complexities.

How would the young science of traumatology conceptualize the nature of trauma such as in the woman above? Two major streams have evolved (chapter 6). The first is derived from a medical model and sees clusters of symptoms such as nightmares and fears arising from the trauma as posttraumatic illnesses, the current accepted name being posttraumatic stress disorder, or PTSD (American Psychiatric Association, 1980, 1994). Its core symptoms include reliving and avoidance of traumatic events.

The second stream is based on a descriptive experiential model. In it are described wide-ranging, fluctuating, and sometimes contradictory responses. For instance, Raphael (1986) described in the impact phase of disasters numbness and apathy as well as arousal and resoluteness, effectiveness as well as helplessness, and fight as well as flight. Wolfenstein (1977) also described a wealth of responses in the impact phase of disasters and in addition noted how egoism and altruism, anger and guilt, feeling numbed and being too full of emotions, feeling abandoned and feeling very close, and feeling alone and being part of a cohesive group could alternate in individuals and groups. Wolfenstein also noted that people judged themselves and others in disasters, for example, as deserving pity or being spongers. They also extracted meanings such as that the disaster was a punishment for having done something wrong. They developed philosophies such as that fate equalizes all. This stream deals more with the "soul" of catastrophes.

Both streams are seen to be valid (chapter 6) and to complement each other, but they also have their limitations. PTSD does not account for the variety of traumatic stress responses. In other words, it does not tell one what is relived and what is avoided. It ignores a wide variety of emotions, guilts and angers, and moral responses and meanings. It takes no account of social systems outside the individual, and because of its perspective of pathology, it fails to account for adaptive, fulfilling responses. However, the descriptive model lacks an underlying framework against which the responses may be understood. This is why some leaders in the field are calling for theoretical frameworks to better encompass available knowledge (e.g., Weiner, 1992).

However, before proceeding further into theoretical frameworks, I present three clinical cases (a bush fire, a case of chest pain in an emergency department, and a child survivor of the Holocaust). These cases indicate the very different ways in which trauma sequelae come to notice, the wide range of trauma responses, and the need for an orientation and a framework that encompasses the different situations and responses.

CASE 1: THE ASH WEDNESDAY BUSH FIRES

The bush fires of 1983 were one of the worst natural disasters in Australian history. Two thousand homes were destroyed in huge fireballs, and 72 people died. And yet this was a surprisingly small proportion of the people who experienced the engulfing infernos. The following are responses from the impact, postimpact, and reconstruction phases. Disaster phases are examined in the Disasters section in the next chapter. The bush fires are described in greater detail elsewhere (Valent, 1984).

During the Fire (Impact Phase)

For most people the bush fire was the most terrible event of their lives. Some said it was worse than combat.

Within the disaster, people responded of necessity to the exigencies of fluctuating circumstances that could change dramatically and quickly. For instance, a young woman was trapped by flames and thought she would die. She surrendered to the flames as if they were a friendly cloak held open to her by an angel. Just then she was rescued, and within a second she continued her fierce fight for her life. A child went to look for her parents. They were behind a wall of flames that now advanced on her. The child lay down and curled up into a listless ball. Her parents ran through a break in the fire and scooped her up. The child then clung intensely to her father. For most inhabitants, it was at times safer to shelter in houses, whereas at other times it was necessary to escape them in cars. Some hid in swimming pools and dams. Unexpected strengths and resources were mustered. Some lifted heavy drums of water that in normal circumstances would have been too heavy. Back pains disappeared, burns did not hurt. Many people were later surprised at what they were able to do, and how instinctively they had acted, at times quite uncharacteristic of their previous personalities.

Children generally followed the cues of adults and were very obedient. However, above the age of 7 years they could make accurate assessments of danger and act accordingly if need be.

Pets also became very obedient. They gave up their territorial demands when squeezed together. Horses and cows stood stock-still in safe areas even for days. Many animals seemed to be "shocked."

A number of observations may be made already. First of all, considering the enormity of the destruction, most people acted very adaptively to survive and were able to draw on previously unknown reserves. Next, the responses that helped people survive were often felt to be instinctive, and indeed many responses overlapped with those of animals. However, human responses were more flexible than instincts and involved intense social interaction and helping. Thus, the responses were at a level of function above instincts, though subsuming them. This level where strategies of survival could be flexibly applied and that allowed many more humans to survive than animals is called the *survival strategy level* of human function. Not all strategies were adaptive. For instance, some drank alcohol in the hope the disaster would just pass them by; but it did not, and some died. For others, otherwise adaptive strategies were just insufficient under the circumstances. Hence, survival strategies could be adaptive or maladaptive or insufficient.

Last, it may be seen that within the turmoil of the disaster there was a wide variety of survival responses that were often contradictory (such as hosing and fleeing, surrendering and fighting) and that fluctuated rapidly.

People had noticed their emotions and physical responses. However, these seemed to be totally understandable within the circumstances and thus were of quite secondary concern. In association with fear and terror, hearts beat so hard that people could see their rib cages heave. One woman described fear like a tight rock in her chest. Many had severe muscle tension pains. Dragging pains in the womb were common, as were dizziness, weakness, and desire to collapse. At times, these symptoms progressed to illnesses and their threats to life did become primary concerns. Such illnesses included epileptic attacks, angina, asthma, spontaneous abortions, and premature births.

At times, people were at a loss to know what to do. At such times, the mayhem seemed distant, like an unreal horror. "It was like a film, it was not real." "The sky was beautiful and dreadful at the same time." Yet within seconds, people might leap into some kind of concerted action.

People did not only try to save themselves. They often risked themselves in order to seek out and save others. Firefighters did this frequently, but so did parents for their children, and so did neighbors for each other. Sometimes people risked themselves for strangers. Those who were more able rescued the more vulnerable and helpless. Circumstances could reverse roles quickly. Firefighters and parents were rescued at times by civilians and children. One man was rescued by his dog. On the whole, other people's survival was of primary importance. Although firefighters acted in professional helper groups, most people concentrated on helping each other within families, networks of friends, and those with whom their fates were tied at the time. Separation from those one cared about or depended on was extremely distressing. Children, the sick, and the isolated deeply yearned for their caretakers to appear. Reciprocally, caretakers often made frantic efforts to reach them in order to save them.

And yet in some circumstances people acted for their individual welfare and were quite selfish. For instance, within a group huddled in a hotel some previously courageous people refused to hose the outside of the building and risk themselves. Similarly, previously generous people struggled fiercely for a small number of wet blankets. When cars were full, others pleading to be taken on board were callously ignored.

It may be seen that survival responses include intense biological, psychological, and social aspects. Although they are adaptive and there is an understandable connection with events, even most extreme responses are accepted as normal. However, the responses may in some cases be maladaptive and develop into symptoms and illnesses such as angina and asthma. At times, too, when events seem overwhelming, disconnection or detachment from them, and feelings about them, occur. Such disconnections from the outside and inside worlds can be seen as means of coping or as defenses.

The primacy of adaptive social helping and the distress when this impulse cannot be satisfied can also be seen in this excerpt. And yet, as noted by others, here too altruism and selfishness sometimes alternated quickly. However, examination revealed that actions were determined by perceived capacities for optimum life saving. The men who refused to hose the outside of their building believed from previous experience that to do so would mean their own deaths before they could save anyone else. Similarly, stopping a full car for others would menace, not enhance, survival.

Nevertheless, the balance between saving self and others could be ambiguous and be influenced by others' angry judgments and evocation of guilt.

At times, naked anger and guilt guided efforts. A flagging mother was energized by an angry statement, "You must look after your child!" A firefighter hit an old man who refused to be rescued. He would have felt too guilty to leave him to certain death. In circumstances of conflict, anger and guilt fluctuated quickly.

An example was a woman whose uncle left her and her children unattended while he tried to rescue his cattle. He stumbled back burned, needing his niece's help. She was angry with him for his desertion, but her guilt overcame her reluctance to drive him to hospital. However, she cursed him silently all the way there for exposing her children and herself to danger.

Similarly, firefighters sometimes felt angry with those who kept them from rescuing their own families. However, guilt and shame for betraying their comrades and ideals kept them at their posts.

Judgments such as guilt and shame not only influenced the survival strategies but formed part of the nuclei for later conflicts within the higher functions of morality, meaning, values, and identity.

After the Fire (Postimpact)

People felt joy at their own and others' survival. The communal joy and camaraderie were part of the frequent "postdisaster euphoria" syndrome, and journalists were easily seduced into writing how the victims were stoic and cheerful. But people were also struck by grief as they assessed their losses. Some were homeless and dirty, because they had no access to soap and water supply. So losses were not only people and goods but also identity, dignity, a way of life. The sudden changes stunned people, and many absorbed their losses slowly. They kept leaving and returning to the places of their traumas and losses, their emotions slowly thawing.

The sense of safety was gone, too. Survival was felt to be tenuous. People were very sensitive to cues that could herald recurrence of the fires. At the same time, they intensely relived the fires in talk, memories, flashbacks, dreams, and thoughts.

Even as people celebrated their survival and had intense hopes for the future, they also had to start to understand what had been destroyed at different levels in their lives. As they tried to orient themselves to the future, they nevertheless continued to relive the fires and their responses to them. They attempted to assimilate the disjunction and unpredictability of past, present, and future by talking and by various internal cognitive means.

Alternating with these responses, the help and rescue spirit persisted, this time centered around providing resources rather than life. Many were extremely generous and shared their food, shelter, and toilet facilities with those deprived of them. Informal helping organizations sprang up quickly.

Guilt and anger also moved from issues around rescuing life to regulating distribution of resources. For instance, those whose houses still stood felt extreme guilt that their houses had survived when their neighbors' had not. The guilt was so intense that many said, "I wish my house had burnt down, not theirs." This led to generous offers of shelter and facilities. However, after some time the extra visitors seemed to become interminable burdens. The previously guilty hosts became angry: "They just expect everything!"

This movement was reflected in the general community, which also responded with an initial outpouring of generosity, later modified to "You'll build new houses from our taxes!" Similarly, emotional resources initially freely given were replaced with "It's time you pulled your socks up!"

With threats to physical survival receding, strategies of survival were directed to distribution of physical, emotional, and mental resources. However, as victims' survival was assured, people turned to protecting their own resources.

Very quickly people tried to make sense of what happened. "Why?!" "Who was responsible?" "Why me?!" Why did they and others help or not help? Why did they flee? Stay too long? and so on.

These questions were inevitably tinged with emotions and moral judgments of self and others. Some could not make meaning of the injustice. Two Germans who had strictly followed instructions were flabbergasted that their property was nevertheless partially destroyed. A man who had carefully constructed a watering system that was to have withstood any fire was utterly galled that his house had burned while that of his improvident neighbor survived. When he thought of the injustice that he had had to ask for buckets of water from this neighbor, he developed chest pains.

Quickly, too, meanings were extracted by compounding this situation with others. A woman complained that her son had nearly lost the vision in one eye 3 years previously. She linked this seemingly irrelevant concern with her son's horrific car ride through the fire. She compounded the two events through the meaning that she was a bad mother as she allowed her son to have such bad experiences.

In many cases, people's sacrifices and enhanced capacities led to positive assessments of themselves and others. But because the disaster also ruptured assumptions of cause and effect and a just and benevolent world, people tried to understand anew questions of blame, guilt, morality, and justice. They tried to extract meaning from the bad events. However, many emergent meanings were themselves dangerous, such as being a bad mother or being vulnerable in an unjust incoherent world. Such meanings and their preceding contexts could be suppressed (defended against). However, the resultant disconnections interfered with the normal sequencing and processing of events necessary for coherent sense in life. This interference made many relived stress responses inexplicable, which in turn could lead to a sense of going crazy.

People were full of constantly changing feelings such as tearfulness, anger, joy, fear, and a variety of physical sensations such as diarrhea, vomiting, exhaustion and palpitations. Psychosomatic illnesses such as ulcers and dermatitis flared up. Accidents increased. The sense of not being in control of their bodies and minds made people fear that they were going mad. They often immersed themselves into activity or alcohol to suppress feelings.

Children regressed, clung, played fire games and drew fire related drawings. They silently blamed their parents for letting their pets and toys burn and they bore guilt for their parents' suffering and at times even for the fires. Their feelings were usually not noticed, and were even actively suppressed. In part this was because of parental guilt for "putting the children through so much suffering."

Some pets' personalities changed. For instance they became overly anxious or aggressive.

Many outside helpers and bureaucracies streamed into the area. Though resources were gratefully received, they were also resented because they emphasized dependence and loss of dignity. If given with a sense of paternalism or do-goodness they offended dignity. Helpers themselves became stressed, suffering burn-out, minor illnesses, and accidents. (Berah, Jones, & Valent, 1984)

The great variety of physical, psychological, and social symptoms was due to continued arousal associated with (re)living of the disaster, readiness for its return, and disconnections between past and present hindering processing. The latter was not only due to suppression of dangerous meanings, but also to unwanted emotions such as rage and crying, alongside exhortations to not cry over spilt milk and to "get on with it." Hence, reliving alternated with avoidance. Responses nevertheless continued or intruded, with variable degrees of understandability. They ranged in depth from physiological arousal to morality and meaning.

Adding to the complexity of the many responses themselves was a growing complexity of "cultures" of the responses. They had different "cultural expressions" according to phases of disasters, social system (individuals, families, groups, helpers, general community) under consideration, and age of the victims.

Reconstruction Phase   Briefly, similar principles apply as they did to previous phases, though the culture was now predicated by the goal of increasing margins of safety and resources. Along with rebuilding their lives, people still kept referring back to the fires and made ever deeper meanings of them. Yet some who could not connect and integrate the events developed relatively more entrenched illnesses, both mental and physical.

An old man became severely depressed a month after the fire. He had believed that he had no right to cry as his house had been preserved. As he was allowed to grieve for the surroundings that would not regenerate in his lifetime, his depression lifted.

An elderly couple's house was destroyed, and they lost all their belongings. The wife soon died of heart disease complications. After prolonged depression, the widowed husband developed a heart complaint on the anniversary of the fire, and he died on the anniversary of his wife's death.

Morbidity and mortality persisted in a higher proportion than usual for at least 2 years. Delayed symptoms came to notice even beyond that time. Both nature and people regenerated, but scars and vulnerabilities remained.

Taking the disaster as a whole, it may be seen that many varied, often contradictory events and responses were established in the first searing impact phase and thereafter. They developed in the later phases and then reverberated with earlier and later events. Together they made increasingly complex meanings and blueprints for later survival contingencies and coherent views of the world. If resolution or coherence could not be achieved, symptoms and illnesses developed or the groundwork was laid for their later development. Characteristic responses occurred at different social levels and ages.

CASE 2: A CASE OF ANGINA
IN THE EMERGENCY DEPARTMENT

Although the bush fire was a traumatic situation that could be followed prospectively to resolution or illnesses such as heart disease, in this case, the heart disease presented initially as an end point, and the traumatic situation had to be found by retracing the traumatic response process.

The patient was a 48-year-old woman who presented to the emergency department with chest pain that turned out to be angina. Her presentation seemed to be unremarkable for that diagnosis, and she was not referred because of any stresses. She was approached routinely by the department's psychiatric liaison team, which was itself a recognized part of the department's medical team.

> When asked, "Of all the things that worry you, what worries you the most?" the woman's husband interjected and said, "Stress." The wife nodded. When asked "What is stress?" she answered, "It is like rage you cannot express."
>
> Her angina pains had developed 2 months prior, 1 month after she was dismissed from her work to which she had devoted 25 years of loyal service. However, this was a background to 18 months of "stress" due to thoughts that her husband had betrayed her with another woman (vigorously denied). During this period of stress, the patient suffered a variety of abdominal and chest pains, and the husband suffered head pains and dizziness. Both thought they might have fatal illnesses. Both had attended their doctors on frequent occasions.
>
> Seventeen years prior, the husband had been a passenger in a car that collided with another car. The couple had two daughters, and the younger, 8-year-old one who happened to be in the car suffered head injuries and died. The patient strongly blamed her husband for the death, unjustly, as she came to see. The couple then had two further children, replicating their initial first two, as if to try again. However, when the second of these children approached 8 years, the stresses mentioned started. The patient and her husband burst into sobs when the poignancy of that age was raised. The patient came to see that her blame of her husband was a revisiting of the original rage with him for betraying her trust in him with their daughter. Together with the dismissal, the patient now anticipated the second daughter to die and saw 25 years of mothering and work, indeed her life's purpose, about to fail. The suppressed rage that reached its peak with the dismissal may well have contributed to the angina. For the husband, his self-blame in the accident led to him identifying with his daughter, feeling he would die of something in his head.

The case illustrates the need for a general biopsychosocial approach and an open mind to prior stresses both in medicine and in traumatology. With a purely biological or psychiatric–PTSD approach, the hidden preceding trajectory of relevant stresses and traumas is likely to not be recognized in many people with traumatic process end states.

The case also indicates that not resolving postimpact griefs, judgments, angers, guilts, and meanings can have long-term effects, even if they are latent or delayed for a long time. It can also be seen that stressors can be symbolic (a child turning 8) and cumulative (unresolved grief and sacking). Compounded together, the stressors may lead to superordinate meanings about oneself and life (failed mother and worker).

Last, the same trauma may be highly but differently significant for each family member, as was seen for the mother and father. However, even the 8-year-old, currently living, replacement daughter could be a hidden victim, being a potentially stressed central figure in a drama she could not understand. So stressors may even be transgenerational.

CASE 3: A CHILD SURVIVOR OF THE HOLOCAUST

The complexity of the above cases may be multiplied when considering early and multiple traumas. In the previous cases, there were single traumatic situations. In situations of long imprisonment and torture, the Holocaust, or childhood sexual abuse, traumatic situations keep occurring over long periods. Many may have the force equivalent to a bush fire or a bereavement. The complexity is further expanded when the victim is a small child who is helpless, may depend on the perpetrator, and cannot understand what is happening. The following is an abstract of a child's experience of the Holocaust and associated sexual abuse. The story is described in detail elsewhere (Valent, 1994).

> Anne said, "I have been depressed for years, but I used to be able to come out of it. Now I am depressed all the time. None of the drugs help now. In the past, I worked and I was devoted to my children. Now they do not need me, and I do not work as much. In my everyday life, I can be the life of the party. At most, my friends see me as a bit moody and prone to minor illnesses, perhaps.
>
> "The Holocaust keeps coming back to my mind lately. I kept it out of my mind somehow for years. My parents and two sisters died in it. I had many caretakers."

As often happens in such cases, Anne expanded on her story over a long time, returning to the same events with ever greater vividness.

> "We came to Paris when I was 3 or 4. One day I went down to play and I saw men in uniforms. I was not worried. When I returned home my whole family were all gone. I thought, 'Doesn't mean much. They'll be back.' The first family made me kneel on wooden chairs, another made me lie in prickles in the garden, I had to have sex with men, I was threatened with being burnt in the oven. I kept going because I was going to see my parents. But when I was 7 I was told that they had been killed.
>
> "I suffered malnutrition and bronchitis. Once I tried to kill myself by cutting my wrists with secateurs. But what upsets me most is that I feel sorry for myself. I

am upset that I cry a lot. I am letting my family down. . . . I have never told any of this to anyone—ever."

Over the next years, Anne went over this summary of her story in ever greater detail with ever greater sense that it belonged to her and that it was important. The therapist became a tangible part of her story telling.

The fragments were revealed without cohesion of time or meaning. Yet this fragmentation was how Anne had survived. To have acknowledged the overall meaning of her existence at the time would have plunged her into despair and death. Anne would not piece her story together until she had faith that it was safe to do so. The therapist was to offer that security and faith in her and her future.

"When I was being taken to another family, I imagined that I was going on holiday. As the weeks dragged, I fervently reconstructed every detail of how things were before I left to play. I clung to this memory, it was what enabled me to keep going for years."

After leaving hospital for tuberculosis and pneumonia, Anne was told her parents had died. "I was sick again, but this time mentally. I do not know which was worse. I had this really severe headache suddenly, and I developed mental blocks. I was angry with my family, but then I became very depressed and moody, like I have stayed till now."

Anne started to relive her abuse in more vivid ways.

One day she confessed, "I hear these voices, I cannot get rid of them. In a way they have always been there, but now they are real." For a long time she would not tell more. "They are the men's voices. I feel like I am betraying them if I tell you. They threaten me with death like they did then if I tell what happened." Anne looked terrified. "I have never told because they would get me." Anne struggled between her terror and strange loyalty to the men and the reassurance that she was safe from them. Anne came to speak more freely of her abuse. "The first family tied me in a kneeling position on a wooden chair. They warned me that they would beat me if I soiled or wetted myself. So I did not. Even now I can be constipated for weeks in spite of stomachaches.

"In another family, a man took notice of me. One day he took my singlet and pants off. It was nice that he paid attention to me. But then he threw himself on me and crushed me, I hated it, I thought I would die. I developed coughs, headaches, and stomachaches. I told the woman something about what this man was doing to me. She became very angry and said that I was very bad. She said that she would get rid of me, picked me up, and she opened the oven door. I thought I was going in. So I did not object anymore."

And again in another family,

"In this family, the man invited me to his bed so I went. I thought he would be nice to me. I saw nothing wrong or abnormal with that. I thought it happened everywhere. But he was rough. I had to do it with my mouth. I felt sick, and he became angry. Obviously, I was doing things wrong. Then he did it from the other end. He threw me this way and that. I bled, I cried, but no one took any notice. I stopped eating." Anne was shriveled in her seat. "How I wanted my parents!" She had a violent headache. "I still have these headaches often," she commented.

Distress, relief, and understanding alternated with new symptoms and new cycles. Long-experienced phobias and nightmares such as about fire were slowly peeled back through later associations to their fundamental traumatic sources. The fire-and-ovens phobia was first linked to a recent threat of being scalded with hot water. The oven was later linked to Auschwitz crematoria, then to a synagogue where Jewish children had been burnt. Eventually, Anne connected the symptoms to the time when she believed that she would be incinerated in the wall oven. Working through this alleviated the phobia.

Anne tried to make sense of her story and herself.

"What is it about me that makes all these things happened to me? Maybe I deserved everything. I did seek affection from the men."

Anne gave her testimony. For the first time, she gave a coherent sequential story of her experiences. After reading her story (Valent, 1994), she said, "It got through to me that this was me, really me . . . , I see it all now, I feel it, I taste it. I feel the rip, the blood, the fist up, I thought I'd die." She said, "It is strange, but I feel as if I am giving up a child . . . In the past I made up episodes, it was not me it was happening to, but to another child. I told this child that she was naughty and she needed to be punished, that is why all the bad things were happening to her. I am losing that child."

More cycles of symptoms and relief and understanding occurred. Anne's depressions associated with her parents' deaths were relieved by grief for them. Anne found a cave of feelings. There she found deep cutting sorrow, followed by heart-rending sobs. After many sobs she said, "I am out of the cave now. It is because my feelings found words for the first time." She also found words for anger, gratitude, and love. The headaches subsided.

Anne reconnected with the nice little girl to whom so many bad things happened, leaving her badly scarred. But that nice girl survived and produced a family. She started to enjoy life and seek happiness, to enter a path of fulfillment.

Early and severe childhood traumas may have major effects on every aspect of the child's life and its development. Initial major inabilities to deal with situations may be associated with more primitive intense and global disconnections (defenses) than some adult ones described above. This may be further exaggerated by adult threats against disclosure. The victim thus may have only partial, fragmented memories of traumas. Some of those partial memories may be represented in biological, psychological, or social symptoms.

The reconnection with earlier, often hidden traumas may be long and arduous as each antecedent is clarified and integrated into a more hopeful current view. The pathway to the clarification of the original traumatic context may require retracing across a number of way stations (such as the symbols representing the original trauma in Anne's fire phobia). Many deeply entrenched meanings may need reinterpretation, such as Anne's conviction that it was her fault that these things happened to her.

THE WHOLIST PERSPECTIVE TO HELP ORIENTATE AND UNDERSTAND TRAUMATIC STRESS RESPONSES

The above cases indicate complexity in orientation (different stressor cultures, disaster phases, age of victims, physical symptoms, problems of meaning and purpose) and contents of the responses (biological, psychological and social, adaptive and maladaptive, and so on). These posttraumatic responses could be conceptualized as PTSD, as patients–victims did relive and avoid their traumas and did experience arousal phenomena in relation to them. The responses also corresponded to the second viewpoint, which described a wide variety of fluctuating and often contradictory responses at different levels of meaning. However, both approaches need further orientation and framework for the seemingly limitless variety of human responses.

It is suggested that the *wholist* perspective helps to make sense of traumatology responses. Its components are the *triaxial framework*, which helps in orientation of responses (section 2) , whereas s*urvival strategies* (section 3) help to categorize and make sense of them.

THE TRIAXIAL FRAMEWORK

The following are the three suggested axes of the triaxial framework.

Axis 1: The Process (Stressors → Illnesses) Axis A process occurs wherein stressors evoke stress responses that include biological, psychological, and social aspects. Each may be adaptive or maladaptive. If stress responses do not resolve the traumatic situation, the process may progress to disconnections (defenses), traumas, and illnesses. They may include PTSD, but also a range of illnesses such as angina, phobias, depression, and persecutory hallucinations.

Axis 2: The Parameters Axis Each case has its own parameters that give it a particular flavor or culture. Parameters include nature of the traumatic situation, age of the victim, social levels under consideration (such as individual, family, group, community, secondary victims, helpers), and disaster phase to the event (before, during, immediately after, or 50 years later).

Axis 3: The Depth (Levels of Human Functioning) Axis In each case, immediate individual survival necessities interacted with survival necessities of others. Actions were influenced by reciprocal judgments facilitated by emotions such as anger and guilt. These moral judgments could later be as distressing as the original events. So could the varieties of meanings arising from the judgments. Also, people quickly became concerned with questions of justice, dignity, and philosophical questions about the sort of world in which they lived. This perspective provides the depth axis of traumatic situations.

Survival Strategies: A Framework for the Variety of Traumatic Stress Responses

Although the three axes provide orientation for stress responses, survival strategies provide a framework for their content. They relate to the questions "What is experienced?" and "Why?"

Survival strategies are postulated to be distinct evolutionary templates serving specific types of survival needs (chapter 7). They are stress responses a level above instincts, which they subsume. They are integrated biological, psychological, and social functional units. Fight and flight are two well-known survival strategies, and flight, for instance, was quite prominent in the bush fires. However, eight survival strategies are postulated in the coming chapters (8–15). In addition to fight and flight, there are rescue, attachment, assertiveness, adaptation, competition, and cooperation. Evocation of alternate and even opposite survival strategies in the context of rapidly changing circumstances can result in a wide variety of fluctuating and sometimes opposite responses.

The wholist perspective with the triaxial framework and survival strategies contains powerful tools that can provide a framework for understanding, making sense of, and categorizing both survival and fulfillment phenomena. For the first time, there is a way to see coherently the wide variety of and often contradictory traumatology responses and to categorize functions most precious to humans such as morals, meanings, values, and other spiritual constituents.

Fulfillment: The Other Side of Trauma

It must be remembered that fulfillment of life is the other side of the dialectic of trauma and the struggle to survive. The life–trauma dialectic is portrayed more fully in chapter 5. Though clinical vignettes of fulfilled persons are almost a self-contradiction, it may be worthwhile to construct a short vignette in order to see for what people strive and what trauma severs.

> The fulfilled person senses satisfaction of all bodily needs, and there is a sense of security in the plentifulness of continued supply of essential resources. The person is in a matrix of loving relationships with parents, peers, and the wider community. Early in life, there is empathy and nurturing toward growth, learning, achievement of natural milestones, and delights for oneself and others in one's skills and achievements. At the appropriate time, one establishes a stable, loving sexual relationship within which framework one nurtures and delights in one's children in the way one was cared for when young.

One is confident of one's worth and similarly respectful and grateful to others. There is also confidence in a just, principled world. Life is meaningful and coherent, dignified, refined, and spiritual. There is a sense that one's life is significant and purposeful, and one fulfills one's special place and talents in the scheme of things.

In summary, this chapter introduced the magnitude and complexity of the field of traumatology. The field includes threats to fulfillment of life ranging from threats to the existence of the body to threats to the meaning and purpose of the soul. A hypothetical case of fulfillment contrasted with three cases that illustrated the range and complexity of the effects of trauma. They included a great variety of adaptive and maladaptive biological, psychological, and social responses in various settings involving varying spiritual depths of human existence.

A wholist perspective was introduced that included two new concepts, the triaxial framework and survival strategies. It was foreshadowed that this perspective would enhance orientation and understanding of the magnitude and complexity in the field of traumatology and the life–trauma dialectic.

Before proceeding to the new perspective in Sections 2 and 3, the next chapter overviews the history of traumatology as it evolved from observations from various traumatic situations. Like cases in this chapter, each situation highlights different traumatic responses. The variety of manifestations from both chapters are conceptually ordered in subsequent chapters.

Chapter 2

Features of Stress and Trauma in Different Traumatic Situations

In the previous chapter, it was seen that different traumatic situations such as natural disaster, psychosomatic medicine, and the Holocaust have different modes of presentation and "culture." Historically, observations on stress and trauma developed in relative isolation in such different cultures. For instance, the literatures on combat trauma, sexually abused children, death and dying, and psychosomatic medicine have often had little contact with each other. In this chapter, the eight major traumatic situations that contribute to traumatic stress are briefly reviewed. Not only does this give some historical perspective to the field, but highlighting special contributions from each situation provides a measure of its wealth. Common themes across the situations are noted, though concepts common to all situations are deferred to the coming chapters.

The traumatic situations examined are wars, the Holocaust, natural disasters, civilian accidents, personal violence and sexual abuse, sexual assault of children and incest, psychosomatic medicine, and bereavement and dying.

I review the traumatic stress of war first because of its recurrent historical impetus to recognition of trauma, as well as the ample documentation of physical medical, psychological, and social consequences of combat trauma.

Though I have attempted to treat them with some consistency, because

different traumatic situations highlight different aspects, headings within sections discussing them are not concordant across situations.

WAR

Early Descriptions

Ancient Greeks and Romans were already aware of the psychological sequelae
of combat. In *The Iliad*, Homer described survival guilt and the pain of betrayal
of what was right in war (Shay, 1991), and Lucretius described the reliving of
battles in dreams. He wrote, "Kings may take cities . . . [but they] fill the night
with piercing screams as though they were writhing in the jaws of a panther"
(Ellis, 1984, p. 168).

The actual sequelae of combat were compiled for the first time by Hofer in
1678 among Swiss troops serving in France. He compiled the symptoms into a
syndrome that he called *melancholia*. It included excitement, "imagination,"
fever and torpor, marked gastrointestinal symptoms, and, finally, a state of prostration and depression (Ellis, 1984). This was the recognized war neurosis for
150 years. Then a variant of melancholia called "nostalgia" was noted in the
American Civil War (Glass, 1966). Added to the symptoms of melancholia were
a longing for home and lack of discipline. In the same war, but separately, Da
Costa (1871) described the "irritable heart" syndrome. Since then, heart and
gastrointestinal symptoms have remained the main somatic symptoms recognized in wars.

In the latter part of the 19th century, the popular diagnosis of neurasthenia
was also applied to soldiers. Its cause was thought to be nervous exhaustion,
and its symptoms in addition to those of nostalgia included a variety of psychophysiological and cognitive symptoms such as loss of memory. In the Crimean
War (1854–1856), the rush of air accompanying cannon balls causing minor
brain damage was offered as an explanation of war neuroses. At last, mental
illnesses related purely to battle stress were first officially recognized and specially treated in the Russo-Japanese War in 1904–1906.

First World War

The importance of the First World War was the final wide recognition of the so-
called traumatic neuroses of war. However, psychological stress effects were
initially recognized only in the form of their psychophysiological equivalents. In
this war, there was much interest in cardiac symptoms, which was reflected in a
range of diagnoses such as Da Costa's (1871) irritable heart, neurocirculatory
asthenia, effort syndrome, and cardiac neurosis. However, gastrointestinal symptoms were still common, too (Glass, 1966).

Nevertheless, the frequent psychological symptoms eventually had to be
heeded. At first, they were described as shell shock (Myers, 1990), following

the earlier concept of brain damage as being due to air pressure from cannon balls. However, as most affected soldiers had not suffered blasts from shells, this theory had to be abandoned (Salmon, 1919). By the end of the First World War, the massive attrition rate due to purely psychological causes forced large-scale recognition of war stress as causing war neuroses (Freud, 1926/1975h). This opened the way to psychological forms of treatment rather than punishment for psychologically wounded soldiers (Salmon, 1919).

The classic work to come out of the First World War was Kardiner's (1941) *The Traumatic Neuroses of War*. Kardiner described early combat responses as having very wide variety and fluidity. Later they could be relived in nightmares and flashbacks, which in turn could become parts of repetitive or intractable traumatic neuroses. They in turn could merge into other neuroses (such as hysteria) and psychoses. Kardiner's examples described a rich plethora of sensory, behavioral, emotional, and somatic symptoms. Kardiner emphasized that they all had meaningful, even if at times unconscious, connections to traumatic events in war.

The importance of Kardiner's (1941) work lay in that for the first time there was a combination of rich biological, psychological, and social descriptions of combat sequelae, with dynamic connections between symptoms and preceding traumas. There was also a flexible phenomenology that nevertheless included specific traumatic diagnoses.

Second World War

The lessons of the First World War were soon forgotten and had to be relearned in the Second World War. Again, this was due to the extremely large number (two million) of combat-related psychological breakdowns (Menninger, 1947). Kardiner's (1941) observations were confirmed and extended, but there also evolved greater refinement in determining the nature of combat stress and the importance of morale.

The Nature of Combat Stress   Combat stress was found to be related to several overlapping factors. They were the intensity of the threat of death, the duration of combat exposure, the number of comrades killed, and unit demoralization.

Intensity of Combat   The more intense the combat, the higher was the psychological attrition rate. For instance, infantry regiments in combat had seven times the rate of psychiatric admissions as compared with the army overall. Those in severe situations such as the North African rifle battalions had casualty rates 30–40 times higher than the general rate (Appel & Beebe, 1946). In fact, all men in such battalions eventually became psychiatric casualties. Other jobs such as grave registration and collection of mutilated bodies also predisposed to breakdowns (Futterman & Pumpian-Mindlin, 1951).

Duration of Combat   Estimates of combat time that led to men to suc-
cumb were continually revised downward. From 200–240 aggregate days, they
came down to 14–180 (Bartemeier, Kubie, Menninger, Romano, & Whitehorn,
1946; Swank, 1949). Next, it was estimated that steadily increasing proportions
of psychiatric breakdowns occurred after 4 days of combat (Hanson, 1949).
Finally, Appel and Beebe (1946, p. 1470) concluded, "Each moment of combat
imposes a strain so great that men will break down in direct relation to the
intensity and duration of their exposure."

Attrition Rate of Comrades   Swank (1949) estimated that when the original number of men in a unit was reduced through death or injury by 65%, the
remainder of men suffered combat exhaustion.

Morale   The sophistication of morale literature from the Second World
War has not been surpassed. Morale was a major determinant of the presence or
absence of combat stress. High morale was seen as the antidote to the anxiety
of annihilation (E. A. Weinstein, 1947), psychiatric illness (Strecker, 1945), and
as was what enabled men to expose themselves to death. The components of
morale included motivation to accomplish important goals and the confidence
that one's strength, effort, competence, and skills would enable one to do so
(Grinker & Spiegel, 1945; Renner, 1973). The psychosocial matrix for morale
was the unit. It was like a body of which one was an important organ, but the
body was more important than oneself (Brende, 1983). The leader, the brain of
the body as well as a parent figure, was especially important for morale (S. H.
Epstein, 1944; Nolan, Engle, & Engle, 1954; Menninger, 1947; Shaw, 1983).
But love was the emotional glue and provided impulse to action (Spiegel, 1944).
The love was for comrades, the leader, unit, and task. Comrades were described
as loved beyond any other friends.

A special type of love was for the "buddy," a kind of combat twin, a
microcosm within which every other relationship and valuation of the self was
invested (Bourne, 1970; Brende, 1983). Outside the unit, there was love of
families one defended and of the cause.

Demoralization occurred with defeat of goals and ideals, loss of confidence
in skills and equipment, loss of leaders and members of the unit, especially
one's buddy, and loss of faith in leaders and the cause (Appel & Beebe, 1946;
H. S. Bloch, 1970; Shaw, 1983). Men now felt abandoned, betrayed, and dragged
to their deaths for no good reason (Bartemeier et al., 1946). With fear of death
now intense, lack of discipline, disobedience, killing of officers, and atrocities
occurred (see also chapter 12). Noncombat factors contributing to demoralization were death, such as of a father whose admiration the soldier sought, or
betrayal by a sweetheart (Bartemeier et al., 1946). Soldiers also constructed
individual pessimistic meanings from combat (Grinker & Spiegel, 1945).

The Nature of Combat Sequelae   As in the First World War, psychological symptoms were first reluctantly condoned through their psychophysio-

logical and psychosomatic equivalents. This time gastrointestinal symptoms were given prominence (e.g., Dunn, 1942).

Of the huge psychological literature emanating from the Second World War, Grinker and Spiegel's (1945) *Men Under Stress* was the classic, like Kardiner's (1941) book was the classic from the First World War. The two books are clinically consistent.

Thus, Grinker and Spiegel (1945) also noted in the early phases of combat breakdown a melting pot of responses, or "a passing parade of every type of psychological and psychosomatic symptom, and of unadaptive behavior" (p. 83). Such symptoms included exhaustion, fear, terror, intense somatic symptoms, full-blown hysterias, and psychoticlike hallucinations. As Kardiner (1941) noted, these symptoms could form fluid and interchangeable clinical pictures, such as anxiety, phobic, conversion hysterical, psychosomatic, and depressed states. All could merge with known psychiatric syndromes. Again, both early and late symptoms made sense in terms of war traumas and their meanings.

In their authoritative military overview, Bartemeier et al. (1946) confirmed Grinker and Spiegel's (1945) observations, but they also described the definitive traumatic syndrome of the war, combat exhaustion. Its early features included slowness, fatigue, with discarding of equipment and even food because they were too heavy. Difficulty in concentration, reclusiveness, moroseness, loss of interest, and affective flatness were other symptoms. The picture was reminiscent of neurasthenia. In the full-blown picture, the traumatized soldiers looked like old men, totally exhausted, retarded, and apathetic (Swank, 1949) and walked like burnt-out automatons with bleary eyes (Grinker & Spiegel, 1945). Nevertheless, a closer look also revealed features of demoralization—a sense of failure, memories of killed buddies, and impotent, angry frustration (Bartemeier et al., 1946). This traumatic syndrome depicted one end state. However, there were others, depending on which cluster of symptoms one concentrated.

For the first time after the Second World War, close attention was given to psychological sequelae in returned soldiers.

Postwar Readjustment   It became clear that combat neuroses did not stop with combat or even with the end of the war. First, 30% of returned soldiers suffered combat neuroses (M. L. Miller, 1944). Further, illnesses could erupt months or even years after homecoming (Futterman & Pumpian-Mindlin, 1951). Last, symptoms could last unabated for 30 years or more (Klonoff, McDougall, Clark, Kramer, & Horgan, 1976).

The symptoms themselves varied greatly, but they included reliving traumas as if they were happening currently (Grinker & Spiegel, 1945). At such times, soldiers could be in aggressive and psychoticlike states or suffer psychosomatic or depressive and guilt symptoms. The vividness of these symptoms could become repetitive and stereotyped and merge with variable personality states and psychiatric disorders. Symptoms could be influenced also by other meaningful army and civilian events.

Also in the Second World War, treating personnel became for the first time subject to (not always complimentary) observation.

Treating Personnel   In both the First and Second World Wars, many doctors and psychiatrists collaborated for a long time with the powerful denial ideology of their officers, who called affected soldiers cowards, misfits, slackers, and malingerers. Psychiatrists harangued soldiers, applied pain-not-gain punishment therapies, and proudly returned great majorities of traumatized soldiers to duty. They discharged the recalcitrant ones with pejorative diagnoses in order to patriotically protect the public purse from later lawsuits (Needles, 1946). Even later, more sympathetic, abreactive therapies were still imbued with the ideology of return to duty.

In summary, Second World War literature reconfirmed the psychological noxiousness of combat and acknowledged for the first time that all people could be broken by it. The components of combat stress were examined, an important one being demoralization. Clinical findings from the First World War were confirmed and extended. Returnees were found to suffer combat sequelae, often long term. The clinical bias in psychiatrists was examined for the first time.

The Vietnam War

When it came to the Vietnam War, recognition of war neuroses was again delayed, and old lessons had to be relearned (Figley, 1978). However, perhaps the historical importance of this literature is the first-time documentation of widespread demoralization and atrocities in a war of defeat and the definition of PTSD (Kolb, 1993). The latter stated clearly that severe psychological stressors could lead to illness in anyone.

Demoralization   Symptoms of demoralization such as drug taking and poor discipline were initially blamed on personality disorders. However, by 1971 Heinl, a military historian and Marine Corps colonel, had put demoralization in context (Lifton, 1973, p. 340):

> By every conceivable indicator, our army . . . is in a state of collapse, with individual units avoiding or having refused combat, murdering their officers, . . . drugridden, and dispirited where not near-mutinous.
>
> Intolerably clobbered from without and within by social turbulence, pandemic drug addiction, race war, sedition, civilian scapegoatise, draftee recalcitrance, malevolence, barracks theft and common crime, unsupported in their travail by the general government, in Congress as well as the executive branch, distrusted, disliked, and often reviled by the public, the uniformed services today are places of agony.

Heinl did not mention atrocities, but Lifton (1973; see also chapter 12) described the My Lai massacre as an example. He noted how frustrated and fearful soldiers raped and killed innocent civilians in an effort to feel that they had some control over enemies and that they were avenging dead comrades.

The men brought their demoralization home. Some 43% of soldiers departing Vietnam had used heroin. Of married returnees, 38% were divorced within 6 months of their return. In 1975, 30% of federal prisoners were Vietnam veterans. By that time, too, 100,000 returned veterans had died (Boman, 1982b).

Psychiatric literature of the war was slow to emerge. However, Shatan (1973) described the post-Vietnam syndrome, which was really a syndrome of demoralization. Its features were brutalization and psychic numbing, rage and violent impulses, guilt and self-punishment, alienation from self and others, inability to trust and love, and feeling betrayed and scapegoated. Drug taking was common. Lifton (1973) added the existential depths of demoralization such as loss of a sense of justice and morality, meaning, and purpose.

PTSD and Other Combat Sequelae   Vietnam veterans mounted pressure to have their psychological anguish recognized. Some highly decorated veterans committed spectacular crimes, and others, without historical precedent, demonstrated en masse for acknowledgment of their sufferings. Eventually, the American Psychiatric Association (APA), which had removed gross stress reaction from the second edition of its *Diagnostic and Statistical Manual of Mental Disorders* (*DSM–II*) at the beginning of the Vietnam War, now reinstated a stress diagnosis in its third edition of the *DSM* (the *DSM–III*; APA, 1980). It specified PTSD as a disorder of extreme stress, such as combat. This gave soldiers a label by which their distress could be recognized legally and medically. However, PTSD did not describe what was relived or avoided. It removed the sting of defeat, and demoralization symptoms and existential meanings of the post-Vietnam syndrome were ignored. The only symptom referring to such dilemmas, guilt, was left out in the revised *DSM–III* (the *DSM–III–R*; APA, 1987) and in the fourth edition of the *DSM* (the *DSM–IV*; APA, 1994).

Even so, the more restricted PTSD confirmed observations following other wars. Like previous war neuroses, PTSD was common in returning veterans. Weiss et al. (1992) estimated the lifetime prevalence of PTSD as 30.9% for men and 26.0% for women. Further, the prevalence of partial but significant PTSD added 22.5% and 21.2%, respectively. If somatic and social symptoms outside of PTSD were added, the long-term prevalence of Vietnam War–induced disorders was very high. Also, as with previous war neuroses, PTSD can have delayed onset and is often chronic. Schlenger et al. (1992) estimated the prevailing prevalence of PTSD among American veterans 15 or more years after their Vietnam service to be 15.2% for men and 8.5% for women, that is, nearly half a million veterans.

As in previous wars, a clinical stream (e.g., Lindy, 1988) found the same variable, complex, trauma-related biological, psychological, and social symptoms in veterans, as Kardiner (1941) and Grinker and Spiegel (1945) did before them. The PTSD literature has recently also acknowledged a range of symptoms under comorbid diagnoses. For instance, Sutker, Uddo, Brailey, Allain, and Errera (1994) described PTSD as well as depression, anxiety, physical symptoms, and anger in a high proportion of Gulf War grave registrant returnees.

In summary, Vietnam War observations replicated those of previous wars but added to knowledge of symptoms of demoralization. Though psychiatry was again seen as susceptible to political influences, PTSD with all its limitations also became the carrier of much energy that is still invigorating the trauma field.

Israeli Wars

After ignoring war neuroses for a long time as other armies had done, the Israeli military had to take them into account after the 1973 Yom Kippur and the 1982–1985 Lebanon wars (Z. Solomon, 1989). As in other wars, initially high morale, coping, and successful return to duty were emphasized (e.g., N. A. Milgram, 1986). Next in emphasis were the acute, more fluid, potentially more recoverable war neuroses, this time called combat stress reaction (Z. Solomon, 1989, 1993; Z. Solomon, Laor, & McFarlane, 1996). For Israel, wars are not yet over. Perhaps because of this, demoralizing topics such as frequent and refractory illnesses and actual symptoms of demoralization such as alienation and loss of meaning are not emphasized. Nevertheless, Z. Solomon (1989), for instance, noted that combat stress reactions could lead to PTSD, which could persist for at least 3 years.

Children

Children between the ages of 6 and 16 have been forced into being soldiers and guerrillas (including performing atrocities) in countries like Lebanon and Mozambique. Such children developed combat responses similar to those of adults, including PTSD, but they also developed deep personality disturbances consistent with complex PTSD, such as identification with their captors (Shaw & Harris, 1994; see also chapter 6).

In summary, wartime psychological wounding is frequent and intense in spite of repeated reluctance to accept such facts. Effects of combat stress and trauma are initially widespread and fluid physical, psychological, and social responses that may develop in a continuous or delayed manner into specific traumatic or more orthodox somatic, social, and psychiatric diagnoses. Whether obviously or not, symptoms and illnesses make sense in terms of original traumas and their meanings, which are relived and defended against in a variety of ways. Like war itself, denial and recognition of trauma and subsequent diagnoses may be subject to political forces. The repeated enforced recognition of the high incidence of traumatic illnesses in previously young, healthy soldiers has led to waves of stress and trauma research.

Civilian Wartime Populations

There was initial denial in the Second World War that the bombing affected the British population. It was thought that immersion in the war effort and the cohesive defiant spirit distracted people from their problems. However, statistics to prove this turned out to be artifacts due to decreased mental health facilities. It was not that morale was not important in protecting people against breakdowns, similar to the army. But it was a significant factor only where there was a relatively low proportion of casualties and near miss experiences, such as in London. Those who were actually bombed suffered so-called acute emotional shock akin to combat reactions, and these could develop into chronic syndromes. More widely, war strain was evident through increased incidence of accidents, absenteeism from work, and delinquency (A. Lewis, 1942).

More intense and prolonged bombing that resulted in more destruction and loss of life resulted in proportionately more trauma sequelae. For instance, in both Germany and among allied countries, following a major air raid more than a third of people suffered both acute and permanent psychological effects (Janis, 1951). Concurrently, they suffered increased incidence of a variety of physical illnesses such as digestive disorders (especially peptic ulcers), angina, myocardial infarction, and cerebral hemorrhage.

Following the atomic bombing of Hiroshima, Lifton (1967) found almost universal acute and long-term ill effects up to 16 years after the event. Early effects included psychic numbing and a wide range of psychological symptoms. The later widespread "A-bomb disease" included a wide variety of psychological and physical symptoms.

Prevalence studies confirmed widespread civilian suffering due to bombing and uprooting. In the town of Onitscha during the Biafran Civil War, 48% of respondents were found to be psychiatric cases (Ejiofo-Mbanefo, 1971). In an evacuated Vietnam community during the Vietnam War, the prevalence of psychiatric cases was 65% (Murphy, 1975). Anecdotal evidence has suggested a wide prevalence in the traumatized populations of Bosnia and Rwanda. There were wide-ranging responses to threats of poison gas attacks and Iraqi SCUD missile hits in Israel arising from the Gulf War (Lavee & Ben-David, 1993).

Children Though children's reactions are influenced by those of adults, they have their own traumatic responses, too. In Bristol, England, in the Second World War, bombed children manifested an eightfold increase in apathy, anxiety, and regressive symptoms (Janis, 1951). Similarly, Dyregrov and Raundalen (1992) found that more than two thirds of the children exposed to heavy bombing in Iraq in the Gulf War suffered PTSD and emotional, cognitive, behavioral, and existential problems. For instance, they expected their parents and themselves to die prematurely. Children expressed similar pessimism during peak times during the Cold War.

THE HOLOCAUST

Though the world has been confronted with other genocides in recent times such as in Cambodia, Bosnia, and Rwanda, the Holocaust still stands out as the most total and widespread persecution of a people in history. Reflecting this, the literature in this area (Krell & Sherman, 1997) is a kind of benchmark of the magnitude and intensity of both stressors and sequelae. Of further importance is that the literature spans 50 years among victims of different ages, and down the generations.

During the War

There is little contemporary psychiatric documentation on the effects of the miseries of ghetto life, roundups, and deportations of Jews by the Nazis. Nevertheless, in a rare study Stovkis (1951) described a steep rise in psychiatric illnesses, suicides, hypertension, and angina in the Jews of Amsterdam when they were rounded up to be deported to concentration camps. He noted that some responses, even those that were psychotic, had survival value, as they stopped immediate deportations.

Concentration Camps   On entering concentration camps, people experienced ubiquitous anxiety, shock, closing off, and depression. Of prisoners, 20%–50% just died within weeks. According to Bettelheim (1960), this was not only from the physical conditions, but also from a lack of desire to live.

Over time, many died in such circumstances of starvation and the markedly increased incidence of illnesses. Frankl (1959) and Dimsdale (1974) noted that hope and meaning were essential, though of course not necessarily sufficient, to survive the excruciating conditions. As well as hope, survival required luck, stamina, and every possible strategy and ingenuity (Levi, 1979).

An unusual piece of research concerned the so-called *musselmen* (Ryn, 1990). These people hovered in the area between having given up hope and death. They were emaciated, starved, old-looking people with major cognitive deficits and emotional numbing, except for hunger. They seemed to be silhouettes of people. Their survival reflexes disappeared, and most died. This syndrome seems a level further in the progression from combat exhaustion (chapter 2).

Long-Term Sequelae

Sequelae of the Holocaust were denied for many years, even in Israel (Solomon, 1995). However, they were first registered in the 1960s because of German restitution law requirements. At first, psychological effects were minimized or ascribed to brain damage due to starvation. However, it became clear that there were major psychological sequelae in almost everyone who had been incarcerated in a concentration camp for any amount of time, irrespective of starvation (Bychowski, 1968; Hocking, 1965, 1970; Klein, 1968). After the war, Holocaust survivors suffered excess mortality and morbidity rates over a wide range of biological, psychological, and social illnesses in each postwar decade in comparison to the rest of the population (Eitinger, 1973). This included depression and schizophrenia.

Clinical descriptions followed of what came to be known as the survivor syndrome (Krystal & Niederland, 1968). Its features include anxiety, phobias, expectations of further persecution, hyperalertness, disturbances of sleep, chronic tension and tiredness, startle responses and reliving of experiences, and disturbances of concentration and memory. These symptoms correspond to PTSD. However, other common symptoms are passivity alternating with overwhelming rage and despair, a wide spectrum of depressive responses, survivor guilt, numerous psychosomatic illnesses, and hypochondriasis. The symptoms and illnesses evolved clearly from wartime experiences with variable conscious connections. The survivors often attempted to overcome their losses and symptoms through quick marriages, having children, and continuous work.

However, more important than the symptoms, Holocaust literature is pervaded, as are the survivors themselves, with the suffering and torment of irreconcilable losses and loss of a sense of human meaning and purpose, both in their own lives and in the world. Survivors suffer to the present day, sometimes with unabated symptoms. In fact, there is a tendency toward a resurgence of symptoms in aged persons as they develop illnesses and face death again. This time, building families and work are not available to them, and their aging brains may further erode their characteristic defenses.

Children

Nine tenths (1.5 million) of Jewish children were annihilated in the Holocaust. The survivors were not recognized until quite recently, in spite of having been the most vulnerable of the Holocaust victims. A more extensive review of the following is published elsewhere (Valent, in press, b).

During the War   Children were not spared any adult suffering. They carried the added burdens of not understanding situations, not being able to make decisions, being dependent on adults, and suffering separations from parents. Very few survived concentration camps. However, in a rare family camp they were noted to manifest irritability, anxiety, bedwetting, and aggression (Tas, 1951). Many children survived in hiding. In all situations, their survival was helped by numbing their feelings, supreme obedience, living day by day, and hoping for the future.

Long-term Sequelae   In some early studies, concentration camp child survivors were noted to have psychosomatic and personality disorders (Krystal, 1971). Later studies indicated that throughout their lives child survivors suffered a great variety of symptoms and illnesses similar to adult survivors. Even if outwardly they seemed to be well, their Holocaust experiences pervaded these survivors' lives (Dwork, 1991; Valent, 1994; 1995a). Memories were important in the organization of later suffering. Those over 7 years of age during the Holocaust had clear memories, and their later disorders resembled those of adults. Younger children tended to relive their traumas through emotions and physical and behavioral manifestations. The lack of memory or only fragmentary memory helped their acquiescence to parental views that they had not suffered and should be well.

It was often not till their 50s that many child survivors recognized themselves as actual survivors. This was a time to integrate their lives. However, to do so they needed to find out objective information about their earlier experiences; retrieve their memories; reconstitute traumatic events, including their meanings and feelings; and finally achieve new views on themselves and their lives (Valent, 1994; 1995a). The nature of survivors' memories and tasks necessary to reintegrate meaningful lives were very similar to that of survivors of childhood sexual abuse (Valent, 1995a; see also chapter 1; Valent, in press, a).

Second-Generation Survivors   Following Helen Epstein's (1979) pioneering book *Children of the Holocaust,* much literature (e.g., Bergmann & Jucovy, 1982) has described the unique problems of second-generation Holocaust children. Although they did not have any direct memories of the Holocaust, they were nevertheless greatly influenced by it. These children grew up with idiosyncratic emotions, roles, world views, and symptoms whose sources they could not identify and that they therefore seemed to carry for no rational reason. They were also otherwise enmeshed with their parents, who were, for instance, excessively concerned about their children's survival. The children also sensed their parents' fragility and protected them, for instance, against normal adolescent rebellions and separations. In complex ways, children often enacted contradictory parental desires, for instance, to counteract the Holocaust, while living out various roles and missions from within it.

Nazi Perpetrators and Their Children   There have been few, but very important, studies on Nazi perpetrators (Arendt, 1963; Browning, 1992; Goldhagen, 1996; Lifton, 1986; Staub, 1989). These books alerted people to the possibility of the escalation of evil in ordinary men in circumstances of fear, deprivation, group pressure, dehumanization and opportunism. This concurs with examination of Vietnam atrocities (chapter 12).

The literature on second-generation perpetrators (Posner, 1991; Sichrovsky, 1988) has indicated that they have surprising similarities to second-generation Holocaust survivors. Both groups had difficulties in integrating and making meaning of their parents and themselves.

Other *in Extremis* Situations

Some traumatic situations overlapped significantly with the Holocaust and exhibited similar sequelae. For instance, survivors of Japanese prisoner-of-war camps in World War Two also suffered from survivor syndrome and had higher than control mortality and morbidity rates for a variety of illnesses over the decades (Beebe, 1975; Goulston et al., 1985). Similarly, child survivors of the Cambodian genocide have been shown to suffer PTSD and other widespread symptoms for more than 10 years, in proportion to the severity of their earlier traumas (Realmuto et al., 1992).

In summary, the Holocaust was consistent with and extended other wartime data. Thus, the Holocaust literature indicated that all can be affected by extreme stressors and that trauma sequelae can continue for 50 years to death, though some symptoms and illnesses may be delayed in their onset even for decades. Similarly, even the most extreme traumatic sequelae can be unrecognized and denied indefinitely.

The development of sequelae over decades was described in Case 3 (see chapter 1). The Holocaust literature confirmed and highlighted the potential for widespread presence of illnesses over decades following extreme stress, and the suffering over existential and spiritual issues. It was confirmed that children were hampered by their added vulnerability and later by their continued defenses and lack of memories. Some wartime sequelae were extended to a different order. As well, parental traumas could be transferred in complex ways to the next generation.

The extreme Holocaust circumstances extended acute emotional shock, psychic numbing and exhaustion noted in soldiers to dying of "shock," "giving up," and musselmen manifestations. To survive, one needed luck, flexible use of every survival strategy and defense, suppression of emotion, yet hope of reconstituted love.

NATURAL DISASTERS

In contrast to previous situations, disasters are single, short-lived events that affect only circumscribed populations and are not results of human violence. Perhaps for these reasons, disasters are the most recognized of traumatic situations. Help pours in quickly, even from around the world. Even so, sustained sequelae tend to be denied. The disaster literature has highlighted proportionate sequelae to intensity of stressors, observed evolution of sequelae, the concept of phases of traumatic situations, and helper (secondary) traumatic stress.

Proportionate Nature of Responses

As in previous traumatic situations, the intensity of stressors determines subsequent sequelae. In the 1968 Bristol floods in England, those in the same street who were flooded, as compared with those who were not, had 50% greater rates of psychiatric symptoms, general hospital referrals and admissions, and mortality due to heart disease and cancer (Bennet, 1970). Weisaeth (1985, 1994) found that the degree of exposure in an industrial fire was highly correlated with acute and long-term development of PTSD. In disasters where a significant proportion of the population is killed, 80% or more of survivors may suffer traumatic syndromes and significant somatic disorders over the ensuing years (Leopold & Dillon, 1963; Titchener & Kapp, 1976).

Nature of Responses

As already noted in the introduction and for previous traumatic situations, one stream concentrates on phenomenological diagnoses. The main current one is PTSD, though the frequency of other diagnoses, especially major depression, is increasingly acknowledged (McFarlane & Papay, 1992).

The second stream already started with the first modern literature on disasters. In the Cocoanut Grove nightclub fire in which 450 patrons were killed, Cobb and Lindemann (1943) and Lindemann (1944) described wide-ranging symptoms in the acute phase. They included confusions, delirium, psychotic reactions, sighing, choking, and apathy. In the later phases, some of these symptoms often developed into grief or depression. Although intrusive memories and fears of fires and cues reminiscent of them were prominent, so were conflicts from the situation and difficult personal meanings. Activity was used as a defense against mental pain.

Titchener and Kapp (1976) noted following a major disaster long-term psychic numbing, survivor guilt, unresolved grief, survivor shame, impotent rage, hopelessness, alienation, and struggle for significance and meaning. These resembled responses described earlier for previous extreme traumatic situations. Wolfenstein (1977) and Raphael (1986) described a wide variety of individual symptoms (chapter 1). Valent (1984; see also chapter 1) organized a great variety of responses according to their biological, psychological, and social aspects and disaster phases. He also foreshadowed that responses belonged to specific survival strategies. As well, symptoms and illnesses evolved according to whether memories of events and their meanings were relived, processed, or defended against (chapter 3).

Children   Responses and illnesses in children, especially older ones, often paralleled those of adults. Older children could even reverse rescue roles with adults (Valent, 1984). PTSD-type intrusive images and startle responses were estimated to occur in between 30% (D. A. Bloch, Silber & Perry, 1956; Silber, Perry, & Bloch, 1957) and 60% (Frederick, 1984) of children. Valent (1984) noted a wide variety of responses in children akin to those of adults but strongly influenced by adult responses and protectiveness. Intense distress in children may be often masked by disturbed and overprotective parents (Yule & Williams, 1990). Children's developmental phases influenced their response. Also children suffered anxiety and phobic states and child-sepcific symptoms such as as playing disaster games, regressing, being clingy, and wetting the bed.

Disaster Phases

Glass (1959) introduced the concept of disaster phases, each with its own typical responses. For instance, in the impact phase Glass estimated that about 15% of the population reacted appropriately and a similar proportion responded quite inappropriately. The rest were tense and anxious, suggestible, and docile. The recoil phase included the disaster syndrome. Its features were being stunned, dazed, apathetic, and bewildered, reminiscent of responses on entering concentration camps. The postimpact phase included what came to be called postdisaster euphoria, a sense of joy at having survived, and excess hope. Recovery and reconstruction phases included anger at authorities, hard work to rebuild, and integration. Though the phases should not be taken too literally, disaster literature had highlighted the different culture of responses, depending on the survival challenges at different times. These were described in more detail in the introductory cases.

Secondary Traumatic Stress

Secondary traumatic stress and compassion fatigue (chapter 8) are the inevitable sequelae of empathic caring (Figley, 1995a, 1995b). Secondary traumatic stress may occur in families and friends of victims, but has been most researched in helpers. In an early study, Berah, Jones & Valent (1984) found that team members who helped in a bush fire suffered shock, fatigue, sleep disturbances, restlessness, physical symptoms, colds and flus, accidents, and changes in drinking and smoking habits. In severe cases, helpers may suffer secondary traumatic stress disorder, paralleling PTSD in victims. Valent (1995b) suggested that specific secondary traumatic stress sequelae could be understood in terms of identification with, or responses to, victims' survival strategies. The widespread occurrence of secondary traumatic stress in helpers led to almost routine preventive debrief procedures among them (R. C. Robinson & Mitchell, 1993; Valent, in press, a).

Last, it must be noted that a sociological stream in disaster literature sees psychological ill effects as artifacts manufactured by pathology-minded helpers (Quarantelli, 1985). This view sees disaster communities as basically healthy and resilient sponges that absorb disasters by reshaping themselves. However, although adaptive social system responses are important, so are individual maladaptive ones. Further, the bias against pathology ignores the fact that even sponges can be torn. The above views have retarded examination of posttraumatic social disorders.

In summary, disasters have allowed a more "leisurely" in vivo examination of previously described responses. This allowed a provisional formulation of specific responses having survival value. Their evolution across time and person was also noted.

ACCIDENTS

More than 100,000 people die in motor accidents in the United States annually, and there are millions of disabilities and tens of billions of dollars in annual cost. More Americans are affected by accidents than natural disasters and wars put together (Malt, 1994; Mattsson, 1975). Yet the history of this literature is not so much examination of accident sequelae but of legal wrangles about whether psychological sequelae are "real" and therefore compensable. Indeed, the accident literature has highlighted prejudices against traumatized victims. Another contribution has been the examination of perpetrators.

Controversies and Prejudices

Since the Prussian government offered compensation to victims of railway accidents in 1871, legally sanctioned prejudice has arisen against those presenting with symptoms following accidents. Nevertheless, neurotic symptoms after accidents were first described by Erichsen in 1866, 5 years before the first compensation laws (Mendelson, 1988; Parker, 1977).

The term *traumatic neurosis* was first coined for postaccident symptoms by Oppenheim in 1889. Both Erichsen and he believed that the symptoms were caused by spinal concussion or molecular disturbances of neurons in the spine. This stream of thinking continued over the decades, for instance, in the formulation of a postconcussion syndrome (Bennett, 1969). Like shell shock, these labels indicated a medical organic bias. Thus, if there were any real symptoms at all, they had to be neurological.

For the rest, a string of pejorative diagnoses indicated views on posttraumatic symptoms. The diagnoses included compensation neurosis, first used by Rigler in 1879. Railway spine was also knowingly used at the time as a means for victims to obtain money. Unconscious malingering and profit neurosis followed, among many others (Mendelson, 1988).

Miller's (1961) categorical statement that all neurologically unsubstantiated symptoms were financially motivated and resolved after compensation carried much weight for decades in Britain and Australia. Yet apart from doubtful statistics, Miller's own clinical descriptions exposed his prejudice. He denied the validity of all nonneurological symptoms such as dizziness and nightmares relating to the accident, and he claimed that asking for a glass of water during the interview was pathognomonic of malingering. He ignored the fact that most compensation seekers returned to work before their court cases. Certainly, subsequent studies have disproved the "cured by verdict" supposition (Mendelson, 1988). Nevertheless, to the present day quasi-diagnoses such as secondary gain are used to diagnose symptoms suspected to be motivated by financial gain. The diagnosis is a corruption of conversion hysteria, in which primary gain and the symbolism of the symptom are important clues to major hidden distress.

Nature of Responses

Clinical descriptions of postaccident symptoms were sparse over the decades of this century. Parker (1977) described wide-ranging nonspecific symptoms following accidents. Reminiscent of army psychiatry, Lishman (1973) concluded that every psychiatric symptom and diagnosis could occur after accidents. More recently, Malt (1994) found the same in the first few days in about half his sample. In the longer term, PTSD occurs in only 1%–15% of cases (Horne, 1993; Lundin, 1995; Malt, 1994; Mendelson, 1988). More common are psychosomatic and guilt sequelae and a variety of diagnoses such as adjustment, anxiety, depression, and psychogenic pain disorders.

Children have been noted to manifest problems in sleep, separation, concentration, memory, having a sense of a shortened future, and PTSD symptoms.

Perpetrators and Victims of Traffic Incidents

Traffic incidents may have quite different meanings for victims and those who cause them. The word *incident* is used instead of *accident,* which forecloses on the dynamics of the event. For instance, desired crashes may not be traumatic.

Among causers of incidents, a significant proportion, though not a majority, has been consistently shown to be young, alcohol-affected men, especially those with sociopathic personalities. Though alcohol has been prominently featured as cause of incidents, Donovan, Marlatt, and Salzburg (1983) have shown that it adds little to accident predictability over personality, stress, and emotions, which seemed to be the primary determinants. With regard to stress, M. R. Weinstein (1968) and Hirschfeld and Behan (1969) showed that accidents could serve as means of resolving relational stresses and unacceptable emotions, especially in people who could not think through their conflicts. In addition, Chan (1987) found emotions immediately before incidents to be important. Such emotions were frustration, hurt, anger, fear, anxiety, inadequacy, and depression. In addition, Isherwood, Adam, and Horn-blow (1982) found that, though not formally depressed, 10% of incident victims in an emergency room had preceding suicidal intentions. Symptoms could be maintained postincident as continued means of resolving conflicts and emotions. Incidents and subsequent symptoms could thus serve primary gains. All these factors combined may explain the relatively low incidence of postincident PTSD and the relative importance of premorbid personality over threat of death in subsequent outcomes (Malt, 1994).

Valent (1993) teased out further victim and perpetrator incident aspects and sequelae. He separated 65 consecutive referred patients into two groups, 40 victims and 25 perpetrators. Of the victims, 8 (12%) cases satisfied PTSD criteria, and 12 (19%) suffered typical posttraumatic symptoms. These 20 cases consisted of half the victims. For the other 20 victims (31% of cases), the incident reopened past vulnerabilities such as childhood physical illnesses. These patients suffered a variety of mood and somatoform disorders colored by their past vulnerabilities.

Of the perpetrators, 8 (12%) of patients were the classical young, male, antisocial alcoholics who drank before the incident in order to resolve current stresses. In the other 17 incidents (26% of cases) incidents served as a means of resolving major life stresses. Together, the causers of incidents suffered significantly more major recent stresses, such as bereavements and relationship disruptions, than had victims. The incident could attempt to force the return of a partner, exact revenge, or be a way to join the dead. The emotions just before the incidents were anger, revenge, depression, desire to evoke pity and care, and anxiety.

Some perpetrators had had previous recent incidents. Across the two groups, 18 (28%) of cases had a family history of serious incidents, including deaths. In half (mainly perpetrators), the current incident was linked to the family incident through identification. For a few families, incidents were almost a way of communicating anger and distress. Though this was a clinical, not a prevalence, study, it indicated the need to keep in mind various categories of both victims and causers and the potentially complex dynamics in what are called accidents.

In summary, legal wrangles over financial compensation and prejudices distracted from examining and treating "accident" victims and perpetrators. Once noted, of true victims, about half suffered the acute and later trauma sequelae noted in previous groups. However, many symptoms could be explained by the incidents' uncovering past vulnerabilities. Perpetrators did not suffer similarly, for incidents could achieve for them expression of emotions and primary gains. Yet they were also victims of their griefs, emotions, and inability to deal with their stresses adaptively.

PHYSICAL ASSAULT, RAPE, AND TORTURE

Willful violent attacks on one's body by others carries high risk and virulence, especially if the damage is inflicted by those one knows, trusts, and depends on. Therefore, as well as PTSD and other symptoms, the literature has emphasized relational and existential sequelae.

The prevalence of the problem became evident in the early 1980s. Millions of people annually noted to be were victims of violent crime in the United States. Of college women, 15.4% had experienced legally defined rape (Hartman & Burgess, 1988). Two million cases of child abuse and neglect were reported, and 3.3 million children witnessed spouse abuse annually (Pynoos & Nader,

1990). The prevalence of political torture had also been exposed as unexpectedly high (McFarlane & de Girolamo, 1996).

Nature of Responses to Personal Violence and Kidnappings

Personal violence and kidnappings may lead to PTSD and a wide range of symptoms, including depression as well as survivor guilt and diminished self-esteem (Kleinman, 1989; Ochberg, 1988). Similarly, battered women suffer PTSD as well as severely affected core beliefs about safety and trust of others and self (Dutton, Burghardt, Perrin, Chrestman, & Halle, 1994).

Particularly unfortunate is stigmatization of victims and, even worse, victims' frequent own self-blame. Though objectively wrong, both allow some coherence of cause and effect and a sense of a moral universe (Holloway & Fullerton, 1994). But for the victim who deep down knows the truth, violence shatters core assumptions of invulnerability, a benevolent meaningful world as well as a worthwhile self (Janoff-Bulman, 1988).

Nature of Responses to Rape

Associated with the rise of feminism came a redefinition of rape. From a sexual act with a range of collaboration, it came to be seen as a violent act in which women feared for their lives. Not unlike combat soldiers, they develop flashbacks and nightmares (Burgess & Holstrom, 1974), and, indeed, rape trauma syndrome was an original contributor to PTSD in *DSM–III*.

However, rape on top of violence is especially virulent because it shatters sexual associations of fulfillment, intimacy, love, and creativity. As well as PTSD, victims suffer existential problems of trust, betrayal, shame, worth, and identity, especially as women (Hartman & Burgess, 1988). Rape victims have also been much blamed and stigmatized. They may also blame themselves and feel like "dirty sluts" (Lebowitz & Roth, 1994).

Nature of Responses to Political Torture

Political torture is especially pernicious as it is a willfully inflicted and cynically engineered assault to achieve political domination and intimidation. It has reached such sophistication that it could produce PTSD and break anyone. In one study, almost all prisoners in an Irish prison developed delusions, hallucinations, depression, PTSD symptoms, and psychosomatic illnesses such as peptic ulcer soon after imprisonment (Watson, 1980). As well, through techniques of terrorization, subjugation, defilement, sexual torture, and rape, torture willfully induces shame and self-blame and undermines the core of victims' and society's identity and values (Ochberg, 1989).

Long-term effects include PTSD as well as a variety of cognitive and somatic symptoms, major depressions, despair, and sexual and relationship problems. Survivors live in a "joyless world in which [there is] little personal meaning and fulfillment" (Turner & Gorst-Unsworth, 1990, p. 478).

Children

Physically abused and kidnapped children, especially older ones, manifest responses akin to adults, including PTSD symptoms and wider consequences (Green, 1985; Terr, 1983, 1990, 1991). In the impact phase, children are vigilant and in a state of frozen watchfulness like adults could be. However, they can act almost normally because they can numb, split, and deny their terror, helplessness, and rage. Later, the traumas come to permeate the dreams, fantasies, and relationships of the children. They can experience shame, guilt, and unresolved grief like adults.

However, children's responses are also influenced by their developmental phases. These result in misappraisals and misinterpretations, including time distortions and even hallucinations. Age-appropriate fantasies could be added to the events; for instance, young boys tend to have fantasies of revenge. Unlike adults, younger children have fewer flashbacks and repetitive dreams, and children under 2 have no reliable memories or dreams. However, they can still depict parts of their traumas in play and drawing and physical symptoms. Children also tend to exhibit developmental regression and see their futures as more foreshortened than adults. Last, repetitive and severe traumas result in massive use of dissociation, denial, self-anesthesia, and other defenses. Subsequent memories are less clear, and symptoms are more severe and varied. These responses were consistent with those found in children in disasters and in the Holocaust.

In summary, the literature on personal violence forces one to recognize the virulence of human-induced trauma and its social and political aspects. Violence, torture, rape, and child abuse violate basic expectations, identity, and values. They may be especially perverse when violence is perpetrated by those on whom victims rely for protection and justice. This is shown to be even more salient in the following group.

SEXUAL ASSAULT OF CHILDREN AND INCEST

Though sexual abuse of children overlaps with their physical abuse, it is examined separately because it has been seminal in trauma literature and has lately been seen as contributing to many psychiatric diagnoses. Further, sexual abuse of children and combat sequelae in adults may be seen as the two ends of the see-saw of trauma literature and conceptualization. Research on combat trauma led to adult phenomenological PTSD-type conceptualizations. Research on childhood sexual abuse examined numerous widespread sequelae and spawned the birth of psychoanalysis.

Sexual abuse of children is also marked by waves of discovery and massive denial. Although this is common in other situations, such as combat, some of the psychodynamics of the denial may be accessible through the example of Freud himself, who both discovered and suppressed knowledge of the sexual abuse of children. Freud's dual contribution is examined in relative detail below because it demonstrates individual denial and its potential influence on institutional denial.

Waves of Recognition and Denial of Childhood Sexual Abuse

The first wave of recognition of the frequency of child sexual abuse started in the 1860s in France. The government pathologist Tardieu concluded from postmortems that there was widespread sexual abuse of children in that country. Bernard confirmed that there were 36,000 reported sexual assaults and rapes of children in France over 40 years (Masson, 1940).

Freud and the Second Wave of Recognition

Freud was introduced to traumatic neuroses and hysteria (in current terms, conversion hysteria and borderline personality disorders) by the famous neurologist Charcot (Freud, 1886/1975n). Freud added that with careful listening, hysterics revealed that their trauma was childhood sexual abuse. On the basis of 18 cases (12 women and 6 men), Freud (1896/1975b, p. 203) stated unequivocally in *The Etiology of Hysteria* that the "determining factors . . . of hysteria are *one or more occurrences of premature sexual experience* . . . in the earliest years of childhood." These sexual experiences were "stimulation of the genitals, and coitus-like acts" (p. 206). In two cases, Freud had outside corroboration of the events. Two cases involved father–daughter incest (Freud, 1893/1975p, pp. 134, 170). In arguing for the truthfulness of his patients' stories, Freud noted that they derived only pain and no pleasure from the telling. They came to remember the events during treatment with reluctance and shame. Further, in the process they suffered both the original distress and their later symptoms.

Freud was not a stranger to hysteria in his own family. In his letter to Fliess of September 1897 (Freud, 1897/1975a), though already recanting his theory Freud noted, in reference to hysteria in his sisters, that he had believed that in "every case the father, not excluding my own, had to be blamed as a pervert" (p. 259). Freud himself suffered hysterical symptoms throughout his life (Schur, 1972), and he relied on Fliess, his confidante–psychoanalyst to reassure him that they were due to sinusitis. Fliess, a possible molester of his own son (Masson, 1984) had idiosyncratic theories of the cause of hysteria being located in the nose.

Freud himself may have had precocious sexual experiences in the context of an unusual family background and multiple deaths in the family (including Freud's younger brother) in Freud's first 2 years of life. During this time, Freud was cared for by a nursemaid, who might well have sexually abused him (Reder,

1989). At this time, too, Freud might have witnessed his mother commit adultery with his brother (a son from his father's previous marriage), who was his mother's age (Krull, 1987).

Soon after Freud had formulated his sexual trauma theory of hysteria, he suffered two traumas. The first was witnessing the near death from a nosebleed of his first patient, Emma Eckstein. Worse, the bleed was obviously due to Fliess's incompetence. Having operated on her nose, supposedly to cure symptoms resulting from early masturbation, Fliess left masses of gauze in her nose. Freud described fully his traumatic state when he witnessed this (Masson, 1984). The second trauma was Freud's father's death at a time when Freud was troubled by his suspiciousness of his father and his own incestuous wishes toward his daughter (Rush, 1977). Freud was threatened with the loss of two fathers and extreme disillusionment in fathers, including himself.

There is a clear description of how Freud increasingly repressed and rationalized the trauma with Fliess, exonerating him and blaming the local doctors instead (Schur, 1972). At the same time, he repressed the notion of fathers abusing their children. Blame was shifted from adult sexual perversity to child sexual perversity. Children's constitution was polymorphously perverse (Freud, 1905/1975q). Hysterical symptoms came to be products of patients' early masturbatory fantasies (1906/1975o). The Oedipal conflict, in which the child desired the parent sexually, became central. For instance, in the case of Schreber, Freud (1911/1975d) deliberately did not look at the historical father who had published a book in which he advocated what could only be seen as instruments of torture to treat children's behavior problems; rather, he analyzed the son's delusions of his father's persecution on the basis of the son's Oedipal complex.

It may be said that having repressed his traumas, Freud reenacted them. He abused his own child, psychoanalysis, by repressing its creative life force. It is only in recent times that psychoanalysis is refinding the importance of trauma.

As a codicil, Freud suppressed recognition of the importance of trauma in the nonsexual traumatic neuroses after suffering a number of bereavements, including the death of his favorite daughter, Sophie. Three weeks after this death he first used the term *death instinct* (Freud 1920/1975c; Reder, 1989). Rather than adults mourning the traumas of loss (perhaps compounded with those in early life as with Freud), once again the child's constitution was blamed, this time as the carrier of death.

The *third wave* in the post–World War Two decades was relatively silent, consisting of five studies, including the Kinsey Report. The studies consistently found that one fifth to one third of ordinary women had had a sexual encounter with a male in childhood. Four percent to 12% were with a relative and 1% were with father or stepfather (Herman, 1981, 1992).

In the current *fourth wave* of recognition, these figures have been vindicated (Finkelhor, 1986; Russell, 1986; Herman, 1992). For instance, Russell (1986) reported that among 930 college women, 16% had been sexually abused by a relative before the age of 18. If extrafamilial abuse was added, the figure rose to 38%. Of those abused within the family, 10% reached sexual inter-course, and another 10% had attempted it. Forty-two had been sexually abused by their fathers. Half the biological fathers had sexual contact only once, though a quarter perpetrated severe abuse. Stepfathers were more frequently forcible perpetrators.

Long-Term Sequelae

The damage of sexual abuse goes deep and wide. Herman (1981) noted that 37.5% of father–daughter incest victims had attempted suicide, 60% had suf-fered major depressive symptoms, 35% had abused drugs or alcohol, and most had sexual problems manifesting in adolescent pregnancy, promiscuity, subse-quent rape, and homosexuality. The closer the relative and the earlier, more severe, and more prolonged the abuse, the worse the outcome. Herman (1992) noted that later manifestations of such abuse are misdiagnosed under various psychiatric labels, and yet, if asked, 40%–60% of psychiatric inpatients and outpatients report childhood physical or sexual abuse or both.

Yet neither statistics nor diagnoses can convey the wide variety of symp-toms described by Freud, or exemplified by Anne in the preceding chapter. Sequelae of childhood sexual abuse are even a step further than those of other violations in their pervasiveness and attack on the person. Further, the victim feels guilt and shame as a whore, someone worthless, betrayed, and unlovable. She feels isolated, unable to trust or be intimate, and expects further abuse. Ordinary aspects of morality, fairness and justice, and general human expecta-tions are perverted. Herman (1992) suggested that PTSD could not describe these complex emotional and existential sequelae. She suggested that they be gathered under the term *complex traumatic stress disorder,* which is described in more detail in chapter 6.

Perpetrators

Masson (1984) noted how already in the last century Bernard described of-fenders as often educated, mature men. Herman (1981) also described incestu-ous fathers as outwardly conventional, competent and even admirable, and meek and ingratiating to outside authority. However, inside the family they are very dominant and controlling, especially of the females, and often use physical force to maintain their positions. The fathers themselves have often been deprived and abused in their childhoods. They are often undergoing stresses at the time of incest. They see their daughters as sources of fulfilment of all their infantile longings and privations. Force and dominance give them a sense of power over this resource. The mothers are often ineffective and often psychiatrically dis-abled. They are treated with contempt, and the daughters often replace them as "little mothers."

In summary, childhood sexual abuse is more noxious and pervasive than other traumas because it may occur from an early age for long periods, the perpetrators are the child's natural protectors, and the trauma deeply perverts basic morality and values and corrodes all avenues of love and fulfillment. Childhood sexual abuse indicates the extent to which trauma may be suppressed and repressed and even perversely reenacted, often on a new generation of victims. The example of Freud indicates the potential psychodynamics of such repression based on unprocessed personal traumas and guilt. Repression may be institutionalized, and victims may be blamed. In the past, hysterics were burnt.

PSYCHOSOMATIC MEDICINE

The psychosomatic literature highlights the noxiousness and cumulative effects of "everyday" stressors and their physical, as well as psychiatric expressions. All the cases in the introduction manifested stress-related physical symptoms or illnesses. Case 2 highlighted delayed and symbolic expression of trauma in the body.

Hippocrates, the founder of scientific medicine, had already noted the connection between stressors and illnesses. He wrote, "It is changes that are chiefly responsible for diseases, especially the greatest changes, the violent alterations" (Dubos, 1968, p. 67). The incidence of stress-related physical illnesses is very high, with many estimating them to involve over half of physician attendances (e.g., Folks & Kinney, 1992). Nevertheless, medicine has also had waves of recognition and denial of psychosocial stressors as precursors to medical illnesses.

Once biopsychosocial medicine (Engel, 1977) is acknowledged, it is seen that almost no symptoms or illnesses are free of psychosocial input. Arguments over the decades have been around whether the input is general or specific or a result of a variety of inputs into a system (Stoudemire & Hales, 1995).

General Stress Effects

Around the middle of this century, it became clear that a variety of stressors led to physical illnesses. Further, the number and severity of such stressors (physical, psychological, or social) highly correlated with the number and severity of physical, psychological, and social illnesses (Thurlow, 1967). Holmes and Rahe (1967) quantified psychosocial stressors in order of virulence. Death of a spouse rated 100; marital separation, 65; taking on a small mortgage, 17; and so forth. The higher the aggregate score, the more, and more severe, the illnesses that followed. The generalist epidemiological approach has maintained its validity. For instance, there are very significant increases in mortality and morbidity rates due to various illnesses among widows and widowers compared with controls (Parkes, 1972; Parkes & Weiss, 1983).

In line with the generalist approach, Selye (1936) postulated that there was one general physiological response in stress, the general adaptation syndrome (chapter 7). He postulated that its activity, together with local vulnerabilities, leads to a great variety of illnesses.

Specificity Studies

As against Selye (1936), Alexander (1950) held that specific emotions have specific physiological correlates. Their overactivity, along with specific physical vulnerabilities, leads to specific psychosomatic illnesses. For instance, rates of peptic ulcer in army inductees were successfully predicted according to the intensity of dependency emotions and pepsinogen levels (physiological vulnerability; Weiner et al., 1959). Other specific emotions have been associated with certain illnesses. For a long time, an association was noted between Type A (driving, time-urgent) personality and coronary artery disease (Friedman & Rosenman, 1959). However, the emotion of sustained unexpressed hostility was honed out of this personality as more predictive of the illness (Goldstein & Niaura, 1992). Schmale (1972) noted hopelessness and helplessness as precursors to cancer and other illnesses, and Grossarth-Maticek, Kanazir, Schmidt, and Vetter (1982) found suppressed crying when feeling abandoned to be a predictor of cancer. However, many suggestive connections between particular stressors and illnesses are hampered by inexact research concepts and tools (Stoudemire & Hales, 1995).

It has been counterintuitive to modern science that nonphysical psychosocial events could lead to physical pathology. And yet such events evoke, very sensitively, responses in the autonomic, endocrine, immune, neurotransmitter, and neuromodulator systems (Cohen, 1981). Emotions may be the intermediaries between stressors and physiological pathology. For instance, suppressed hostility may then lead to overactive sympathetic nervous system activity, which predisposes one to coronary artery disease (Goldstein & Niaura, 1992, 1995). Depression as can occur after bereavements may lead to suppression of immune system components, which in turn may contribute to development of infections and cancers.

Other emotion-evoked physiological overactivity may contribute to many symptoms such as dyspepsia, heartburn, dizziness, tiredness, palpitations, muscle pains, and so forth. Such symptoms often parade under organic quasi-diagnoses. In the digestive system, examples are esophagcal motility, hyperacidity, and irritable bowel syndrome.

In summary, psychosomatic medicine highlights a wide variety of physical sequelae of stress and trauma outside PTSD. It also brings to notice that everyday stressors can nevertheless threaten life, and can do so cumulatively and with delays. The challenge is to conceptualize the different ways illnesses may be manifestations of physiological overactivity, effects of general arousal on vulnerable organs, more specific attacks on particular organs, as well as conversion symptoms or symbols of conflicts. There is a great need to find both overarching concepts and more specific means of connecting stressors and illnesses. It is suggested that the wholist framework contributes to meeting this need.

DYING AND BEREAVEMENT

Although everyone needs to face death, scientific examination of bereavement and incipient dying (thanatology) is only a recently established science. The literature highlights a wide variety of sequelae in relation to death and dying. It also highlights that even though traumatic stress may be defined by threat of death, what is really threatening is its contextual purposelessness.

Responses to Bereavement and Incipient Death

Descriptions of bereavement and loss include sadness, grief, mourning, and depression. These states may occur in overlapping phases (Bowlby, 1981; Parkes, 1972; Raphael, 1984; see also chapter 11, Adaptation: Goal Surrender). Initially, there is shock and denial reminiscent of the impact phase of disasters. This is followed by pining, yearning and searching for the lost person, then anger, anxiety, shame, blows to self-image and dignity; then grief and depression; and eventually, one hopes, acceptance and a new meaning in life (Marris, 1991). These responses apply to other losses, too, such as those of body parts (Krueger, 1984). Valent (1980) distinguished biological, psychological, and social responses as well as defenses across the phases of mourning.

Losses (ultimately of one's own life) that are not expected or according to the life cycle; that are massive and mutilating; meaningless; and purposeless; absurd deaths without honor, morality, point, or rounding out constitute some of the core visions of trauma (chapter 1). Such traumatic losses are difficult to grieve and lead to chronic, pathological, and unresolved grief, depression, and a variety of other illnesses (chapter 9). A variety of losses constitute many of the everyday stressors that are followed by illnesses (chapter 2).

Kübler-Ross (1969) broke a taboo by talking to dying patients about their dying. She found that they passed through phases similar to those of normal bereavement. This applied to concerns affecting the rest of their lives. This included striving to achieve a meaningful death.

Similarly, Valent (1978) found that it was not death itself that was feared but traumatic drawn-out painful illness, loss of faculties, incontinence, dependency, loss of dignity, helplessness, and loneliness. Such states resembled earlier traumatic situations such as childhood helplessness and abandonment, and they prevented a meaningful and wholesome death (Valent, 1979).

Children

Though a child's death is severely traumatic to parents, children have the capacity to adjust to their shortened life cycles through dying processes similar to those of adults, but they are also beholden to parental responses and needs. With adequate support, children are capable of creating purposeful meanings out of their dying and to achieve individual constructions of universality and immortality. As with adults, they can use secular, magical, or religious views. For instance, some may see themselves helping science to help other children. Others may see themselves joining previously deceased friends or pets or preparing the way for their parents who will later join them.

In summary, bereavement and dying are major challenges requiring huge readjustments in life. Failures in adaptation lead to varieties of symptoms and illnesses. Dying patients highlight the overriding importance of purpose and meaning in life. Traumatic deaths and losses without such meanings negate not only physical life but everything of human value.

LESSONS FROM ACROSS DIFFERENT TRAUMATIC SITUATIONS

In this chapter, the three traumatic situations described in the introduction (bush fire, death of a child, child in the Holocaust) were put in context within eight major traumatic situations from the stress and trauma literature.

Different traumatic situations highlighted different aspects of trauma. For instance, combat psychiatry emphasized trauma in adults whose memories allow cognitive reliving and avoidance of known traumas. Research on childhood sexual abuse has emphasized childhood trauma, and unclear and unconscious relivings in emotional, physical, and action fragments, rather than clear reliving of specific events.

Psychosomatic medicine highlighted the somatic aspects of stresses and traumas. Disasters drew attention to disaster phases and secondary victims. The Holocaust drew attention to transgenerational effects. The Holocaust, violence, torture, and sexual abuse highlighted the pervasiveness and depth of trauma sequelae over long times. They also highlighted the social and political dimensions of personal traumas.

The historically fragmented recognition of trauma in different traumatic situations may reflect the fragmentation of trauma generally and in individuals. Each fragment seems to be "it," "the" problem. Yet each fragment highlights only part of the problem, the whole being too overwhelming. And yet there is gradual assimilation of the whole.

Thus, common themes emerge across traumatic situations. For instance, each situation tended to be denied and victims were blamed. Initial recognition was frequently through physical symptoms. With full recognition, each traumatic situation was eventually seen to manifest acute and long-term biological, psychological, and social stress responses, symptoms, and illnesses. Acute responses tended to be a passing parade of a wide variety of symptoms. These gelled not only into PTSD, but into many other symptoms and diagnoses.

In some traumatic situations, it was observed that children's responses resembled those of adults. However, children's greater vulnerability, poorer ego development, and dependence on adults led to proportionately more diverse and deep effects whose origins were later often not obvious. Within some traumatic situations, perpetrators were often noted to have been abused themselves and were stressed when causing traumas. Some traumatic situations highlighted treaters subject to secondary stress effects, as well as personal and political pressures in their conceptualizations and treatments.

In summary, as with the individuals, the literature from traumatic situations indicates the magnitude and complexity of stress and trauma effects, ranging from threats to survival to existential meanings. The latter may be more important than symptoms, or even life. Responses have been described in wide-ranging, often conflicting varieties, as well as in diagnostic clusters. Both types of organization are examined more closely in chapter 6.

The next three chapters of Part 2 examine concepts common to all traumatic situations. This is done in the context of the triaxial framework, which orientates the concepts within the field of traumatology.

Part Two

The Triaxial Framework: The Process, Parameters, and Depth Axes as Coordinates for Orientation of Concepts in Traumatic Stress and Fulfillment

Whereas the previous section examined clinical and historical aspects of particular traumatic situations, this section investigates concepts applicable to all traumatic situations. It is suggested that traumatic stress concepts fall naturally into three axes (Figure 1).

Axis 1: The Process (Stressors → Illnesses) Axis

The process axis is the one that has been most studied in traumatic stress and therefore receives the most space here. This does not mean that it is the most important axis. The process referred to is from stressors to illnesses, with appraisals, stress responses, trauma, defenses, memory, and strengths and vulnerabilities influencing the process (Figure 2).

Axis 2: The Parameters Axis

The components in this axis, it is suggested, set the context or parameters of traumatic stress, that is, what happened where, when, and to whom. Parameters include nature of stressors, disaster phases, social system units affected, and times in the life cycles of victims.

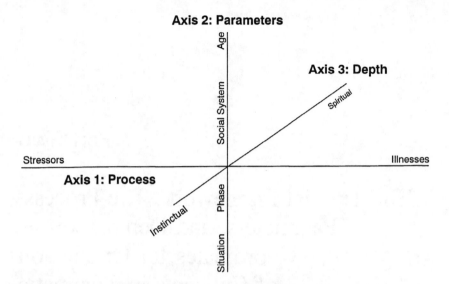

Figure 1 Triaxial view of traumatic stress.

Axis 3: The Depth (Levels of Human Functions) Axis

This axis refers to the levels of human functions whose fulfillments are disrupted by trauma. Levels of human function refer to evolutionary and developmental levels that range from the physiological to the existential and include morality, meanings, values, principles, religion, ideology, the sacred, creativity, and wisdom.

The components of the three axes are concepts summarized below.

Axis 1: Process (Stressors → Illnesses)

The components of the process axis are

- stressors
- appraisals

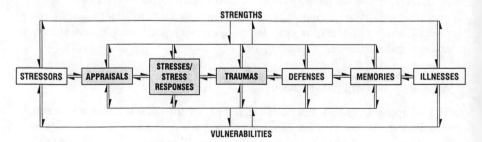

Figure 2 Components of process axis.

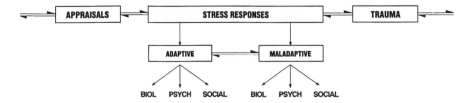

Figure 3 Stress responses.

- stress responses (see Figure 3)
- strengths and vulnerabilities
- trauma
- defenses
- memories
- illnesses

Axis 2: Parameters Axis

The components of the parameters axis are factors in traumatic situations

- factors in traumatic situations
- phases of traumatic situations
- social system levels, including helpers
- developmental phases

Axis 3: Depth; Levels of Human Function Axis

The components of the depth axis are

- instinctive and survival needs
- basic social needs
- spirituality, early spirituality, magic myths
- morality, including good and bad, worth and justice
- meanings
- ideals, values, and principles
- codes, dignity, rights, and ethics
- religion, ideology, and beliefs
- symbols
- identity
- creativity and aesthetics
- sacredness
- wisdom, knowledge, and truth

The three axes are examined in the next three chapters. The life–trauma dialectic is delineated at the end of chapter 5. A proposed triaxial view of illnesses and fulfillment is considered in chapter 6.

Chapter 3

Components of Axis 1,
the Process Axis

The process axis examines what happens to people affected by severe circumstances. Its components are represented in Figure 2. It may be seen that although each component encompasses aspects of all prior ones, the components are part of a complex interacting system, with each component affecting all others.

Briefly, it is suggested that stressors are events that disturb current life-enhancing equilibria, whose purposes are survival and fulfilling one's life according to the life cycle and helping others to do the same (chapter 5). According to appraisals of the disturbances, particular stress responses are evoked to deal with the stressors. The organism is now in a state of stress. Stress responses may be adaptive or maladaptive and may have biological, psychological, and social aspects (Figure 3). Indeed, it is suggested that all components of traumatic stress have concurrent biopsychosocial aspects. Adaptive stress responses resolve stresses and form the basis for continued survival and fulfillment. Maladaptive stress responses manifest increased stress and strain, which may progress to trauma. Trauma means that some kind of damage has occurred. Traumas are mitigated by defenses. Together, they mold events and memories that become parts of illnesses. Illnesses are less stable and less life enhancing compromise equilibria, in comparison to the relatively more life enhancing original disrupted equilibria.

The process axis is typically examined in individual adults at the level of survival. However, the other two axes should be borne in mind for perspective. I now examine each component of the process axis in more detail. Some components such as defenses and memories are quite complex and are given relatively more space.

STRESSORS

Stressors are life challenges with potential noxiousness for the organism (Lazarus, 1966). However, the definition of stressors has been historically confused with that for *stresses*, which are their consequence. For instance, traumatic stress would be more logically called *traumatic stressor*. Stressors have also been confused with change, so that even holidays have been considered to be stressors (Selye, 1973). However, holidays are only potentially noxious when associated with loneliness and separation.

Some have attempted to distinguish classes of stressors according to the degree of noxiousness (Eisdorfer, 1985; Lazarus & Cohen, 1977). The most noxious group is cataclysmic events outside the realm of normal human experience, such as war and rape (Davidson, Fleming, & Baum, 1986), which have been called traumatic stressors (see below). The next group, called personal or "everyday" stressors, includes bereavement, marital conflicts, migration, and retirement and has been thought to have less impact. The last group, that with the least impact, is called chronic background stressors or "daily hassles" and includes overcrowding, role strains, and social isolation. The disadvantage of these distinctions is that they were externally determined by researchers, not subjectively determined by the stressed. Thus "everyday" stressors such as bereavement, marital conflict, and work stressors could lead to heart attacks and suicide and could be subjectively as noxious as, say, an earthquake. Further, observer-determined stressors do not recognize invisible psychological or social stressors such as neglect, humiliation, persecution, and other disruptions of fulfillment such as inability to fulfill life's developmental goals (chapter 4). Yet such stressors could also be sufficiently noxious to endanger life, for instance, in Case 2, the patient with angina (chapter 1).

Four other factors add to the complexity of the stressor concept. First, Khan (1964) introduced the concept of cumulativeness in which stressors could add up (akin to life-change units, chapter 2). In such cases, a seemingly innocuous stressor could "break the camel's back." Second, an event might become a stressor only retrospectively. For instance, the significance of a sexual act as abuse and betrayal might only reveal itself years after the event. Third, apparently innocuous symbols (such as in Case 2, a child's turning 8; see chapter 1) could represent major life threats. Last, stressors may be secondary (Figley, 1995a, 1995b) or even transmitted from previous generations (chapter 2).

In summary, stressors may be cumulative, retrospective, symbolic or secondary, or objective or subjective. In each case, they have the potential to disrupt life's purpose, that is, to survive and fulfill oneself according to the life cycle and to help others do the same. The following definition is offered: *Stressors are events whose effects actually or potentially interfere with the purpose of life, that is, survival and fulfillment.*

Traumatic Stress

Traumatic stress is a very frequent term in traumatology. It was seen that initially traumatic stress denoted cataclysmic stressors outside the range of usual human experience that led to serious distress in almost everybody. As currently defined in *DSM–IV* in axis 1 of PTSD (APA, 1994; chapter 6), it involves threat of death or serious injury to self or others and is associated with intense helplessness and horror. Hence, the intention of the term is to denote a major stressor that almost inevitably leads to trauma and PTSD.

Though the term traumatic stress helped to put PTSD and trauma on the psychiatric map, it is tautological, that is, defined by its result. It is also exclusive, as it ignores the potential damage from subjective "everyday," chronic, cumulative, retrospective, and symbolic stressors. The confusion over the term is increased because it is almost synonymous with PTSD, and it also denotes a field of study (Figley, 1988).

It is suggested that the term traumatic stress eventually be restricted to denote a stressor concept. The following definition encapsulates this: *Traumatic stress refers to severe stressors that commonly threaten life and often result in trauma.*

To follow common usage, traumatic stress is also used to denote a field of study, though the newer term *traumatology* is preferred. Traumatology, as described in the Preface, is more encompassing.

APPRAISALS

Appraisals interpret the significance of stressors and mediate between them and stress responses (Lazarus, 1966; Lazarus & Folkman, 1984). They help explain why different people react differently to the same stressors. Like stressors, appraisals may be biological, psychological, and social. For instance, the immune system appraises foreign intruders in the biological arena. The media influence social appraisals.

However, appraisals usually refer to the psychological arena. Cognitive psychologists describe different levels of apprehension of the world (definitions are sparse, and they overlap). On the basic level, perceptions facilitate sensing the environment according to specific modalities such as sight and sound. At the next level, cognitions subsume perceptions and are ideations with pictorial or verbal content that make up the person's "stream of consciousness" (Beck, Rush, Shaw, & Emery, 1979). Appraisals or cognitive appraisals comprise the third level of complexity. They are evaluations of the significance of information for survival and well being (Lazarus & Folkman, 1984). Meanings further order and evaluate significance (Lazarus & Folkman, 1984) and are incorporated into higher level structures called *schemas* (chapter 4). Experiences are then categorized and evaluated through a relatively stable matrix of schemas (Beck et al., 1979).

This cognitive hierarchy reflects cognitive evolution and serves increasingly complex human function levels (chapter 5). In traumatic stress, appraisals are affected by both basic and complex levels of apprehension. Sometimes factors that affect appraisals are divided into situation and person factors (Lazarus & Folkman, 1984; Raphael, 1986).

Situation Factors

Intense sensory information such as raging fires and means of dealing with them are usually appraised unambiguously at an almost reflex-instinctive level. Unambiguity, imminence, and predictability lead to immediate evocation of stress responses. Ambiguous appraisals such as husbands missing in action could be more stressful than knowledge of husbands' deaths (Lazarus & Folkman, 1984).

In ambiguous situations, people may depend on past experience. For instance, if past warnings were not followed by catastrophes, current warnings may be denied. Alternatively, previous catastrophes sensitize people to future cues and warnings (Janis, 1962). The former situation may lead to overassurance and hypovigilance, whereas the latter may lead to a background state of arousal and hypervigilance (Janis, 1962; van der Kolk & Greenberg, 1987). In the latter state, or when stressors accumulate, an objectively small last straw may be appraised as a major stressor.

Next, in ambiguous situations people may need to depend on others' appraisals. They, and orders issued on their basis such as to evacuate, may be trusted according to current relationship of trust and hierarchical status with respect to these others, their perceived expertise, and past experience of their appraisals (Hill & Hansen, 1962).

In the absence of reliable appraisals or reasonable hope for protective action, people often deny danger or become hypervigilant, indulge in magical thinking and rituals, believe rumors, and may even take undiscriminating action (Janis & Mann, 1977).

In traumatic situations, certain factors disable appraisals from evoking hopeful responses with adaptive outcomes. Such factors include closeness to stressors; unexpectedness; surprise and shock; lack of preparation or training for the event; deaths, especially of close persons, ones with whom one identifies, young people, or children; presence of mutilated bodies and body parts; and unnecessary and intentional injuries and deaths (Ursano & McCarroll, 1994; Weisath & Eitinger, 1993).

Person Factors

Person factors in adults include commitments and beliefs. Commitments correspond to higher level functions such as morality, values, ideology, and the sacred (chapter 5). Threats to commitments may be appraised as dangerous to all that makes life meaningful, and people may die for them.

Cognitive beliefs are considered to be higher level schemas that may or may not overlap with commitments. They inform about how things are within oneself, the world, and the future. A belief that one has the capacity to control the environment (internal locus of control) may lead to appraisals of stressors as challenges. A belief to the contrary (external locus of control) may appraise the same stressors as major threats (Seligman, 1974). Nevertheless, Lazarus and Folkman (1984) concluded that beliefs are likely to be important only if situations resemble the original one where the beliefs were first formed or in ambiguous stressor situations. However, in new acute traumatic situations, people frequently act in unexpected ways, contrary to past beliefs and personalities. This was noted in Case 1 (chapter 1).

Last, appraisals are continuous and have feedback. Lazarus and Folkman (1984) distinguished primary appraisals, which assess current threat, harm, and challenge to action. Reappraisals give feedback on the efficacy of the coping options.

In summary, appraisals register stressors and elicit stress responses. Appraisals are influenced by environmental and host factors in interaction with each other. The following definition is suggested: *Appraisals are processes that register the quantity and quality of stressors in order to elicit appropriate stress responses.*

STRESS

Stress in the physical sciences is the tension or strain in a body resulting from external force. Analogously, stress in the biological arena is the tension or strain on the body's physiological equilibrium. The latter was called *milieu interieur* by Claude Bernard (1878/1930), and later homeostasis by Cannon (1939). These terms implied a relatively static equilibrium. Currently, biological equilibrium is conceived as dynamic, changing with circumstances and life phases.

Psychosocial stress, like stressors, has been an enigma (Eisdorfer, 1985) and difficult to define. However, definitions usually include a sense of potential danger, threats to one's well being, unpleasure, tension, strain, and being taxed (Eisdorfer, 1985; Davidson et al., 1986; Lazarus & Folkman, 1984). These definitions are parallel to the physical concept of stress as a buffer zone of strained equilibrium in which the noxiousness of external forces is resisted. They also indicate that threats to both survival and fulfillment can be stressful.

Some consider that stress can be beneficial or harmful. Selye (1973) suggested that without stress there is no life, but that stress can lead to death, too.

He suggested a triphasic response in stress. The first phase is alarm, or hardship, but a fast resolution of the stress is possible. The second phase is adaptation or resistance, when one gets used to the new strenuous challenge. This is a situation of strain, however. Nevertheless, the stress is so far reversible. The third phase is exhaustion, or "having had it." Reversal from the first phase, and even from the second, may indicate responses to stress having been adaptive (see below), and the ultimate result may indeed result in greater reserves and fulfillments. In this sense, stress on living beings differs from stress on inanimate objects. However, in the third phase the state has gone beyond the original equilibrium being retrieved, or stress being beneficial. In fact, in our terminology, trauma occurs.

An overlapping concept of stress is found in crisis theory (Caplan, 1964). Crisis is seen as a disturbed homeostasis that can have adaptive or maladaptive outcomes. Beneficial outcomes (aims of crisis intervention) are consistent with the Chinese symbol for crisis, representing both danger and opportunity. Crisis concepts stop short of potential contiguity with trauma, whereas stresses are often linked with it.

It is suggested that the following definition captures the tension of stress, yet its potential adaptive and noxious outcomes: *Stresses are states of tension resulting from challenges to life-enhancing equilibria. They may be resolved adaptively, or they may lead to compromise of life.*

Because following stress prior equilibria can be retrieved, unlike following trauma, some suggest that the field of stress and traumatic stress are different (Shalev, 1996). However, it may be countered that just like physics and medicine incorporate forces that at times lead to stress and at other times to trauma, so should traumatology. Though a broken bone may be very different from a stressed, unbroken bone, it may be artificial to ignore the forces and circumstances just before the break.

STRESS RESPONSES

Stress responses are evoked to counter the effects of stressors. They are part of the buffer state of stress between stressors and trauma. They are extremely variable, and it may be best to define them early, in order to give their descriptions a context: *Stress responses are processes that counter the noxious potentials of stressors.*

Adaptiveness and Maladaptiveness of Stress Responses

When stress responses counter the effects of stressors successfully they are called adaptive. At such times, they restore previous life-enhancing equilibria and may even contribute to further enhancement of life. When stress responses are insufficient or are wrongly applied and unsuccessful in countering the effects of stressors, they are called *maladaptive.* They may then contribute to the continuing tense and strained equilibrium of stress or be parts of progression to trauma. In reality, adaptive and maladaptive responses often fluctuate or are in an uneasy equilibrium with each other.

Biopsychosocial Nature of Stress Responses

Stress responses act simultaneously in biological, psychological, and social arenas. Though they are described separately, their essential biopsychosocial unity should be remembered.
The nature of stress responses is summarized in Figure 3.

Biological Stress Responses   Biological stress responses fall under anatomical and physiological headings.

Neuroanatomical Substrate   The level of the brain where stress responses are generated is the "old mammalian" brain, which includes the limbic system and the primitive cortex. This area elaborates emotional feelings that guide self-preservation and preservation of the species (MacLean, 1973). It initiates strategies of survival at the level where basic biological, psychological, and social responses can be coordinated (see also chapter 7). It is at a higher level of evolutionary development than the "reptilian" brain, which includes the upper brain stem, reticular formation, midbrain, and basal ganglia and which is involved with ancestral memory and reflex and instinctive behavior. This part aids the "old mammalian" brain in its more basic instinctive survival goals.
The old mammalian brain also both radiates its information and is in turn regulated by the more evolved "new mammalian" brain, which includes the neocortex and involves the higher level functions of the depth axis.
Early thinking postulated specific centers in the old mammalian brain for specific emotions and behaviors. Currently, too, specific centers arouse interest as important way stations of features of PTSD. For instance, the locus coeruleus (van der Kolk & Saporta, 1993) and the hippocampus (Bremner, Krystle, Southwick, & Charney, 1995; M. Lewis, 1995) are thought to be important in norepinephrine depletion, dissociation, and memory disturbances.
Recently, pathology of the hippocampus has been extended further. Some workers found that its volume was diminished in PTSD sufferers. Van der Kolk (1996a) suggested that the damage led to failure to assess and organize emotional impressions from the amygdala, which then continued to have emotional and sensory lives of its own. A further consequence was diminished processing through Broca's area, resulting in diminished symbolic, verbal, and analytic thinking of the left hemisphere. Together, the result was domination of the right hemisphere with its emotional, intuitive, and nonverbal thinking—a feature of PTSD.
Nevertheless, the overall trend in current thinking is overall more systems oriented. Although it acknowledges that sites and subsystems exist whose

functions may be disrupted, they are parts of very complex systems (Smith, 1991). Within them there are "many avenues of cross-talk between brain circuits" (Panksepp, 1989a, p. 6). Thus it may be reductionist to think about centers for PTSD, just as it was earlier for emotions and behaviors. There are many way stations on different levels that are organized in complex ways to achieve the organism's functions. Often, higher level goals determine which areas, circuits, and patterns of interactions are used. Hence, dissociation and other defenses (chapter 3, chap-ter 16) may be influenced by messages from the neocortex.

Physiological Responses   *Autonomic nervous system.* Cannon (1963) described sympathetic nervous system stimulation in the fight–flight response, manifested by arousal and decreased digestive motility. Gellhorn (1970) expanded Cannon's symptoms to very widespread effects, which included dilated pupils, rise in heart rate and blood pressure, and increases in sweat gland activity, adrenomedullary secretion, and the tone of striated muscles. This was accompanied by cerebral excitation and behavioral arousal. Gellhorn called the combination of sympathetic nervous system responses and its psychobehavioral correlates the *ergotropic* response.

Conversely, parasympathetic nervous system activation was accompanied by relaxation of striated muscle, lessening of somatic responsiveness, and tendency toward sleeplike electrical synchronization of the cortex. These responses Gellhorn called the *trophotropic* response. The two systems were finely tuned to each other. Because of the ubiquitous innervation by the autonomic nervous system, the two systems could produce a wide variety of opposite effects in all body systems. Gellhorn's views are still current (Henry, 1986).

The endocrine system. Mason (1968) noted that a great variety of hormones were very sensitively evoked in a great variety of stress situations such as combat (Bourne, 1969) and examinations (Meyerhoff, Oleshansky, & Mougey, 1988). The hormones included cortisol, epinephrine and norepinephrine, thyroxin, growth hormone, and male and female sex hormones. However, it was not clear which hormones were secreted in which particular stress.

Nevertheless, some workers gave preeminence to specific hormones. Selye (1936) believed that cortisol was the universal stress hormone, secreted in what he believed to be the ubiquitous general adaptation syndrome (chapter 7). Yehuda, Southwick, Mason, and Giller (1990), however, saw cortisol as shutting off biological stress responses (such as epinephrine and norepinephrine). Yet others at different times have seen epinephrine and norepinephrine as *the* stress hormones (Friedman, 1991; van der Kolk, 1996a).

As with stressors, Mason (1968) called for a framework to make sense of the prolific secretion of hormones in stress situations. He believed that patterns of hormonal secretion would ultimately be understood through psychological goals. He drew an analogy with muscles. Although most muscles respond in most movements, special patterns of contraction such as of flexor or extensor muscles occur according to higher psychological goals. Such goals may be a variety of survival strategies.

To date, perhaps a rough start has been made. Thus epinephrine and nor-epinephrine, but not cortisol, are secreted in the fight-and-flight or in the ergotropic response (Henry, 1986). Rather, cortisol is more a distress hormone associated with a trophotropic response in helplessness, grief, defeat, illness, and the need to learn new behaviors (Sachar, 1975a, 1975b; Panksepp, 1986b).

The immune system. The immune system also responds very sensitively to stressors. For instance, even not being able to escape noise, or imagining extremely negative experiences, led almost immediately to disturbed natural killer cell and mitogen (anticancer) activity (Kiecolt-Glaser, Cacioppo, Malarkey, & Glaser, 1992). A variety of stressors in both animals and humans have been shown to have longer term effects, depressing both humoral (B, antibody) and cell-mediated (T, white blood cells) immune responses (Stein, 1981). This is not even, and at times parts of the immune system show elevated responses.

Though immune responses occur in as yet heuristically unclear patterns, diminished immunocompetence seems to be associated with trophotropic-evoking circumstances and possibly enhanced immunocompetence with ergotropic ones (Fleshner, Laudenslager, Simons, & Maier, 1989). In one study, the immune response in aroused combat veterans was overall enhanced (Burges-Watson, Muller, Jones, & Bradley, 1993).

Since Bartrop, Lazarus, Luckhurst, Kiloh, and Penny (1977), compromised immunocompetence has been noted following bereavement in both immediate and later phases. The presence of depression has especially been associated with suppression of parts of the immune system such as natural killer cells (Calabrese, Kling, & Gold, 1987). Irwin, Daniels, and Weiner (1987) speculated that part of the increased morbidity and mortality after bereavement was due to diminished immunocompetence. This could lead to illnesses such as infections, cancer, and autoimmune illnesses. However, other stressors such as social defeat in rats (Fleshner et al., 1989) and maternal separation in infant primates (Coe, Luback, & Ershler, 1989) could also could lead to diminished immunocompetence in both short and long term and could possibly contribute to similar illnesses.

In spite of the demonstrated trend, simplistic notions of cause and effect need to be discouraged because many factors influence the immune response. They include stage of life cycle, previous physical and psychosocial experience (which may sensitize subsequent responses), feedback mechanisms, current emotional state, and the presence of a variety of hormones, neurotransmitters, and neuromodulators (Rogers et al., 1979).

As with the endocrine system, here too there is a call for psychology to furnish the goals and emotions that may characterize immune system response patterns (Calabrese et al., 1987). Further, it is also likely that higher level conceptualizations may demonstrate overarching patterns of autonomic nervous system, endocrine, and immune systems.

Neurotransmitters and neuroregulators. In recent years, there has been an explosion in the capacity to discover and assay a wide variety of amines and peptides in circulation and at their receptor sites. Their levels can be correlated with a range of stimuli and behaviors. As in the preceding areas, there were initial hopes that individual dysfunctions led to specific psychiatric disorders. Hence originated the amine depletion theory of depression, the dopamine theory of schizophrenia, the norepinephrine theory of anxiety disorder, and the acetylcholine theory of Alzheimer's disease (Smith, 1991). Similarly, a variety of neurohormones have been suggested to be if not the cause of PTSD then key markers of it. They include increased cortisol and opioid secretions (Bremner et al., 1995; Glover, 1992; van der Kolk & Greenberg, 1987), increased norepinephrine secretion (this time with suppression of cortisol and opioids; Friedman, 1991), and norepinephrine depletion (van der Kolk, Boyd, Krystal, & Greenberg, 1984).

However, again recent thinking has seen neurotransmitters and neuromodulators in their roles as parts of various transmitter and modulator systems facilitating higher level goals (Smith, 1991). For instance the norepinephrine system facilitates integration of neural, sensory, hormonal, autonomic, and cognitive responses to imperative environmental challenges. The serotonin (5-HT) system, with almost identical brain distribution, inhibits and modulates a wide variety of physiological processes. The dopamine system facilitates behaviors such as exploration, acetylcholine systems mediate cholinergic activity as well as learning and memory, and the endorphins possibly inhibit memory consolidation, as well as mimic morphine functions.

Many of these substances are sensitively evoked or suppressed in a wide variety of stressful situations. They also act in concert with each other and the endocrine and immune systems. Again, there is a need for a higher level framework to explain their patterns and significance.

In summary, each newly discovered biological stress component has held hope that it might be "the" stress pathogen, which could then be controlled, probably with drugs. But each time, components fell into more complex stress responses whose goals needed higher order clarifications.

Psychological Stress Responses

Psychological stress responses include cognitions and emotions. Though in life they are inextricably linked, for clarity they are described separately.

Cognitions   Cognitions that mobilize stress responses have been described under appraisals. Cognitions in trauma and in defenses are considered below. In this section, cognitions are considered specifically as parts of stress responses.

Cognitions may be influenced by survival needs at the time. For instance, during fight or flight people may be impervious to the pain of wounds. Further, there may be distortions of time, space, and person. Time distortion includes expansion of time for waiting victims, for whom minutes may seem like hours. For busy helpers, time shrinks. During long imprisonments, time may collapse (Terr, 1990). Space may expand if distance between danger and security seems unattainable (Nader, 1993). Person distortions include focus on personal security needs and ignoring peripheral concerns.

Cognitions are affected by developmental stages. Children tend to not attribute malignant motives to parents and authority figures (Terr, 1990). Atavistic distortions can occur at all ages, such as with the woman who saw the fires as an angel about to embrace her (chapter 1), though perceptions of monsters, predators, and angels may be weighted toward the young. The illusion of being the center of a disaster (Wolfenstein, 1977) or feeling abandoned when not being personally attended may be part of childhood preoperational thinking or regression to it.

In summary, there is a variety of cognitive stress responses that both focus clarity and distort cognitions in the service of survival.

Emotions   Emotions are subjective feelings that are associated with physiological arousal and motivation to action. Perhaps they especially indicate the biopsychosocial nature of stress responses as well as the mechanisms of translating outside stimuli to inner responses.

Yet emotions have been shunned since the ancient Greeks, who separated the passions from reason. The former were seen as instinctive, irrational, animal, and clouding reason and the attainment of truth. At most, they were in the domain of the lower gods such as Dionysius. However, philosophers' reason included introspection of emotions such as love and justice. In fact, it was unwelcome emotions such as lust and violence that were shunned as animallike passions.

Modern science has also shunned emotions because they are outside the scope of methodological rigor that demanded that constructs be visually observable and measurable (chapter 6). However, Panksepp (1989b) noted that behavioral science without emotions lost a central essence. For the sake of ideology, scientists "chose to conceptually cripple themselves" (p. 32). The vacuum of scientific study of emotions has been ameliorated by psychoanalysis and researchers influenced by ethology and evolution.

Psychoanalysis   From its beginning, psychoanalysis has been vitally concerned with emotions. In fact, it was splitting off from consciousness of unwelcome feelings in trauma and the blocking of their subsequent discharge that was seen initially to be the cause of hysterical symptoms. Abreaction or discharge of these repressed emotions was then the treatment for these symptoms (Breuer & Freud, 1895/1975). Freud considered the repressed emotions to be sexual desire and aggression. Each had derivative emotions; for instance, pleasure, tenderness, love, and creativity derived from sexual emotions.

Freud also contributed to the emotions of grief and depression and fear and anxiety. In *Mourning and Melancholia* (Freud, 1917/1975k), he contrasted grief with its conscious painful giving up of a lost object, with melancholia (depression) in which neither loss nor the need to give it up were in conscious awareness. Next, although current dangers evoked fear, anxiety was a universal signal for the imminent reemergence of internal or external dangers (Freud, 1926/1975h). Depression and anxiety are the two affects that have rated clinical psychiatric diagnoses. It may be interesting to contemplate whether had Freud taken more interest in other emotions, we may have inherited other diagnoses, such as rage, jealousy, and betrayal disorders.

In fact, later psychoanalysts described a variety of emotions. Melanie Klein (1952/1975a) concentrated on what she saw as the derivatives of the aggressive or death instinct. They included terrors of persecution, hatred, frustration, greed, sadism, and envy (Klein, 1957/1975b). She also added derivative emotions of the life or sexual instincts. They included love, trust, gratification, guilt, need to make good, and gratitude. Klein maintained that all these emotions were already present in infants, derived from innate life and death instincts. The alternative view here was that these emotions are inborn signaling capacities that help to enhance life and avoid trauma for oneself and one's own (chapter 7).

Most feelings have been examined somewhere in the scattered psychoanalytic literature. Socarides (1977) and M. Lewis and Haviland (1993) compiled chapters on around 40 emotions. In addition to depression and anxiety, they included happiness, pride, enthusiasm, embarrassment, shame, arrogance, jealousy, and some less well-known ones such as gloating and pathos. Others paired positive and negative emotions. Bowlby (1971, 1975, 1981) contrasted security and separation anxiety and, akin to Freud, grief and depression. Erikson (1965) contrasted trust and mistrust, autonomy and shame and doubt, and ego integrity and despair during progression of the life cycle.

Even so, emotions have not been systematized or conceptualized by the discipline. But its recognition of their importance has been helpful in psychological treatment and to traumatology.

Interdisciplinary Research In recent times, ethology and comparative neurophenomenology have suggested that emotional feelings may be "read" through behaviors that may be "natural metaphors" for them. Nonverbal communications such as facial expressions may be such metaphors that use complex programs to enable exchange of emotional information.

As well, modern technology such as computer digitization can correlate central motivational role of emotions with specific neural circuits and physiological accompaniments (Panksepp, 1989a). Panksepp described five such neural circuits, each associated with specific survival needs and specific emotions. The emotions were expectation, anger–rage, anxiety–fear, grief–panic and play–joy (see also chapter 7).

Plutchik (1980, 1993) similarly postulated a small number (eight) of primary emotions that evolved to evoke specific survival behaviors (see also chapter 7). Plutchik organized them in four pairs: fear–flight and anger–fight; joy–mating and grief–reintegration; trust–affiliation and loathing–rejection; and anticipation–exploration and surprise–orientation. All other emotions were postulated to be derivatives of these primary emotions.

Entrenched emotions could contribute to characteristic personality traits, such as timidity or aggressiveness. Further, primary emotions together with presumed characteristic defenses could lead to specific clinical diagnoses (Kellerman, 1980). For instance, disgust (loathing), together with projection, led to paranoia, ,whereas anger together with displacement led to clinical aggressions.

Panksepp's (1989a, 1993) and Plutchik's (1980, 1993) ideas organize emotions according to survival needs. This accords with their place in survival strategies to be described later. However, issue is taken with specific strategies of survival and the one-to-one correlation of emotions and illnesses.

In summary, the literature is recognizing emotions as central mediators of appraisals and biopsychosocial stress responses. Pleasant and unpleasant emotions may signify enhancement or otherwise of life-enhancing equilibria.

Social Stress Responses

Every psychological and biological stress response is associated with an action in the social environment. However, because of an antipathology bias in much sociological literature, only a random selection of sociological responses has been studied.

Antipathology Bias Much sociological literature has seen communities and their organizations as sponges that could become distorted in disasters, but if left to themselves could find their own resilience and always spring back to shape (Quarantelli, 1985). Maladaptiveness and pathology were seen as artifacts of pathologizing and consequent harmful mental health interventions (Quarantelli, 1985; Quarantelli & Dynes, 1972, 1977). The rarity of panic, looting, and psychological illness was used to testify to communities' ubiquitous adaptiveness. The literature emphasized positive effects of disasters such as postdisaster cohesion.

However, this perspective ignored the fact that cells of the sponge (individuals, families) could be irretrievably changed. Further, in major disasters even sponges could be ripped apart. Last, increased rates of accidents and drug intake and major maladaptive social responses such as riots, persecutions, and war were ignored. Nevertheless, sociology has been helpful in elucidating the following common disaster responses.

Common Social Responses
Panic Though often mentioned, panic is rare. People only panic when they feel trapped and powerless and the only escape is through congested exits

(Quarantelli, 1954). This was the situation in the Cocoanut Grove nightclub disaster (Veltfort & Lee, 1943), where people trampled and crushed each other.

Convergence   This is the phenomenon in which masses of people converge on a disaster area. They may seek loved ones, want to help, or just look on in fascination, possibly in order to learn about trauma (Raphael, 1986).

Altruism   Although parents' sacrifice for offspring and soldiers' for their comrades is accepted, similar sacrifice in wars, such as in the London blitz (Schmideberg, 1942) and in disasters, evokes surprise and admiration. However, a postdisaster phase marked by optimism (postdisaster utopia) and social cohesiveness and generosity (the altruistic community) is common (Dynes & Quarantelli, 1976; Siporin, 1976).

Altruism is sometimes explained by the nobility of human nature coming to the fore when the chips are down. However, at other times ruthless struggle for survival is claimed as human nature. Perhaps each occurs in different survival situations. In Hiroshima, there was little London-type spirit and no postdisaster euphoria.

Information Communication   As noted earlier with warnings (chapter 3), information continues to be believed or not according to people's trust in those who convey it (Dynes & Quarantelli, 1976). The media can be very helpful in diffusing correct information. However, they may deny threats of disasters, sensationalize and exaggerate the tolls once disasters occur, and then overemphasize courage and again deny longer term effects.

Rumors and False Beliefs   Rumors tend to occur where information is necessary but unavailable. Rumors may have superstitious and magical qualities. They may exaggerate dangers or satisfy belief needs, such as that all will be well. The latter beliefs may help explain why disaster-prone areas are reurbanized to ever greater extents after disasters (Mileti, Drabek, & Haas, 1975).

Scapegoating is based on a particular type of rumor that enables people to (falsely) believe that the cause of a catastrophe can be pinpointed, blamed, and eliminated. This gives a sense of control where otherwise there is none (Mileti et al., 1975; Valent, 1984). Scapegoats can be individuals, as occurred in the Boston Cocoanut Grove nightclub fire of 1942 (Veltfort & Lee, 1943); groups, as in the Vietnam War My Lai atrocity (Lifton, 1973; see also chapter 12); and communities, such as Jews, who have been the traditional scapegoats in Europe.

Relationships   Different intense relationships develop in traumatic situations. They include cohesive high-morale relationships (chapter 2), rescuer–victim relationships (chapter 8; Valent, 1995a), and perpetrator–victim relationships (chapter 2). A paradoxical example of the latter, in which hostages come to identify with their captors, has come to be called the Stockholm syndrome, after such an event in Stockholm (Ochberg, 1988). Children who identify with abusive parents present a more common version of such relationships (Herman, 1992; chapter 2).

Other General and Specific Social Responses   Tyhurst (1957) distinguished certain common social responses in different disaster phases. They included returning to homes that were abandoned in danger, reestablishing family connections and retrieving possessions, then a transient community prostration, followed by spontaneous group formations, emergent leaders, and increased community cohesion, which are later followed by irritability and social strain.

Specific responses occur in specific circumstances, such as the evacuation of the Titanic by women and children first, followed by hierarchy according to class. Another example is extreme passivity and going to sleep in an airplane hijack, alternating with rumors such as that elderly persons would be raped first (Jacobson, 1973).

In summary, sociology has contributed knowledge of specific social stress responses such as panic and rumors and has drawn attention to social system levels wider than individual and family. However, many social stress responses— especially negative ones such as competition, greed, loss of dignity, destructiveness, and persecution—have not yet been examined in detail. A taxonomy of social responses and their association with biological and psychological stress responses is lacking.

In conclusion, biological, psychological, and social stress responses are wide-ranging complex phenomena that may be adaptive or maladaptive. Specific types of responses and specific individual stress responses may highlight features of later illnesses. Therefore, it is important to understand the patterns, functions, and malfunctions of the earlier coexistent biopsychosocial stress responses.

VULNERABILITIES

Vulnerabilities and strengths (Figure 2) may be important in determining whether stress proceeds to trauma and beyond.

Vulnerability has usually implied an explanation of why some people respond more adversely than others to the same stressors (van der Kolk, 1987). In the past, the term vulnerability was used in a pejorative way to indicate inability to cope, whether through genes (bad stock) or inadequacy of personality. Either could be used to deny victims care and compensation. Once it was accepted that everybody was vulnerable and had a breaking point (Freud, 1919/ 1975i; Hocking, 1970), vulnerability could be examined with less prejudice. Two categories of vulnerability may be abstracted from the literature—general and specific.

General Vulnerability (Across Populations)

Vulnerabilities are also biological, psychological, and social (Lazarus & Folkman, 1984). However, they are more commonly summarized in the literature according to disaster phases. Raphael (1986) summarized predisaster factors as early and late stages of the life cycle, being female, and low educational and socioeconomic status. Disaster factors corresponded to traumatic appraisals and were stressor destructiveness, death and mutilation, suddenness, unpredictability, nearness, and being "manmade." Postdisaster factors included poor coping styles, social isolation, or inability to avail of help. Shalev (1996) noted that the above factors have been claimed to predispose one to PTSD.

Yet some findings were inconsistent. For instance, although some studies showed previous personal psychopathology to predispose a person to PTSD (McFarlane, 1988), Emery, Emery, Shama, Quiana, and Jassani's (1991) review of the literature contradicted this. Similarly, although some found that an antisocial family history predisposed one to PTSD, van der Kolk (1987) suggested that a negative family history could act as a shield against further hurt and PTSD.

Gibbs (1989) questioned the validity of some common beliefs on vulnerability. For instance, in some disasters it was middle-aged people who were most affected, possibly because of threats to their young children and burgeoning property. At other times, older people coped better with disasters because of what they had learned from previous ones. Similarly, women's vulnerability could be an artifact because psychometric tests measure what women typically exhibit, such as anxiety and depression. They do not measure the more common male responses such as alcoholism, belligerence, and somatic illnesses. As well, symptoms in women may be aggravated postdisaster by their relative responsivity to higher levels of social demands placed on them.

Even the consistent lower socioeconomic and education vulnerabilities came into question. First, women were not affected by them to the same degree as men. Second, low income and education could already have provided a background of higher pretraumatic stress. Indeed, if pretraumatic levels of stress were controlled, individuals of lower social class did better in disasters than those of higher social class.

Similarly, social support was not always protective. For instance, isolation could be less distressing than intrusive or insensitive family members or helpers (S. D. Solomon, 1986). Gibbs (1989) concluded that all the above factors were adaptive or not according to circumstances and needed more sophisticated assessments.

In their own approach, Emery et al. (1991) showed that deeper meaningful structural life themes such as unreliability of the environment and lack of control over affects and behaviors were better indicators of vulnerability than previous simplistic concepts. For instance, 90% of veterans with PTSD had experienced these factors in their backgrounds, as opposed to only 20% of veterans without PTSD.

In summary, demographic factors make for vulnerability in particular circumstances. However, vulnerability is more predictable when deeper meaningful structures are taken into account.

Specific Vulnerability (Individual)

In individual cases, past wounds, fractures, traumas, and illnesses and traumas are sources of future weakness or sensitivity (especially to stressors similar to the original ones). Such vulnerabilities may be latently present for many years (Cohen, 1981; chapter 9). For instance, chronic handling and adverse early life experiences made mice and rats relatively vulnerable to developing cancer in adulthood (Ader, 1980) through the early negative sensitizing effect on the immune system (Stein, 1981). Similar vulnerabilities may be significant for cancer development in humans, too (Grossarth-Maticek et al., 1982). Other inadequate attunements early in life may lead to specific psychobiological dysregulations, which may predispose to later illnesses, such as asthma (G. J. Taylor, 1987).

There are analogous psychological vulnerabilities. Vulnerability and sensitivity to cues of past trauma are central features of PTSD. As well, early maternal loss predisposes to later loss and depression (Bowlby, 1981). Early sexual abuse predisposes to a variety of later symptoms and further sexual assaults (Kilpatrick, Veronen, & Best, 1985). Earlier specific illnesses may be (over)compensated for by a variety of defenses. When the latter are punctured, aspects of the original illnesses may become overt again. This was seen in a group of vulnerable patients who suffered traffic incidents (chapter 2).

Specific transgenerational vulnerability may also occur, such as through identification with a family member who was killed in a traffic incident (chapter 2). Alternatively, a soldier whose father or older brother was killed in combat may volunteer for dangerous missions. Holocaust survivors' children may be vulnerable to cues reminiscent of their parents' traumatic stressors (Kestenberg, 1992).

In summary, though in one way vulnerability is a universal human condition, as used here it is what facilitates the noxious influences of stressors. General vulnerabilities considered in the past have been demographic factors such as young and old age and being female, as well as deprived family histories. Deeper concepts of personality damage are more likely to be heuristically useful. Specific vulnerabilities include specific earlier damage. They may predispose a person specifically to certain symptoms and illnesses or recurrences of the original illnesses.

The following definition of vulnerability is offered: *Vulnerability is any factor that facilitates the noxious effects of stressors.*

STRENGTHS

Strengths are the opposite of vulnerabilities. Again, in a general way everyone has natural endowments that protect against stressors. However, as used here strengths are particular resources and equipment that make organisms better able to resist stressors. They may be general, such as stable and nurturing family background, or they may be specific, such as training to deal with stressors (McFarlane, 1988), sense of control, ability to avail oneself of social help and networks (e.g., Shalev, 1996), well-developed capacities to predict and regulate external and internal turmoils, and ability to recognize and modulate affects. The following definition of strengths is offered: *Strength is any factor that resists the noxious effects of stressors.*

TRAUMA

Trauma comes from the Greek word denoting wound, or penetration, as in stabbing. Trauma in medicine to this day includes wounds and fractures. There is an implication that though wounds and fractures can be healed, scars, sensitivity, and vulnerability remain at least to some degree. Thus, if trauma does not result in death, it does result in some damage and a less life-enhancing equilibrium.

Freud (1888/1975g) followed Charcot's view on trauma and introduced it as a seminal concept in psychoanalysis. Trauma involved splitting of consciousness and led to illnesses such as hysteria and other neuroses. Freud (1896/1975b; chapter 2) became explicit that the nature of trauma was sexual abuse. Though he recanted this idea, he elaborated in the context of nonsexual trauma on three further ideas.

First, akin to biological trauma, in psychic trauma an event penetrates the equivalent of the skin of the mind—the stimulus barrier (Freud, 1920/1975c). The event then comes to be surrounded by masses of energy that try to contain it, akin to a foreign body inside the skin. A contained traumatic event can then act as an abscess of the mind.

Second, in traumatic neurosis recurrent reliving and repression alternates as means to master the trauma (Freud, 1896/1975b, 1920/1975c). One could say that the abscess is both a constant reminder and an encapsulator of the traumatic event from the rest of the mind. This concept presaged the reliving and avoidance criteria in PTSD.

Third, the traumatic event is molded by a variety of defenses, leading to a variety of neurotic and psychotic illnesses. This presaged Figley's (1985) description of trauma as a central event, like a pebble breaking the stillness of a pond. The ripples can then be molded by a variety of defenses, leading to a wide variety of possible trauma sequelae. This view represents the psychodynamic view of illnesses (chapter 6).

Some psychoanalysts (Solnit & Kris, 1967; M. M. Stern, 1953) tried to explain what actually happened in psychic trauma. Descriptions included psychic shock, mental paralysis, immobilization, and deprivation of autonomous function. They came to be designated in the concept of overwhelming of the ego, a concept still current today.

Nevertheless, with Freud abandoning trauma the concept became emasculated (Benyakar, Kutz, Dasberg, & Stern, 1989). The term *psychic trauma*, like *stress*, came to be used in a diffuse way, denoting at different times stimulus, response, and consequence. The confusion is still reflected in the term *traumatic stress* and in PTSD.

Some workers attempted to restore trauma as a central and germane concept. For instance, Horowitz (1992/1976; chapter 5) and van der Kolk, Brown, and van der Hart (1989) suggested that trauma disrupted established meanings. Trauma meanings stayed recorded in unintegrated fragments until they could be integrated in new homogenous meanings and life narratives.

Benyakar et al. (1989), however, saw trauma collapsing the structure of the self. As the self integrated, mediated, and regulated emotions, psychological and social relationships, and behavior, its collapse included intense uncontrolled emotions; loss of mastery; shattered assumptions, meanings, and identity; and the horror that oneself and the world would never be the same again.

These views advanced the view of trauma from a conceptual black hole to making it a concentrated, multifaceted examinable event from a level of shock and numbness to function levels of meanings and identity. However, the biological, psychological, and social aspects of trauma were still not cohesively addressed, and a structural view fell short of being able to answer why which manifestations occurred at particular times.

It is suggested that the complexity of trauma can be understood by its capacity to disrupt all levels of human functioning from the anatomical to the spiritual; by its location in different disaster phases and individual and social parameters; and by its including aspects of all preceding components in Figures 2 and 3. That is, trauma includes features of particular stressors (traumatic situations), stress responses (biological, psychological, and social; adaptive and maladaptive), strengths, and vulnerabilities (it may also be modulated by defenses as well as feedback from illnesses). Last, survival strategies will be seen to explain the greater variability as well as specificity of stress responses and their contributions to variable yet specific trauma categories (chapter 16).

Although Figure 2 may seem to imply a stable equilibrium, trauma is in fact a major watershed following which it is impossible to return to the previous equilibrium. Hence, the reader should imagine a step down at trauma in the figure.

In summary, trauma is a complex state beyond the strained state of stress, where there is a fracture with a previous equilibrium. This results in some damage at least, though it may lead to illnesses of varying severity, and even death. The following definition encapsulates this: *Trauma is a state in which a previously life-enhancing equilibrium is irretrievably lost.*

To clarify some of the terms around trauma, it is suggested that a traumatic state is the state of an organism at the time that trauma is occurring. A traumatic situation or traumatic event is the external situation in which an organism is traumatized. Traumatization is the process of production of trauma.

Trauma is a central, crucial, and germane concept, being the essential pro-
tagonist in the life–trauma dialectic (chapter 5).

DEFENSES

In ordinary language, defenses deflect and eliminate threats or mitigate their
damage. Skin and the immune system are biological defenses. The army is a
social defense organization. In traumatic stress, it is psychological defenses that
are given prominence. The implication is that when stress responses cannot
prevent traumas, one can at least adjust the mind to make them more bearable
and mitigate the damage. Psychological defenses can also prevent repetition of
the trauma when, akin to the immune system, they are evoked in a very sensitive manner by cues reminiscent of the trauma. In such cases, defenses may be
imagined in front of traumas in Figure 2.

It is suggested that defenses can be divided into primary and secondary
ones.

Primary Defenses: Dissociation

From the first descriptions of psychological defenses, Janet (van der Hart &
Horst, 1989) and Freud (Breuer & Freud, 1895/1975) were interested in the
basic mechanism by which the mind protected itself in trauma. This was by
fragmenting the integrity of its functioning, often called fragmentation or disintegration. However, Janet's term *dissociation* has recently been revived. It
has been defined as a loosening of associations between cognitions, emotions,
somatic sensations, and behavior (Braun, 1993; van der Hart & Horst, 1989; van
der Kolk, 1996c). These are core mental functions present in basic nodal organizations of the mind (chapter 4). The clinical hallmarks of dissociation are
fragmentation of affective and cognitive experience, depersonalization and derealization, being "spaced out" (van der Kolk & Fisler; 1995), change in the
state of consciousness, a mental paralysis, and psychic numbing (Herman, 1992).
Dissociation may involve awareness or expression of any one of these symptoms or a combination of them.

Some workers (van der Kolk, McFarlane, & Weisath, 1996) have differentiated the initial fragmentation of mental functions as primary dissociation, and
they called depersonalization and derealization phenomena secondary. Dissociation at the time of trauma has been called peritraumatic, and found to be
an important precursor and predictor of PTSD (Marmar et al., 1994; Shalev,
Orr, & Pitman, 1993; van der Kolk, 1996c; van der Kolk & Fisler, 1995).

On a parallel track to the above mainly cognitive stream, Breuer and
Freud (1895/1975) described the basic defensive fragmentation of the mind as
splitting of emotional consciousness. Here incompatible emotions led to the
unconscionable one being split off from consciousness (Freud, 1894/1975l).
Psychoanalysis continued its interest in splitting as a basic defense where

only one aspect of ambivalent emotions (such as good and bad) was in awareness.

Actually, both Janet (van der Hart & Horst, 1989) and Freud (Breuer & Freud, 1895/1975) acknowledged emotional, cognitive, and contextual fragments that were disconnected from conscious awareness. Both maintained that the unconscious fragments had psychic power and could return in characteristic symptoms and illnesses. This basic tenet has held up for over a century.

It may be seen that the process of disconnection of mental functions has been called by different names such as dissociation, splitting of consciousness, fragmentation, and disintegration, according to the vision of the process and optimism or pessimism with regard to it. Defenses have also been labeled, it is suggested, according to where splits of awareness occur and which fragment(s) are observed. Thus, dissociation (using this term) of feeling is called *psychic numbing*. Together with cognitive awareness, it may be called *detachment* or *isolation of affect*. Lack of cognitive representation may be called *disavowal*. Disavowal of one's person while acknowledging external reality is *depersonalization,* and acknowledgment of self but not of external reality is *derealization.* Dissociation of all but somatic representations is *somatization*, whereas actions being sole remnants in awareness is *acting out.*

It may be that primary defenses are parts of a higher level concept. In other words, dissociation may include a variety of strategies of arranging awareness in traumatic situations so that one's actions promote maximum survival and fulfillment. This could explain why different manifestations of dissociation come into play in different traumatic situations.

In the biological arena, too, one can find disconnections of inner parts to promote survival of the rest of the body. Such disconnections may involve sequestering (as in abscess formation), dissolving, expelling, sloughing, and separating.

Secondary Defenses

A number of other defenses came to be recognized that could usefully be regarded as secondary, as they did not fragment core mental functions. Anna Freud (1936) was the first to compile a list that included such defenses, such as repression, regression, reaction formation, undoing, turning against the self, sublimation, and identification with the aggressor. Repression has been sometimes seen as a primary defense and been used synonymously with splitting of consciousness. However, repression can obliterate from awareness whole organized events after traumatic situations and is thus less basic than dissociation.

Analysts came to differentiate early or psychotic, later or neurotic, and more mature or benign defenses. Klein (Segal, 1975) included among the early psychotic defenses projection, introjection, splitting, fragmentation, and projective identification. She called them defenses of the "paranoid position," common in the first year of life. They are followed by more mature defenses of the "depressive position," common between 6 and 24 months, thus overlapping with the paranoid position. The latter defenses are against loss and included denial, manic defenses, and fantasies of control, triumph, omnipotence, and contempt. Vaillant (1993) also categorized defenses as psychotic, immature or neurotic, but added mature ones. Psychotic defenses correspond broadly to Klein's. Immature and neurotic defenses include hypochondriasis, acting out, intellectualization, and reaction formation, whereas mature defenses include altruism, sublimation, avoidance, worry, and humor.

Implied in the differentiation of defenses was the notion that psychotic defenses are integral to psychotic illnesses and neurotic defenses to neurotic ones. The specific defenses used then determine which particular psychoses and neuroses result (Vaillant, 1992).

Clinically, primary and psychotic defenses predominate at young ages and in severe traumas and become parts of severe illnesses such as dissociative, somatization, borderline, and psychotic disorders. In less straitened circumstances, immature defenses could contribute to less disintegrated illnesses such as obsessional neuroses. Mature defenses could even enhance fulfillment (Vaillant, 1992). The concept of specific defenses contributing to specific illnesses is explored further in psychodynamic views of illnesses (chapter 6). A wholist perspective view of defenses is presented in chapter 16.

Once again, in the biological arena there are parallels to defenses contributing to the nature of illnesses. For instance, they determine whether a streptococcal infection leads to a mild tonsillitis, abscess, septicemia, or rheumatic fever.

Mechanisms and Functions of Defenses

As noted above, it may be that defenses are mental capacities used to arrange information and ways of being for maximum survival and fulfillment. Examples of the latter include the use of dissociation by children in play and fantasies (van der Kolk, 1996b). Similarly, denial, repression, and inhibition can enhance prioritization and adaptive channeling of impulses. Projection, introjection, splitting, and projective identification may be the only means of conveying emotions and stories that have not been synthesized into verbal narratives.

Alternatively, in traumatic situations defenses may be combined and elaborated in quite complex ways to suit circumstances. For instance, scapegoating may use dissociation, projection, and displacement. Similarly, primitive defenses such as dissociation may be subsumed and elaborated at higher function levels, for instance, into dissociative identity disorder, previously known as multiple personality.

In fact, it may be best to see various capacities of registering, categorizing, and expressing as normal mental functions that can be used for fulfillment purposes or as defenses to mitigate and prevent trauma. In the latter case, it is suggested that they should be called defenses and accord with common usage. In line with this, the proposed definition of defenses is the following: *Defenses mitigate the potential and actual effects of trauma and its recurrence.*

Defenses contribute to compromise equilibria that involve strain and cost. Part of the cost is obfuscating reality. If on balance defenses are cost effective, they are often called adaptive, or coping, strategies, and people may be described as coping. For instance, "I cope by not thinking about the past. I keep very busy, thinking about the future." When defenses are not cost effective, they are maladaptive or pathological, and people are said to not cope. "It drives me crazy not to be able to relax. If I do I get anxious, then I have to drink to settle down."

One may speculate that primary defenses "dis-integrate" or stop integration of awareness at more basic levels, whereas secondary defenses use more complex means to keep out of awareness more integrated information. It may be that trauma disconnects or, in the young and very traumatized, prevents connection of information. It may further be that for survival purposes in either case, integration stops short of knowledge of trauma and the perceived danger of its repetition. At such times, defenses precede (further) trauma in Figure 2. It is suggested that there may be as many ways of unawareness as awareness, or as many troughs as salient points in the ripples of trauma (see also chapter 3).

In summary, defenses mitigate sequelae of traumatic situations and their recurrence. In the psychological sphere, they do this by diminishing awareness. Defenses become integral parts of memory (or its lack), and they contribute to the specific nature of illnesses.

MEMORIES

Although defenses mitigate trauma by diminishing awareness, in later reviews of the trauma this may manifest as deficient memories. The question of memories includes all the complexities of defenses.

Being buffeted by fragments of memories of the trauma leads to a sense of irrationality and madness and a hindrance to progression in life. However, to remember fully may be sensed as endangering life. The dialectic may be experienced in the various intrusions and forgetfulness of traumatic events.

An internal dilemma may be set up. For instance, in child survivors of the Holocaust there was on the one hand typically hunger for memories as if life depended on them (Kestenberg, 1988). On the other hand, they were feared, as if they "might unleash the demons of remembrance to haunt the already haunted" (Krell, 1985, p. 400). Janet (van der Kolk et al., 1996) called this phobia of memory.

Traumatology has been able to contribute recently to the nature of memories (e.g., Reviere, 1996) and their obfuscations through prospective and retrospective clinical observations. What follows concentrates on psychological memories. However, one should remember that humans have a complex biological genetic memory (D. N. Stern, 1984) and physiological memory that records early events and attunements (chapter 3, chapter 9), as well as memories transposed by parents (Kestenberg, 1989; chapter 2) and the wider culture.

Memories are examined along a process of perception, appraisal and encoding; consolidation; and retrieval.

Perception, Appraisal, and Encoding

Events perceived by sense organs are transmitted through the midbrain to the limbic brain, which is concerned with survival issues. There cognitive (facts) and emotional (feelings) aspects are processed separately by the hippocampus and the amygdala, respectively (Bremner et al., 1995; chapter 3). They are reprocessed and integrated in the higher brain centers in nodes of information (chapter 3, chapter 4).

However, in traumatic situations, it has been suggested, such integration may not occur. Events stay in their fragmented dissociated modes and are encoded as such. The lack of processing of such memories gives the impression of a photographic etching on the mind of the different modes and have therefore been called "flashbulb" memories. Tinnin (1994) noted accurate encoding of somatic and emotional events from birth. The younger the child and more traumatic the event, the more only dissociated somatic and emotional fragments may be encoded (Terr, 1987, 1991).

Factors other than dissociation have been shown to influence traumatic memories. Immature brain function leads to younger children perceiving relatively more somatically and being more prone to time skew, faulty sequencing, condensation of events, and atavistic images (M. Lewis, 1995; Pynoos, 1993; Pynoos & Eth, 1985; Pynoos, Steinberg, & Goenjian, 1996; Terr 1987, 1990; Valent, 1994, 1995a). As well, verbal and complicated events can be misinterpreted by the young. In some situations, such as prolonged traumatic ones, children can also add wishes (even hallucinations) and other defenses. These can be encoded as an amalgam, or in different memory fragments. Additional obfuscation can result when adults impose appraisals different to children's perceptions. For instance, frightening and painful genital perceptions can be labeled as pleasant. Opposing appraisals can then be encoded in separate fragments.

Overall, encoding occurs according to available mental capacities and their defensive arrangements. It may range from solely somatic and emotional fragments to complex, integrated, and verbally meaningful events.

Consolidation

Consolidation is thought to occur over weeks to form permanent engrams. In nontraumatic circumstances, new schemas are added to older ones, and one derives a richer average of particular objects akin to Plato's forms or molds. Desires and distortions may be added for psychological and social consistency.

Desires and defenses may be added to traumatic memories, too. For instance, children may create heroic fantasies or a fantasy where they say goodbye to a dead friend. They may develop retrospective omens to make them feel that they had predicted the unexpected (Pynoos & Eth, 1985; Terr, 1990). They may desire that what father is doing to them during sexual abuse is somehow good or will turn out to be so. However, unlike nontraumatic memories, relatively little molding occurs. Rather, memories remain stable in bigger or smaller dissociated fragments.

It may be that the traumatic amalgam is imprinted in stable engrams according to the intensity of the traumatic event and the receptivity and maturity of the brain. This imprinting may be similar to attachment imprinting of young animals to their first caretakers (K. Lorenz, 1968). However, nontraumatic events may be molded in a more plastic manner. Even stressful events may be appraised and reappraised according to survival needs of the time and the final appraisals remembered relatively more clearly. It is possible that such differential remembering serves survival. Traumatic events must be remembered as they were, to recognize future cues reminiscent of them.

From this time on, traumatic memories are also distinguished quantitatively, by hypermnesia and amnesia. The former are experienced as intense intrusions of traumatic memories in dreams, flashbacks, thoughts, fantasies, and actions. In amnesia, the opposite occurs. The two can vary in degree and fluctuate. Amnesia, though counterintuitive, has been observed after every type of traumatic event. For instance, 10% of soldiers have no memory for recent combat (van der Kolk & Fisler, 1995). Retrospective (Elliot & Briere, 1995) and prospective (Williams, 1995) studies of sexually abused children indicated a range of 18%–59% who totally forgot their abuse at some time over the years. Those who forgot tended to be at the time of the abuse relatively younger, more frightened, more threatened if they told, and less supported by their mothers. Yet even those who remembered the whole time remembered the events in similarly fragmented ways to those who had not remembered them for some time (see also case 3, chapter 1). This may indicate the ubiquity of primary defenses at times of trauma.

Different degrees of amnesia and hypermnesia together with different types of defenses used determine degree and type of awareness. For instance, described levels of awareness ranging from total unawareness through fugues; reliving fragments of experience biologically, psychologically, or in action; to ever more coherent and owned narratives.

Traumatic experiences may be triggers to previous forgotten memories (van der Kolk et al., 1996; chapter 1). Thus, trauma may remind one of previous traumas. Though emotional recounting of traumas from long ago may seem irrelevant to the observer, it allows victims to try to make overarching meanings of their traumas.

Retrieval

Nontraumatic memories that have been consolidated into other schemas form part of a coherent self. They may be retrieved through will and communicated verbally as part of one's narrative. They are called declarative memory. Traumatic memories resemble procedural memory of automatic skills and habits in that they are outside will and time sequence. Rather than resembling logical left brain expression, they are said to resemble emotional responses of the right brain. They also differ from declarative memory for reasons relating to the previous phases.

First, traumatic memories may have been encoded and consolidated at an age prior to the person's having had the capacities of cataloguing, time sequencing, verbal symbolization, and a sense of self, all of which are needed for verbal, narrative autobiographical recall (M. L. Rogers, 1995). Thus, only dissociated mental imprints of somatic and emotional or iconic (isolated visual images) memory may be available for retrieval.

As well, there may have been regression to earlier functioning at the time of the trauma. Hence, memories that may eventually return are often first retrieved as visual, olfactory, affective, auditory, and kinesthetic experiences (van der Kolk & Fisler, 1995).

Second, retrieved memories may reflect traumatic experiences together with the perceptual distortions and defenses from the encoding and consolidation phases mentioned above. For instance, memories may be admixed with atavistic images. Such memories tend to be highly accurate for traumatic events (M. L. Rogers, 1995), but in the way they were experienced initially.

Last, people may be rejected, blamed, shamed, and punished for their memories, which then may become suppressed. In Case 3, as Anne (chapter 1) was about to tell of her abuses in detail, she reexperienced men threatening her with death if she talked. Among child survivors, remembering the Holocaust broke the "conspiracy of silence" and evoked much suffering in the survivors' parents. If a current listener is not sympathetic, the initial suppression of memory may be reenacted.

The following case summarizes some of the above points. Amnesia provided a cushion for trauma, self-blame, and life's lack of meaning. Retrieval was allowed when therapy gave hope of a moral and meaningful life. The case also illustrates that perpetrators as well as victims can suffer amnesia.

A young, intoxicated man drove into a woman crossing the road. Her decapitated torso landed in the passenger seat. He gave a clear deposition to the police of the event. In the emergency department the next day, while complaining of some pains, he expressed some casual puzzlement about whether he had had a passenger with him or not. Over the weeks, he totally forgot the circumstances of the incident. In therapy, he slowly retrieved a clear memory for the event. He said the memory was really always there, but it was only in the context of hope beyond his deed that therapy had given him that "I allowed myself to remember." During his court appearance, he had full memory and remorse. [*I thank Tony Catenese for allowing me to quote his case.*]

Veracity of Memories

There are few social problems regarding veracity of retrieved memories in adults such as soldiers and disaster victims. Even retrieval of incomplete memories in children, such as child survivors of the Holocaust or those bereaved in early life, are accepted as the facts become known. However, when it comes to similar surfacing of memories of sexually abused children, there has been a recurrent outcry. Usually, individual children are blamed as mad or bad. However, there has recently emerged a movement blaming therapists for supposedly implanting false memories of childhood sexual abuse into their clients' minds. They thus supposedly created a "false memory syndrome" (*The New York Review,* 1994). The emotional heat of the argument reaches into denial of trauma, amnesia, and the psychodynamics of mental illness.

The scientific argument draws on laboratory studies that indicate that people are suggestible (Loftus, 1993). However, the studies were on nontraumatized college students whose suggestibility of memory was for events that did not threaten them. Such suggestibility is part of nontraumatic memory, which includes desire to please and have consistency. However, traumatic memory is different. For instance, Lewis (1995) found that although children were suggestible for peripheral details, this suggestibility was absent for centrally significant events. Similarly, Valent (1994) found that hidden Jewish children in the Holocaust older than age 3 remembered their Jewish identities in their cores no matter how great the influence to forget and to whatever degree they lived a convincing double identity. In a literature search, van der Kolk (1996a) found no reports of suggestions distorting traumatic memories. Leavitt (1997) found that those who recovered memories of sexual abuse were significantly less suggestible than a control group of psychiatric patients.

Nevertheless, it must be remembered that the very young can misinterpret and misattribute their experiences. It is also possible to speculate that they absorb their parents' experiences as their own to some degree (Valent, 1990). Nevertheless, memories of sexually abused children greatly resemble those of child survivors of the Holocaust whose traumas are well documented (Valent, 1995a).

As well, threats to survival on the one hand and promise of safety on the other can induce defensive splits in past and current awareness that allow survival at the time. This can occur in brainwashed prisoners, cult members, intimidatory suppression by perpetrator adults of children in their power, and in some cases, no doubt, by unaware or unethical therapists. However, it is more likely that false positive sexual abuse fantasies are far outweighed by false negative ones.

In fact, most memories of sexual abuse are usually retrieved outside therapy (van der Kolk, 1996a; van der Kolk & Fisler, 1995; Williams, 1995). They are retrieved in the context of cues reminiscent of the trauma, reaching life phases where the trauma can now be assimilated or needs to be assimilated to fulfill progression in one's life. When memories are retrieved in therapy (such retrieval is commonplace in psychotherapy from all kinds of traumas), the result is more coherent thoughts and less depression (Foa, Molnar, & Cashman, 1995). Memories are felt deeply as belonging to oneself, unlike imposed thoughts, which may be deprogrammed relatively easily. Invalidation of retrieved memories can reevoke the traumatic event when it was originally invalidated (Herman, 1992; Pearlman & Saakvitne, 1995), whereas validation of memories is very therapeutic, with the discovery that certain apparently crazy fragments of oneself belonged to real past events.

> Bernadette remembered a cherry tree behind the house where she was hidden as a Holocaust child at the age of 4. She felt major distress, as if her whole past was in question, when told there had never been such a cherry tree. She felt great relief when she found the tree in the orphanage from which she had been taken to the house in question. (Valent, 1994)

> Litzi felt that her returning images of a river of shit with a boot poking out were crazy until she realized that this was a childhood memory of the latrines at Teresienstadt camp. (Personal communication, L. Hart, 1990)

Perpetrators are usually older and know and remember more clearly. However, they can also arrange their minds to suit their survival. When confronted with their actions, they tend to explain them with the appraisals and defenses (such as detachment or "doubling"; Lifton, 1986), used at the time of abuse or atrocity. In everyday life, they also use these defenses and continue to double as innocents or victims. They suppress knowledge in themselves and others more or less violently and impose a conspiracy of silence (Herman, 1981; Posner, 1991; Sichrovsky, 1988). Vietnam veterans who did not need to worry about punishment and were treated sympathetically could confess their atrocities and live their trauma and consequent remorse.

In summary, declarative memories serve fulfillment by putting together a coherent and ever expanding and deepening narrative, or life story. They are tools of a constructive process of expanding organization and satisfaction. Traumatic memories, however, concentrate on survival needs. On the one hand, they may command central attention and be very sensitively evoked. On the other hand, memories may be sensed as dangerous, and awareness of them is fragmented by a variety of defenses. Hypermnesias and amnesias become parts of new illness equilibria. The following may be a definition of memory in traumatic stress: *Traumatic memories are reverberations of traumatic events and their defenses.*

It may be that in evolutionary terms declarative and traumatic memories are chosen in proportion to demands to survive and fulfill. It is also possible that they may be to some extent interchangeable according to current needs and life meanings. For instance, traumatic memories may be worked through and assembled in testimonies. When traumatic memories persist in spite of current safety, a sense of irrationality is added to illnesses. Sense can only be found in the original traumatic situation. To determine veracity of memories, the different natures of both declarative and traumatic memories must be kept in mind.

Last, memories are a complex capacity of the self that help it to adjust to the world in as rational, consistent, and meaningful a way as possible. When the world is rent asunder, so are rational, consistent, and fulfilling memories of normal times. Healing restores connections of memories to events and their times and meanings, allowing life's narrative to continue.

To summarize this chapter, it may be seen that the process axis contains extremely complex components whose own subcomponents and interactions make the system even more complex. Nevertheless, the system clarifies the nature of the process from the happening of a traumatic event to its later sequelae, for instance, how physiological, psychological, and social stress responses may be influenced by defenses, strengths, and vulnerabilities in the final expression of physical, psychological, or social symptoms.

Components of the other two axes are looked at in the next two chapters. Although illnesses are noted on the process axis, they are considered separately in chapter 6 because of their importance, in conjunction with the other two axes.

Chapter 4

Components of Axis 2,
The Parameters Axis

The parameters or context of traumatic stress includes the nature of the traumatic situation, disaster phases, social system levels, and developmental phases
of the victims. If the process axis is the length axis of traumatic stress, the
parameters axis is its breadth. The next chapter describes its depth.

FACTORS IN TRAUMATIC SITUATIONS

Because there are only limited avenues of basic human responses to traumatic
situations (Weisaeth & Eitinger, 1993), a relatively small number of concepts
are universal to them all. However, the endless variety within each trauma is
contributed to by the nature of the traumatic situation and the environment in
which it occurs.

Each traumatic situation described in chapter 2 has its own culture. Combat, sexual abuse, psychosomatic medicine, bereavement, and so on have their
own patterns and expressions, and that is why they initially seemed unique and
developed their own disciplines and journals. The nature of the traumatic situation is usually the first parameter used to designate traumatic stresses.

PHASES OF TRAUMATIC SITUATIONS

Phases describe the "when" in the process of traumatic events. Different disaster phases such as impact, postimpact, recovery, and reconstruction and typical events occurring in each have already been described (chapter 1, chapter 2).

Disaster phases have their own challenges and hence their own fulfillments and traumas. For instance, the challenge in the impact phase is to save life, in the postimpact phase to take stock and ensure vital resources, in the recovery phase to consolidate and expand resources and to grieve, and in the reconstruction phase to get back to normal. Stress responses have different "cultures" in different phases. For instance, flight may involve evacuation before a disaster, frantic escape during a disaster, and moving away to escape memories after a disaster.

It is important to know retrospectively which phases are represented in which memories. It is also important to know the history of awareness and memories at different phases of the traumatic situation, for instance, whether subjects dissociated at the time of the trauma or whether their memories were punished and suppressed after it (chapter 3).

SOCIAL SYSTEM LEVELS

Much traumatic stress literature has concentrated on individuals, perhaps because its founders were doctors who treated individuals. However, different social groupings may be just as or even more important. For instance, international violence may be more significant than personal violation.

Traumatic situations—and other stress components such as stress responses, defenses, and memories—often have different subgoals, organizations, and activities at individual, family, community, and national levels. Similarly, the same concept—such as conflict, loyalty, isolation, or persecution—has different expressions according to the social situation. Using the previous example of flight, individual, family, group, and community evacuations and escapes manifest different organizations and activities. A special system unit is the helper–victim one. It is examined in more detail in chapter 8.

DEVELOPMENTAL PHASES

Trauma, it is suggested, is experienced differently throughout the life cycle. Childhood traumas are particularly important because they interfere with early building blocks and lead to lasting distortions. It is fortunate that childhood development and its disruptions have received some attention.

The following paradigm suggested by Bion (1962) may be seen as applicable for more complex developmental fulfillments and disruptions throughout life. Infants were predesigned to root for and recognize an integrated sensory breast, both sucked and seen. Bion called the premonition in the baby's mind before the revelation of the actual nipple a preconception. Finding the nipple enabled a concept to form. Others have called this primitive concept an episode (D. N. Stern, 1984) or a node (Yates & Nasby, 1993). Such nodes already contain feeling states, a proposition, sense of self and others, and context. These nodes or episodes are abstracted and generalized and linked in associative networks called schemas that are the basic "package" of knowledge. When stimuli activate schemas, the whole package is stimulated. The components of the package (cognitions, emotions, self, relation to others, and context) then tend to further activate temporally encoded schemas and previous memories associated with aspects of the schemas.

However, continued lack of the nipple may lead to a traumatic situation. This may affect the quality and quantity of the components of the node and their connections. For instance, cognitions, emotions, physiological feeling states, sense of self and others, and context may be disrupted (see also dissociation, chapter 3). Later, recurrent desires, thinking, and other cues may reevoke the traumatic situation. Such traumatic states can interrupt development of more complex concepts such as two-ness, or the concept of complementarity to one's needs. This may have widespread ramifications in the adult's ways of thought and views of the self and the world. The following case seen in the emergency department illustrates sequelae of another fault in earliest development, not being seen.

> A 34-year-old man developed a terrible hollowness in his chest and abdomen at the moment he lost sight of his girlfriend at the airport. The pain was only appeased when he made contact with a nurse in the hospital who had cared for him during a previous admission. His problem was traced back to an inability to gain security from his mother ever since he could remember. He always tried to keep her and later his girlfriend within sight. Otherwise, he felt he was disintegrating and the somatic equivalents of aloneness appeared. At times he was able to keep an image of eye contact in his mind and then he could function well.

The above paradigm and clinical case may have certain implications, first, that there are deeply desired evolutionary preconceptions according to the developmental phases of the life cycle that, if not fulfilled, act as stressors and may result in major distress and trauma.

Second, what may be minor hassles for most adults (being fed, seen) may be life-and-death issues for infants and for adults in whom the earlier traumas are evoked.

Third, poor early handling and misattunements may be deeply remembered physiologically and emotionally in later life. The manifestations of "remembering" may be variably disconnected physiological responses (such as diminished immunocompetence; chapter 3), emotions, and actings out. These "memories" can also be cued by events reminiscent of early traumas.

Last, akin to memory, thinking and feeling may reevoke trauma. This may be dealt with by interruption of thinking and introspection, which if ingrained as a style is called alexithymia. Such adults may suffer symptoms evoked by cues reminiscent of early traumas but not know their sources.

The younger the child, the more prone it is to not have solid integration of nodes and schematic trees but have immature and fragmented experiences in trauma (chapter 3). Such experiences may also serve as points for regression to earlier more secure developmental phases. Traumatic stress manifestations may indicate current development, developmental phase at the age of the trauma, and levels of regression.

In the previous chapter, it was suggested that human function levels manifest evolutionary progress that is reflected in the developmental phases of individuals. The following is a composite of cognitive (Brainerd, 1978), emotional (Lane & Schwartz, 1987), and moral (Kohlberg, 1981, 1985) developments in children. It is suggested that they are complementary to the evolution of human function levels described in more detail in chapter 5.

Characteristics of Developmental Phases

1   *Sensorimotor* (Substage 1; 0–1 month). The infant has reflex responses to the outside, accompanied by internal physiological responses. Facial expression is present. Emotions are felt as global body sensations and lead to undifferentiated arousal (or inhibition).

2   *Sensorimotor* (Substage 2–6; up to 2 years). Infant learns about the durability of time and space and differentiates self from others. He or she acquires a variety of skills. Emotion is both a bodily sensation and an awareness of an action tendency. Pleasure and unpleasure are differentiated and can be described. Morality thus far is dominated by pleasure and unpleasure. Developmental phases thus far correspond to the physiological and security needs human function level.

3   *Preoperational* (2–7 years). Child learns about individual objects and objects as classes. The child does not have an objective concept of why things happen and that they may occur randomly. In an egocentric way, the child lives in the center of a world of animism and magic where everything is preordained by gods and adults. Emotions are pervasive and either/or. There is greater use of symbolic language. The child may represent its inner world in paintings, action, and other symbols. Morality at this phase is hierarchical or deontological. The child has reached early social and spiritual function levels.

4   *Concrete operational* (middle childhood). Classes of objects and various attributes of single objects are integrated into unified concepts such as conservation of volume. Learning occurs according to the brain's maturational readiness and smoothness of acquisition of necessary structures. Opposite feelings and blends of emotion are now differentiated and can be described. Different forms of virtue, worth, and justice

are learned. Guilt, shame, and conscience develop. The level of moral evolution has been reached.

5 *Formal operational* (adolescence). Mature abstract and symbolic reasoning and speculation occur, and ambiguities are appreciated. Many nuances of emotion can be discerned now in self and through empathy with others. Conflicts in morality can be appreciated. Higher values and principles are sought. The level of ideals, principles, and justice has been reached.

Further Developmental Phases

Biological, cognitive, emotional, and moral development continue throughout the life cycle. Erikson (1965) described eight developmental stages of humans ranging from infancy to maturity. Each had its fulfillment and traumatic equivalents, for instance, autonomy and doubt in early childhood and ego integrity and existential despair in maturity. This range roughly parallels the function levels in chapter 5.

In conclusion, points in the life cycle influence biological, psychological, and social fulfillments and traumas. Such influence then ramifies into later phases and function levels. When under stress, people may relive to previously traumatic developmental phases, and regress to even earlier phases that had offered fulfillment.

In summary, components of the parameters axis contextualize traumatic stress manifestations. Grids of parameter components may be used for fuller descriptions or research purposes. For instance, Mileti et al. (1975) suggested a disaster-phase/system-level grid that looked at various system-level responses at different disaster phases. Valent (1984, chapter 1) extended this when he described biological, psychological, and social responses in a bush fire according to disaster phases, social system levels, and points on the life cycle. It is suggested that all components of all axes can be contextualized according to the above parameters.

The next chapter describes the last of the axes in the triaxial framework, the depth axis.

Chapter 5

Components of Axis 3,
the Depth Axis

The study of trauma forces a study of what trauma destroys, including what is spiritual, the soul. Van der Kolk and McFarlane (1996) referred to trauma as the soul of psychiatry. Previous chapters have indicated, too, that trauma disrupts body and soul, happiness, and the essence of life.

Components of the depth axis have been relatively ignored in medicine and psychiatry. According to the scientific–humanist dichotomy, depth axis components have traditionally been in the domain of priests and philosophers. However, it is suggested that traumatology can provide a valuable observational and prospective perspective on such components. Perhaps for the first time philosophy and traumatology are being combined in a heuristically meaningful way. It is suggested that the combination is exciting and fertile, providing insights and perspectives on what humans consider most important in their lives.

A hierarchy of function levels from the physiological to the spiritual are examined briefly. At the end of the chapter, the concept of the life–trauma dialectic is developed more fully.

A HIERARCHY OF HUMAN FUNCTION LEVELS

Appreciation of biological evolution has been followed by examination of evolution of developmental goals (Erikson, 1965) and capacities. For instance, evolution of cognitive capacities has been described by Piaget (Brainerd, 1978). Kohlberg (1981, 1985) described a parallel moral evolution. A similar hierarchy of function levels from body to "reason" or "soul" has been postulated since Aristotle (D. M. Robinson, 1993). The hierarchy is generally thought to re-capitulate in each human's development evolutionary developments of the species. Both philosophers and psychologists have maintained that happiness entails fulfillment of all evolving potentials.

Perhaps the best known hierarchy of potentials that need fulfillment was described by Maslow (1970). He said that bodily needs and needs for safety are most basic. They are followed by needs of belonging and love, then by self-esteem, followed by needs to fulfill an esthetic sense and quest for knowledge, and finally by actualization of individual talents and potentials.

The hierarchy of human function levels described in this chapter is roughly similar, though it also includes morality, religion and ideology, identity, the sacred, and finally wisdom, beauty, and truth. The latter may be seen as aspects of the soul. Generally, each level is a foundation for those that follow. For instance, good and bad and worth and justice on the judgment level are basis for types of meanings and ideals and values and principles, respectively.

Fulfillments on all these levels are the purpose of life—what life is about. Trauma disrupts all these levels.

FULFILLMENT AND TRAUMATIZATION
AT DIFFERENT FUNCTION LEVELS

Physiological and Security (Survival) Needs:
Pleasure and Unpleasure

Humans share with animals various physiological needs, such as feeding, excretion, sexuality, warmth, and security needs such as being held close. Satisfaction of each need is associated with a specific pleasure. Lack of satisfaction is associated with specific unpleasures. Instincts form parts of more complex drives such as hunting, sexual love, and caring for young. Each is modulated by its more complex pleasures and unpleasures.

Hedonists throughout history have advocated enjoyment of bodily pleasures as ultimate fulfillments. Freud (1915/1975j) and Skinner (1953) also saw bodily pleasures (and avoidance of unpleasures) as motivators of human behavior. The ancient Epicureans saw unpleasure as evil, going against human nature, threatening life.

Instinctual and drive pleasures are associated with biological survival. They form the basic happiness of being alive. When fulfilled, one says, "It is so good to just be alive." In trauma, all bodily processes and aspects of security may be threatened, producing a variety of physical and emotional pains and unpleasures. Survival pleasures and unpleasures can be found in Table 2 (chapter 7).

Evolution of Social Pleasures and Unpleasures

For 99% of their evolutionary existence, humans hunted and were hunted (Laughlin, 1977; Lee & DeVore, 1977), and they evolved various social characteristics with other animals in similar ecological niches. These characteristics served survival of the group. Within the group, they included hierarchy, group loyalty, and territoriality (Ardrey, 1967). Defense and competition were characteristic attitudes to outsiders, comprising the xenophobia principle (Scott, 1989; E. O. Wilson, 1975). Here outsiders were appraised as subhuman and could be killed akin to animals.

In addition to individual pleasures and unpleasures, there were now social pleasures, too. They included belonging to a group and territory and fulfillment of tasks, skills, roles, and status. Dominants had the pleasures of power, wealth, and leadership, subordinates of devotion, order, and security of distribution. Killing and robbing enemies gave warriors the satisfactions of promoting survival of their own group.

Many early social characteristics were carried over to more complex human societies. For instance, tribal chiefs like King Solomon shared similarities with dominant animals in directing defense, acquiring and distributing resources (first taking the royal share), and settling disputes. Though work and positions of power have replaced pleasures of hunting with pleasures of wealth and comforts and territories have expanded to states, earlier mentalities could still be applied to them. Especially in times of stress, societies may return to the jungle mentality. Then group cohesion, territoriality, and the xenophobia principle are accentuated.

Traumatic situations can include collapse of social integrity, networks, and structures. Roles, status, power, and wealth may be disrupted and lost. The social pleasures associated with each of these factors may be replaced by various forms of distress.

Evolution of Cosmology and Spirituality: Magic and Myths

Unlike animals, humans evolved thoughts and imagination that were used to make wider networks of meanings of the world, including life's exigencies and traumas. There were projections from the known to the unknown. Animate qualities were attributed to inanimate matter, human qualities to animals, live qualities to the dead, and inner desires to outer reality. Alongside the objective world ran a cosmology of threatening monsters resembling earthly predators and spiritual allies resembling parents and leaders. They formed a world of magic and myths. Aided by sorcery, rituals, and human mediums, they gave the impression of control over the unknown world.

The sense of spirituality of this world included a pervading significance and connection of all things with a known universe. It included beliefs of eternal survival and fulfillment. The social sharing of these myths increased their power.

This type of thinking is present in children and reflects Piaget's preoperational level of human development (ages 2–7). At this stage the question "Why?" demands an answer that simultaneously includes causes and consequences (Brainerd, 1978). It is as if the universe was a blueprint willfully preordained and devised especially for oneself (or one's group) by parents (ancestors) or God. Hence, everything is knowable and predictable.

Such spirituality, accompanying rituals, prayers, and beliefs of being the chosen children of the universe and of universal significance and eternal life can be highly fulfilling. However, in traumatic situations, both the real and the magic world are torn asunder. A whole cosmology can collapse, leaving widespread demoralization, disillusionment, and fear. It is akin to a child being abandoned to the monsters of the jungle. Magic and myth are subsumed by later religion and ideologies (see below).

The Evolution of Morality

Traumatology and philosophy meet midway in their observations of three types of morality. They are *hierarchical morality,* which determines good and bad; *morality of worth,* which determines worthiness and unworthiness; and *morality of justice,* which determines what is fair and unfair. More than one morality can apply in particular situations.

Although philosophers wonder at the naturalness and universality of these moralities and attribute their source to universal principles or divinity, traumatology may see their naturalness in terms of survival of the group in traumatic situations. The reciprocal evocation of pleasant and unpleasant moral feelings regulates distribution of strategies and resources of survival and ensures maximum survival in a community. Moral feelings reflect the evolutionary fact that other people are often the greatest resource serving survival, and consequent fulfillment.

Hierarchical Morality: Good and Bad   Hierarchical (also called deontological) morality is concerned with obedience—oughts and obligations decreed from above (Bayles & Henley, 1983). It uses praise and anger to evoke feelings of goodness and rectitude or badness and guilt, respectively. It is the oldest morality and is the only one used in the Old Testament. Theological morality depends on it, and it adds virtue to good acts and sin to bad ones.

According to Kohlberg (1981, 1985), hierarchical morality is deeply satisfying at the preoperational level of development described above. Hence, it draws heavily on early social constellations of parents and dominant males, chosen groups, magic and myths, predetermined universe, and heavenly bliss for the good.

In traumatic situations, authorities and rescue workers can take on godlike characteristics, and obedience to them may be life saving. Hierarchies are, however, flexible in traumatic situations and depend on who has the power to rescue others.

Anger and guilt are feedback mechanisms that balance and modulate a variety of rescue efforts. For instance, it was noted that the admonition "Look after your child!" evoked guilt and energized a flagging mother to look after her child. Similarly, an uncle's cries prevailed on a woman's guilt and induced her to take him to hospital and risk herself and her children. And "How can my house stand when my neighbor's is destroyed?!" led to intense guilt that was appeased by provision of shelter to the neighbor (chapter 1).

In trauma, it may not be possible to rescue or give sufficiently. Conflicts may arise between whom to rescue or between preservation of self and others. In such cases, people may feel guilt akin to having killed or robbed. Even when, objectively, choices are limited, people's almost instinctive guilt for not having rescued others may lead to the long-term mental torment of survivor guilt.

Also, trauma may rip away the bases of hierarchical morality. There is no correlation between goodness and obedience and being traumatized. People may assume guilt or sin to try to normalize the events. However, this may be patently impossible. Then comes the plaintive cry, "Why did it happen to me when I was good?" "Why did God allow Auschwitz?" One may lose faith in God and an ordered universe (Rubenstein, 1992). The whole preoperational world may collapse.

Morality of Worth ("Natural Goods"): Worthiness and Unworthiness
Worth (often called *natural goods* or *goods*) is an innately desirable human quality. Worthiness is rewarded by esteem and evokes self-esteem. Unworthiness leads to humiliation and evokes shame. This morality is more recent and may imply self-determining qualities and character. Nevertheless, worth is still judged according to its survival value for self and others.

Examples of qualities that influence others toward one's own survival are lovableness, attractiveness, and likeability. Qualities that enhance survival of others include bravery, self-sacrifice, nobility, munificence, kindness, and charity. Negative judgments such as cowardice, dependence, and selfishness induce people to change behavior to others.

Goods may be variable and contradictory (Bayles & Henley, 1983; Finnis, 1980). Examples are decisiveness and patience, ferocity and meekness. According to survival needs, qualities may be admirable or foolish. Aristotle (1988) acknowledged that courage could be the undoing of men if the circumstances were wrong.

Some have said that philosophers' goods are geared to high-minded pursuits rather than day-to-day survival issues. Yet in *The Prince,* Machiavelli (1513/1988) espoused power as the principal good. In this sense astuteness, shrewdness, and cunning may also be seen as goods.

Fulfillment from appropriate expression of personal qualities results in high self-esteem, sense of worth, and lovableness.

In trauma, one's qualities fail to produce desired results. Negative judgments such as "You're a coward . . . greedy . . . selfish . . . irresponsible!" result in lasting low self-esteem, shame, humiliation, and a sense of worthlessness and unlovableness. People may assume negative qualities undeservedly in order to try to maintain order in a traumatized world. In case 3, Anne decided it must be something about her that evoked her sexual abuse (chapter 1). When this is untenable, one has to accept that trauma occurs irrespective of personal worth and character.

Morality of Fairness and Justice: Right and Wrong   Justice judges the fairness and unfairness of actions and regulates security and resources in the community. It praises correct actions as right and evokes a sense of rightness or righteousness. It uses blame and punishment for unfair actions and evokes a sense of wrong and blameworthiness. Justice in all societies concerns itself with murder, assault, robbery, treason, theft, arson, and rape (Hall, 1960). It also concerns itself with systems that distribute power, resources, and favors.

Fairness and justice are old moralities. Children complain early on "It is not fair!" if hurt or not given their share. The innateness of fairness and justice has been recognized since the Romans as "natural justice" and "natural law." And yet the morality is variable, predicated by perceived survival needs. For instance, killing, slavery, and looting may be heinous crimes in peace but just in war.

Justice contributes to happiness and fulfillment by providing a fair social matrix where security is guaranteed, resources are sufficiently distributed, offenders are punished, and victims are compensated.

In trauma, security and resources are sensed to be arbitrarily and unjustly removed. People ask in pained outrage, "Why?!" "Why me?!" They feel let down by leaders and, in preoperational thinking, by God or Fate. To maintain coherence, scapegoats may be manufactured or people may blame themselves. Otherwise, there may be a collapse of trust in a just and fair world.

In postimpact phases, people are very sensitive to fair dealings, as the disadvantaged may die. The frequent withholding or just indifferent bureaucratic administration common after wars and disasters may be seen as so unfair as to be even more distressing than the original trauma.

Meanings

Though existential meanings are implied in most philosophical discussions, it is traumatology that can contribute to their origins. It is suggested that survival and moral outcomes are compounded into basic positive or negative existential meanings. Examples associated with hierarchical morality are "God was on my side" or "I am a bad brother because I failed to rescue him." Examples associated with the morality of worth are "I have capacities I did not know I had" or "I am a brave . . . cowardly soldier." Examples in association with justice are "It was fair that he helped my family after I helped him." or "The government is not interested in giving me what I deserve."

People quickly connect their experiences with previous and subsequent events and abstract meanings from them. They attempt to make the trauma, their role, and the world coherent. Examples are "People become good when the chips are down." or "Bad things happen to good people." Horowitz (1976/1992) described emergent meaning of justice in a truck driver after a fatal crash. "When I break rules, bad things happen."

Survival responses, moral feelings, and meanings have ramifications for higher level functions. For instance, survival guilt and its belief that another person, not oneself, should be alive, can affect every level of existence. Many problems in traumatology refer back to the levels so far considered—physical survival, morality, and basic meanings made of the events.

Ideals, Values, and Principles of Justice

Ideals, values, and principles are higher level abstractions of hierarchical, worth, and justice streams of morality, respectively.

Ideals   Ideals are enunciated from on high, sometimes, such as in Proverbs and Ecclesiastes, as divine advice. Examples of ideals are honoring God, never letting go of loyalty, and not being seduced. Ideals still require obedience, duty, obligation, and devotion and are rewarded by divine favors in this life or the next. Ideals can be contradictory, covering opposite life circumstances. They may require turning the other cheek one time and repulsing aggressors at another, or preservation of life one time, but its destruction at another. Over time, there have been attempts to abstract overarching ideals. They include Aristotle's moderation or Golden Mean: "Moral virtue is a mean . . . between excess . . . and deficiency" (Ross, 1988) and "Do for others what you want them to do for you" (Matthew 7:12, *Good News Bible*).

Values   It is only recently that there have been attempts to classify values. For instance, Schwartz (1994) suggested 10 types, including hedonism and conformity, but his values ranged from physiological satisfactions to ideologies.

It is suggested that emerging from concepts of worth and goods are a wide variety of often contradictory values. They include honor and humility, equality and knowing one's place, freedom and law and order, and peacefulness and patriotism. Each is appropriate by serving survival according to circumstances.

Principles of Justice   These are attempts to abstract concepts of fairness. Such principles include respect for life and property, equality of all humans, impartiality of judgment, keeping promises, and returning favors. In other circumstances, other principles may contradict them. Such principles may include, for instance, the idea that killing is right to preserve life, one must maintain hierarchies to keep order, one should look after one's own, and promises may be broken if they lead to harm. Breaking specific principles is often explained by pragmatism or realpolitik (or current needs of survival).

Philosophers have attempted to abstract overarching principles of justice. For instance, Kant's categorical imperative (*Metaphysics and Morals*, 1786) stated that one was to act only in such a way that one would wish the action to be universal. Alternatively, the utilitarian principle (John Stuart Mill, *Utilitarianism*, 1863) stated that acts should be judged solely by their achievement of the maximum amount of happiness for the maximum number of people. Finnis (1980) listed nine principles of justice, including pursuit of goods and no arbitrary preferences.

Critics say that higher abstractions of ideals, values, and principles are too removed from everyday issues of survival and are thus unworldly.

However, the variable ideals, values, and principles provide a sense of moral guidance, of morals being modulated through civilization into greater order. Adherence to them can give great satisfaction. Trauma can disrupt them all, and, as it were, make a mockery of these "veneers of civilization." Loss of ideals, values, and principles can rip away faith in civilization.

Codes, Dignity, and Law and Rights: Ethical Principles

Codes, dignity, and law and rights (in the sense of entitlements) comprise ethical principles (ethical conduct, or simply ethics). They subsume previous moral levels and their streams of hierarchical morality, values, and justice.

Codes derive from hierarchical morality and ideals. They are ethical strictures of behavior imbued with much experience and tradition. Codes may be specified in Bibles, or specified for special groups such as warriors and doctors who are responsible for matters of life and death. Usually codes are assumed voluntarily. Punishment may involve extrusion from a special group but seldom includes fines, prison or death.

Dignity includes respect for the physical, psychological, and social worth and values of people.

Laws subsume an innate sense of fairness and justice and its principles. Unlike codes, laws apply to all members of the community, and transgressions may be punished by fines, prison, or death. Laws are meant to be fair across the society and embody principles that give maximum protection and resources to its members. Laws protect people's rights or entitlements. They include right to life, to security and essential resources, to morality, to justice and dignity, and to freedom of thought and expression of personal ideals, values, and principles (if they do not conflict with others). Rights and dignities are often used synonymously, for instance, with respect to rights of children, of sexual freedom within marriage, and to a dignified death.

Harmonious conjunction of personal and social ethical codes, recognition of one's dignity, and its lawful protection in a just and lawful society facilitate personal and social fulfillment. One of the most painful aspects of trauma is the loss of proper and lawful behavior and the loss of dignity and rights.

Religion, Ideology, and Philosophical Beliefs

Major religious and ideological beliefs include all previous levels of function. Though highly variable, religious and ideological beliefs share a harmonious theory of causation of problems, social relationships, right and wrong, status and justice, and action for an imminent fulfillment of essential goals. They can bring together these various components in a simple set of ideas that can hold large masses of people and provide easily absorbed all-inclusive views and hopes of fulfillment (Ingersoll & Matthews, 1986).

Even though inclusive, specific belief systems may have biases toward subsuming one or the other stream of morality. For instance, fundamentalism, whether in religion or politics, emphasizes hierarchical morality. The ideology of fascism incorporates its tribalism, prophetism, purity, righteousness, faith, and commitment (Maxwell, 1984). Alternatively, the liberal ideology incorporates the values of enterprise and ability. The democratic ideology incorporates the justice of equality.

Religion and ideologies can provide a deep and widespread sense of fulfillment of all the social and moral needs that they subsume. They can combine with preoperational magical and mythical thinking, and provide a sense of being part of a positive universal historical development. In trauma, the collapse of all these components and hopes may be quite devastating.

Symbols

Symbols can represent vital aspects of social groupings, morality, and survival through a small number of associative links. For instance, flags, crosses, anthems, and slogans can represent ideologies and religions, and through them moral outlooks and social groups. Symbols can assume the quality and intensity of the components' previous function levels that they represent. For instance, people may devote themselves to representations of their value through symbols of honor, prestige, and reputation. Clothes and expensive items may designate wealth. Bearing and rituals may symbolize status and dignity.

Symbols can provide fulfillment akin to the original functions they represent. Their destruction in trauma causes equivalent pain.

Traumatology teaches that symbols can also act as cues of imminent repetition of past traumas, even when this is objectively not so. Similarly, words like *Catholic, Protestant, communism,* and *colonialism* can serve as cues for alertness to danger, prejudice, displaced hatred, and destructiveness. Koestler (1974) noted that symbols have been reasons for the greatest carnage in history and the greatest unhappinesses of humans.

Identity

Identity is a complex symbol of oneself that encompasses all prior levels. Fulfillment involves their integration, ownership, and expression. A fulfilled person feels secure; enjoys bodily, emotional, and social satisfactions; feels good, worthy, and just; fulfills ideals, values, and principles; bears him- or herself with dignity; has a sense of honor, prestige, and reputation; has wider satisfactions in beliefs and religion; and is surrounded by symbols of all these fulfillments. Such a person lives in harmonious balance with the identities of other individuals and groups at all function levels (chapter 1).

Trauma can shatter every aspect of identity and relatedness. Disruptions may range from basic functions such as a sense of coherence; competence; and control of one's body, mind, and social roles to disruptions of one's ideals, values, and principles; world views; and symbols.

Creativity and Aesthetics

Creativity combines different parts and synthesizes them in new ways. At the biological level, male and female combine in procreation. At each level, components can be looked at from different angles and combined in new ways into future possibilities. Tools of creativity are many and include play, fantasies, dreams, humor, thinking, and science. The arenas of expression of creativity are also many and include medicine, jurisprudence, and art.

Aesthetics is a frequent companion of creativity and adds to its delight. It hones and fashions creative pursuits and connects them with universal beauty, harmony, symmetry, and proportion.

Fulfillment in creativity can be intense. There may be peak pleasures at moments of synthesis and newness, sexual orgasm being a biological paradigm. However, the creative vision may also harness much long-term effort. The paradigm is bringing up a child.

Although stressful situations may spur inventiveness, trauma destroys creativity and aesthetics. Instead of synthesis, there is disconnection; instead of movement into the future, there is backward regression; instead of beauty and delight, there are ugliness and revulsion.

Perversions of creativity use it against life, for instance, in inventing new ways of torture, killing, and perpetrating sexual abuse.

Sacredness

Sacredness subsumes previous function levels but also connects them to a larger universal whole. Czikszentmihalyi and Rathunde (1993) noted that discovery of universal connections may be accompanied by an existential joy, a cognitive holism, and an ethical compulsion. The sacred also evokes a sense of reverence, awe, and humbleness. The intense sense of being, significance, and fulfillment is sometimes called *mystical consciousness*.

A sense of the sacred may be evoked when a function level extends to the universal. This may occur in confrontations with life and death such as in hunt, war, bereavement, and fertility, when ideology or religion are felt to connect with the universe or when philosophers or quantum physicists have a glimpse of its wholeness.

In trauma, the sense of significant connection to the greater universe is shattered. Instead, there is a sense of disintegration, expressed as "Life is shit." A sexually abused patient said, "My father severed me from the universal stream of life."

There may be perverse attempts to connect with the universe by owning it, breaking its taboos, being God. The thrill of having ultimate control, being arbiter of life and death, and dictating morality is, however, desecration of life and breaks connections with nature and the universe. This is often labeled evil. As happened, for instance, with many Vietnam veterans, there is a sense of having lost one's soul.

Wisdom, Truth, and Knowledge

Wisdom, truth, and knowledge (also called reason by philosophers) have long been revered as pinnacles of human potential, the sacred fulfillment of one's essence or soul. They subsume previous levels of function; however, awareness and self-awareness of them allow observations of their patterns, relativity, and limitations. This new perspective may be sensed as higher knowledge of them. Through added discernment of their meaning and purpose, there is a sense of the human mind glimpsing the mind of the outside creator.

Wisdom has only recently become a focus of study. Collating a number of views (Sternberg, 1993), wisdom may be said to have the following components. First, wisdom includes rich factual knowledge about life's universal problems and their contexts and patterns. Along with this, however, wisdom includes knowledge about the relativity of values, and even of the relativity and limitations of current wisdom. Therefore, like Socrates, a wise person questions rather than answers. Second, wise people have qualities of sagacity, perspicacity, empathy, knowledge of self, and ability to communicate. Third, wisdom, in spite of (or sometimes because of) knowledge of the limitations of knowledge, facilitates pragmatic navigation around the exigencies of life toward fulfillment. Wisdom therefore reverberates with survival needs and streams of morality. However, it includes them all in an aware, knowledgeable way and hence controls human destiny and fulfillment a little more.

Knowledge, truth, and wisdom may be lifelong pursuits that fulfill a wholeness of life. They connect personal significance to universal dimensions of time, space, and purpose. They include both personal ripeness and being the vehicle for the propagation of life through one's truth and wisdom. The ripeness and propagation of life are the final fulfillment sought by philosophers but also by all humans.

Yet there is an ambivalence to truth. God's first communication to man was to not eat of the tree of knowledge of good and evil (Genesis 3). Socrates died because he did not relinquish truth. Truth is that along each step to fulfillment of life lurks its opposite, trauma. As well as having universal dimensions, humans are vulnerable, finite, their lives being indeterminate and unpredictable. In trauma, all human aspirations and fulfillments at all function levels, from body to soul, can be damaged.

Religion and other defenses protect from knowledge of trauma. Wisdom, however, learns from it and integrates it. It is not destroyed by the knowledge of good and evil but uses it to learn and propagate life. Through constant and painful questioning, humbly and with awe, but with perspicacity and sagacity, it may learn to help a little to heal and preempt trauma, to shift the balance toward both survival and fulfillment.

In summary, fulfillment and trauma occur along a hierarchy of function levels. The hierarchy reflects biological, psychological, and cultural evolution, with ever wider, more civilized, and more universal perspectives. Morality, and the latter levels that include the sacred and wisdom (reason), are often equated with the soul.

The evolutionary hierarchical view helps to explain some philosophical conundrums. First, the seemingly mysterious or divine naturalness and universality of the moral streams of virtue, worth, and justice can now be seen as feedback mechanisms that have evolved to maximize community survival. The intensity of moral feelings reflects the magnitude of people's needs of other people to survive. Existential meanings and their derivatives similarly help maximum community survival in ever wider and more symbolic ways.

Second, the evolutionary survival view explains the variety and contradictory nature of moral components and their higher function derivatives. This is because different moralities are needed to survive in different circumstances. A taxonomy of morals and components of higher level functions is now possible. Examples are considered in the survival strategy chapters (7–15) and in chapter 16.

The source of morals in survival explains the frequent replacement of their derivatives by what are appraised as pragmatic survival needs of the times. The puzzling, objectively wrong apportioning of moral blame on others or self (such as when a child like Anne (chapter 1) takes the blame for sexual abuse) can now be explained as means of social survival and a coherent view of the world. Last, the view presented here explains evil as the perverse abrogation of sources of life and fulfillment for the purpose of power over them, at the expense of others' lives and fulfillments.

Trauma can disrupt happiness and fulfillment at each hierarchical level. It can disrupt the deepest meaning and purpose of life. It is the opposite of life.

THE LIFE–TRAUMA DIALECTIC: THE PURPOSE OF LIFE

It was noted that it is not death that is the opposite of life. This is because death can be fulfilling either as part of a ripe life or when chosen for the sake of the lives and fulfillment of others. Further, if death is seen to fulfill either or both of these purposes, people may choose to die for their country, ideology, or truth. Death can then fulfill deep existential meaning and purpose of life.

What, then, is the purpose of life, and what is the nature of the "worm at the core of the apple" of human happiness (chapter 1)? Using the apple analogy, the apple is concerned with its own survival and with fulfillment ultimately in a ripe death. However, it is also concerned in furthering other apples' survival and fulfillment. So the purpose of life is its ripening and its expansion into ever more life and fulfillment. Trauma is the worm that disrupts this. The life–trauma dialectic may then be stated thus: Trauma compromises the purpose of life, which is to survive and fulfill oneself according to the life cycle and to help others do the same.

The lower hierarchical function levels are relatively more concerned with immediate survival of self and others. The higher levels reflect ever more ripening and wider dissemination of seeds.

Trauma compromises life's purpose first by endangering survival. It can also disrupt fulfillment or ripening after immediate survival needs are satisfied. This is when trauma makes nonsense of high ideals, leads to disillusionment about the veneer of civilization, and makes the soul absurd (chapter 1). Trauma also includes conflicts between survival of self and others. Perceptions of wrong choices can then lead to prolonged moral and existential torment and distortion of higher fulfillments.

In conclusion, the depth axis provides a consistent schema by which to view fulfillment and its opposite, traumatization at different levels of human function. The understanding of fulfillment and its traumatic equivalents may help to enhance fulfillment and contribute to healing and preventing trauma.

This completes examination of the components of the three axes of traumatic stress. These components encompass the concepts that are found ubiquitously in various traumatic situations. The three axes include the process axis, concerned with the process from stressors to trauma and illnesses; the parameters axis, concerned with the context of the process; and the depth axis, concerned with human issues that trauma disrupts. The next chapter examines illnesses, which are the end product of the process axis and which absorb much attention in traumatology. The triaxial framework is applied to provide a proposed triaxial view of illnesses.

Chapter 6

Illnesses and the Triaxial Framework

Illnesses are often described as clusters of symptoms. The view taken here is that a triaxial view enriches illness concepts and adds etiologic dynamics. This is enhanced further if one accepts transgenerational biological (including genetic), psychological, and social transmission of traumas leading to vulnerabilities and reenactments. It is suggested that all illnesses may be conceptualized triaxially, but some, such as PTSD, adjustment disorders, and dissociative disorders, are more obviously stress- and trauma-related than others. They may be called stress and trauma illnesses, though in a broader sense all illnesses are such. In the following chapters, it is shown how survival strategies (chapters 8–15) as stress responses contribute to the specificity of symptoms within a broad range of illnesses.

Illnesses (Figure 2) generally may be seen to be in the buffer state between trauma and death. They are less stable and less life-enhancing equilibria than those present before traumatic stressors. This can be summarized in the following definition: *Illnesses are compromise equilibria established after trauma.*

It is suggested that most clinicians intuitively use two parallel streams of conceptualizing trauma illnesses (see also p. 4). The two streams are the phenomenological and the dynamic. PTSD is the current flagship of the former in traumatic stress, whereas the latter stems from dynamic formulations. It is suggested that PTSD fits the prevalent scientific paradigms of medicine, and the dynamic view is more consistent with recent nonlinear scientific paradigms. The triaxial framework is shown to encompass and extend both paradigms. As well as enriching illness concepts, the triaxial framework is also shown to help orientate symptoms and be useful in disaster planning and research.

HISTORICAL BACKGROUND

Because views of illnesses are influenced by historical paradigms and the triaxial framework suggests a shift in the prevalent one, a brief look at the major paradigms affecting views of trauma illnesses is warranted.

Soon after Hippocrates declared that illnesses were not visitations by the gods but due to changes, especially major changes (Dubos, 1968), the secular dichotomy between phenomenological and dynamic theories of illnesses started. Platonic ideas of forms in which each disease had a unique prototype influenced a phenomenological view, whereas Aristotelian ideas that each disease was shaped by universal attributes in particular ways influenced the dynamic view.

Phenomenology in Medicine and Psychiatry: Linear Science

As science emerged from the dark ages, it countered witchcraft and superstition by concentrating on the visible and logical. Three principles may be said to have developed that are relevant to current illness theories. The first, starting with Galileo, was mathematical observation. Because the language of nature was mathematics, Galileo said, "Measure what can be measured, and make measurable what cannot be measured" (Gaarder, 1994, p. 157). Newtonian physics confirmed a steady mathematical view of the universe. The second principle was dualism, cemented by Descartes, which separated body and mind. The third principle was reductionism, where smallest components were ultimate causes. For instance, Virchow, the father of pathology, held that altered cells are the basis of disease (F. K. Taylor, 1980). Bacteria, viruses, genes, hormones, and biochemical compounds, leading to specific phenomenological diagnoses, enhanced the reductionist view of illnesses.

Psychiatry, in attempting to gain scientific credibility, modeled itself on scientific medicine. For instance, through the *DSM,* it declared that it too had numerous diagnoses based on measurable scientific criteria, and it too searched for specific genes and chemicals for causes. Klerman (1984) saw the *DSM–III* as a reaffirmation of psychiatry's scientific medical identity.

Others criticized psychiatric scientism. Vaillant (1984) said that *DSM*'s reductionism produced a lot of whats, but no hows or whys. Further, neither patients nor clinicians thought about symptoms and illnesses statistically.

Weiner (1992) said that the reductionist paradigm was like fragments of a broken Humpty-Dumpty. He predicted that the fragments would be reconstituted in a medicine based on systems and nonlinear concepts.

A Shift in the Scientific Paradigm: Nonlinear Concepts

In the past decades, nonlinear paradigms of quantum mechanics (Davies, 1984; Hawking, 1988) and chaos theory (Gleick, 1987) challenged old linear paradigms.

Quantum mechanics maintained that in the epochs of the first seconds of the initial Big Bang, space, time, and matter froze out of a ferment of quantum energy. Their derivatives were greatly influenced by events in the epochs of the first seconds. At a deep level, the axes that froze out and their derivatives continued to influence each other (theory of relativity). Particles, virtual particles, and ghost particles of these cosmic events influenced each other through webs of vibrating energy patterns.

Static Newtonian logic was replaced by an apparently surrealistic dynamic language. To continue, sometimes events reflected aspects of the Big Bang. As a star aged, it could develop a gravity so strong that it imploded on itself, becoming a black hole enveloped in an infinite time warp and a prison of curved space, where time stood still. This could explode in flash of energy called a supernova, resembling a star.

Understanding came from whole views, and yet the whole could not be viewed concurrently. For instance, neither the energy and matter properties of light nor the motion and position aspects of bodies could be observed at the same time. What was observed depended on the observer, and the observations had an innate uncertainty (Heisenberg's uncertainty principle; see Hawking, 1988). The observer became important not only in what was observed, but also in influencing the system. "When someone looks . . . an atom jump[s] in a characteristic fashion that no ordinary physical interaction can mimic" (Davies, 1984, p. 40).

Chaos theory also emphasized the importance of the initial conditions in the "butterfly effect" (E. N. Lorenz, 1979). Theoretically, the flap of a butterfly in Brazil could set off a tornado in Texas. Apparently random events could be represented not in statistics, but simple codes represented visually as infinite complex loops so beautiful as to be described "like grapes on God's personal vine" (Gleick, 1987, p. 221).

Elegance, beauty, harmony, and unity were reflected in nonlinear equations and codes described as the poetry of nature. They evoked awe and delight, search for cosmic meaning, and purpose reminiscent of the sacred (chapter 5). The sterile, soulless Newtonian view of the world gave way to the holistic perspective of the new physics (Davies, 1984). Or poetry and metaphors were added to the language of nature.

PHENOMENOLOGICAL STREAM OF STRESS AND TRAUMA ILLNESSES

PTSD is based on the phenomenological linear-based scientific paradigm. The *DSM–IV* introduced acute stress disorder, which filled the gap before PTSD could by definition become operational.

Acute Stress Disorder

Acute stress disorder lasts 2–28 days following a traumatic event. Its symptoms include the intrusion, avoidance, and arousal of PTSD (see below). The disorder also needs to contain three of the following dissociative symptoms: numbing, daze, derealization, depersonalization, and amnesia.

The PTSD and dissociative group of symptoms may reflect sectional interests of PTSD and dissociative disorders groups (Brett, 1996). Each implies that later PTSD and dissociative disorders gel from their acute manifestations. However, early PTSD symptoms are only partially predictive for later PTSD (Shalev, 1996), and the same may well be true for dissociative symptoms.

Combat stress reaction is the term used for acute stress disorder by the Israeli army (chapter 2). Clinical descriptions of both actually correspond clinically to previous descriptions of acute responses following combat and other traumatic situations (chapter 2). What stands out in them are not only PTSD and dissociative symptoms, but the very wide polymorphous fluctuating nature of the responses. They have an unpredictable potential to develop into PTSD and dissociative disorders, as well as a wide range of other psychiatric disorders (e.g., Z. Solomon et al., 1996).

A tension remains between the polymorphous fluctuating unpredictable nature of acute stress reaction symptoms and the need for reductionist pathological phenomenology in the *DSM*. Such tension reflects a conceptual hiatus of great energy. Indeed, McFarlane and Yehuda (1995), Z. Solomon et al. (1996), and Brett (1996) concluded that the primary task for traumatology was to understand and specify the uniqueness and variability of acute traumatic stress responses in a way that made sense of them and their later developments. This is one of the major tasks of this book (see also chapter 16).

PTSD

PTSD was like a diagnosis waiting to happen. It harnessed the restless energies of the times and gave Vietnam veterans a diagnosis, recognition, and validation of their sufferings. Though the impulse for the diagnosis came from veterans, the diagnosis included observations from rape and domestic violence, too. It rightly came to be considered applicable to all traumatic situations (van der Kolk, Weisath, & van der Hart, 1996). The advantages of treatment and compensation without shame spread from Vietnam veterans to victims of other traumatic situations.

Yet PTSD is the latest phenomenological rendition of previous traumatic diagnoses (Trimble, 1985; chapter 2). For instance, its core contained Freud's description of trauma being relived and avoided. However, it was claimed that for the first time PTSD was scientifically robust as its components could be operationalized and measured (Newman, Kaloupek, & Keane, 1996; J. P. Wilson & Keane, 1996). PTSD was also simple and easily understood across disciplines, such as by lawyers.

The following summarizes the criteria for PTSD in the *DSM–IV* (APA, 1994).

A. The person has been exposed to a traumatic event involving threat to life and has experienced intense fear, helplessness, or horror.

B. The traumatic event is persistently reexperienced in images, perceptions, thoughts, dreams, actions; flashbacks, illusions, or hallucinations. These may be evoked by cues reminiscent of the event, and they evoke physiological reactions pertinent to the event.

C. The traumatic event is persistently avoided by avoiding thoughts, feelings, activities, situations, and stimuli associated with the trauma. This is facilitated by numbing and restricting general responsiveness, emotions, interest, and interaction with others. There is restricted ability to recall and sense of a foreshortened future.

D. Persistent symptoms of increased arousal such as sleeplessness, hypervigilance, startle response; irritability, and difficulty concentrating.

Symptoms between 1–3 months postevent are called acute; after 3 months, chronic; and if they first arise after 6 months, delayed.

Consistent with reductionism in the scientific paradigm (Smith, 1991; Weiner, 1992; chapter 6), different factors have been suggested to cause PTSD pathology. Norepinephrine was suggested to be associated with the intrusive phase, and serotonin and endogenous opioids with the numbed phase (van der Kolk & Saporta, 1993). Recently, hippocampal damage and resultant dissociation have been suggested to be central (chapter 3). Specific psychosocial precedents have included inescapable shock (van der Kolk et al., 1984), helplessness (van der Kolk, 1987), and loss of control (Garber & Seligman, 1980). It is likely that all these factors are significant to variable degrees in different circumstances.

Limitations of PTSD

Though PTSD is without question valid and useful, Brett (1996) noted that its dominance could lead to overlooking other traumatic symptoms and illnesses.

1 PTSD does not list many trauma-related symptoms. They include dysregulation of affect and self, somatization, alexithymia, eating disorders, substance abuse, self-mutilation, and victimization and revictimization (van der Kolk, 1996b).

2 Other posttraumatic syndromes such as complex posttraumatic stress disorder (also known as diagnosis of extreme stress not otherwise

specified) may be ignored. Herman (1992) suggested the latter syndrome arises following severe and prolonged abuse, especially of the
very young. In the syndrome, symptoms are grouped under somatization; dissociation and alterations in consciousness; affective changes;
alterations in perception of the perpetrator; alterations in relationships;
changes in identity; and alterations in sense of meaning and existence.

3 Significance of traumatically determined comorbid diagnoses may not
be appreciated (Fullerton & Ursano, 1997). The majority of trauma victims develop a range of illnesses in addition to PTSD. They include
depressive, panic, and generalized anxiety disorders (McFarlane & de
Girolamo, 1996) and adjustment, dissociative, somatization, borderline,
schizophreniform, and antisocial disorders (Blank, 1993; Herman, 1992;
Rothbaum & Foa, 1993; Threlkeld & Thyer, 1992; van der Kolk, 1996b).
Thus, premature closure of PTSD as the only posttraumatic diagnosis
ignores the possibility that acute polymorphous pictures can develop
into a diagnostically polymorphous array of illnesses.

Some of the criticisms may be due to the high level of abstraction of the
core PTSD criteria of reliving and avoidance. The problem is that they do not tell
what is relived and avoided, how and why, and how it affects the person. The
second problem is its very scientific paradigm. Its reductionist view constricted
it to a single syndrome. Its dualism ignored the biopsychosocial whole. Ignoring
what could not be measured left out emotions and higher function levels. Though
recognizing veterans' sufferings, PTSD lost touch with their rage, guilt (deleted
in *DSM–III–R*), grief, demoralization, alienation, and lost existential meaning.
Trauma, which promised to be the soul of psychiatry (van der Kolk & McFarlane,
1996), was sanitized by PTSD. "PTSD . . . does not begin to describe the
complexity of how people react to overwhelming experiences" (p. 15).

Perhaps scientific psychiatry could not assimilate the new trauma schema
and relegated it to an unobtrusive part of awareness. (For instance, it was not
allowed its own section in *DSM–IV;* Brett, 1996). Perhaps assimilation of the
schema would mean psychiatry having to see the widespread dynamic effects
of trauma in the various, now not-so-separate psychiatric diagnoses, and this
would threaten the scientific paradigm. Threats to scientific paradigms are always strongly resisted (Kuhn, 1962).

DYNAMIC STREAM

Psychodynamically minded traumatologists are not so much concerned with
classifying symptoms as with providing historical meaning to them. They see
trauma akin to a pebble disrupting the stillness of a pond (Figley, 1985, p. xix)
whose ripples range over many symptoms and diagnoses, depending on the
trauma and subsequent defenses. This psychoanalytically derived view (Freud,
1896/1975b; Vaillant, 1992; chapter 3) has recently been reformulated.

Herman (1992), Braun (1993), and Yates and Nasby (1993) noted that particular dissociative defenses determine later dissociative symptoms (such as amnesia, fugues) and illnesses (such as somatization, DID). With addition of further defenses, other comorbid diagnoses could develop (Herman, 1992; Threlkeld & Thyer, 1992). Even so, in clinical practice diagnoses have lost much of their importance, being replaced by cross-diagnostic issues such as appreciation of boundaries, modulation of affects, and acting out of traumas within the therapy.

The dynamic stream was humanist (concerned with emotions and existential issues), nonreductionist (concerned with both minutiae and bigger pictures), and interactional (observing interactions between client and therapist). Nevertheless, relative lack of classification and scientific paradigm made for diffuse thinking and difficulty in communication and explanation. Also, apart from traumatologists, most psychodynamicists denied trauma at the center. That is, they dealt with the ripples in great detail, but denied the pebble in the pond (chapter 3).

PHENOMENOLOGICAL AND DYNAMIC STREAMS IN CHILDREN

The phenomenological and dynamic streams described above for adults are also reflected in the child trauma literature.

Phenomenological Stream

Beyond latency age, intrusion and avoidance phenomena resemble ever more those of adults (Pynoos, 1993; Valent, 1994, 1995a). However, in younger children they were replaced by body symptoms, affects, and behavioral reenactments such as in play and paintings (Pynoos & Eth, 1985).

Pynoos (1993) and Pynoos et al. (1996) warned against reification of PTSD as a kind of platonic form of trauma illness. As for adults, this ignored complex traumatic stress disorder and trauma-related comorbid diagnoses. In addition to adult diagnoses, they included eating, sleeping, learning, attention deficit, and attachment disorders. Pynoos et al. also warned that concentrating on phenomena risked missing their experiential and clinical significance.

Dynamic Stream

In addition to similarities with adults, children in particular may experience trauma sequelae when their innate, developmentally appropriate biopsychosocial expectancies had been unmet. This may include not finding a nipple (chapter 4) or not being recognized (chapter 4). The shattered expectations skew the child's inner plan physiologically, psychologically, and socially.

Developmental phases also limit maturational competencies to deal with trauma. For instance, younger children have limited appreciation of time sequence, emotional fluctuations, and meta-analyses of events into a coherent whole. This may be confused with dissociation (chapter 3).

As with adults, workers expressed the need for a more inclusive paradigm (Gordon & Wraith, 1993; Pynoos & Nader, 1993). Gordon and Wraith (1993) themselves provided a visual analogue of a rope representing a child's life continuum. Its strands represent biological, psychological, and social developments. The strands are surrounded by layers of family and community. Trauma potentially disrupts all strands and layers.

OTHER THEORIES OF TRAUMA ILLNESSES

Psychosomatic Medicine

This view (reviewed in chapter 2) emphasizes that physical illnesses are also part of the posttraumatic picture, encourages a biopsychosocial perspective, and highlights the complementary use of dynamics and phenomenology.

Emotions

Plutchik (1980, 1993; chapter 3) suggested that each of eight basic emotions led to a specific illness when associated with its characteristic defense. For instance, fear together with repression led to a timid personality. Sadness with the defense compensation led to depression. Though highlighting the importance and potential taxonomy of emotions, there may be doubt about the exclusive association of particular emotions, defenses, and pathology.

Cognitive Theories: Horowitz

Horowitz (1976/1992) incorporated Freud's reliving and forgetting of traumatic experiences into a cognitive framework including meanings. According to this view, trauma creates massive new information and cognitive dissonance with established inner schemas and meanings (chapter 3, chapter 4). The function of intrusive traumatic memories is for them to be cognitively processed and assimilated. This is achieved through new, higher order schemas of meaning that successfully assimilate old and new information.

THE TRIAXIAL FRAMEWORK APPLIED
TO VIEWS OF ILLNESSES

It is suggested that the triaxial framework can act as a multidimensional radar map within which can be located combinations and permutations of specific points, lines, areas, and volumes. Examples of points are, say, particular stressors and illnesses, such as angina and PTSD. Lines may connect points, such as between being sacked and angina in Case 2 (chapter 1). Lines may have a number of points on them, so the previous example may be expanded to being sacked leading to rage, elevated blood pressure, cholesterol plaques, artery blockage, and angina. Psychosomatic specificity theories and Plutchik's (1980, 1993) theory of emotions used such lines. It may be said that a line in Figure 2 leading from stressors to illnesses may be used to conceptualize PTSD as the illness at the end of the line.

It is suggested that linear physics and mathematics apply to lines in the triaxial framework. Statistics help to determine sequences and correlations along the lines and relative importance of points on lines and may even correlate points on different lines.

But lines may be expanded to volumes. For instance, adding adaptive and maladaptive biological, psychological, and social components of Figure 3 to Figure 2, or adding to it, as Horowitz did, morality and meaning, expands the stressor → PTSD line along the depth axis. The dynamic stream also uses greater volumes of the triaxial framework, for instance, noting client–therapist interactions. It is suggested that at this stage concurrent use of multiple axes brings complexity, uncertainty, and unpredictability, which requires nonlinear concepts.

Nonlinear Concepts Applied to the Triaxial Framework

Neurophysiologists have already applied nonlinear thinking to brain function. Bergland (1985) said that "hormonal harmonies" and other codes were the stuff of thoughts and the soul. Lonie (1991) and Morstyn (1992) noted applicability of nonlinear paradigms to psychotherapy. In both, layers of meaning brought order to flows of apparently random information. Nonlinear thinking seems particularly applicable to traumatology.

Analogous to the Big Bang, trauma may also be said to be a ferment of energy out of which freeze the three axes of traumatic stress. Like time, matter, and space, the axes and their derivatives "remember" and continue to influence each other. Each of them, too, is influenced by events in the initial epochs of trauma. As with the Big Bang, traumatic events influence unpredictably long-term constellations of illnesses, though as with cosmic constellations with the right codes they can make retrospective sense.

Black holes and supernovas may be analogous to traumatic amnesias and hypermnesias reminiscent of the initial trauma. Black holes may be like intensely compacted traumatic memories imploding on themselves in a time warp where time stands still.

As in quantum physics, neither the axes nor their components can be examined concurrently. For instance, depending on the view of the observer, only one axis, or one of the biological, psychological, or social aspects of an event may be observed at one time. This introduces a principle of uncertainty and, as in nonlinear physics, too, the way the observer observes influences the system observed.

In traumatic stress, too, divergent derivatives along the axes "remember" each other through webs of energy that may be discerned when viewing the whole triaxial framework. For instance, apparently random or chaotic divergent biological, psychological, and social manifestations may be dissociated memory fragments that from a whole perspective can be seen to have core relationships. Such memories within a web of energy may resemble particles, virtual particles, and ghost particles that "remember" each other in quantum physics (chapter 6).

Finally, both nonlinear physics and the triaxial framework contain vast complexities, ranging from physical to ultimate meanings and purpose, that can nevertheless be represented visually and coded in relatively simple symbols and metaphors.

The frequent metaphor of trauma as the pebble in the pond (used in its logo by the International Society for Traumatic Stress Studies) may be expanded by the triaxial view. The expanding ripples represent the process axis. Each ripple is like a memory from the impact and subsequent resistance. Crests and troughs of ripples represent reliving and avoiding, respectively. Points on ripples represent particular symptoms and illnesses, and comorbid diagnoses involve other points on the same or similar ripples. The parameter axis involves the nature of the pebble and the pond, when the pebble was thrown, at what angle, at which part of the pond. The depth axis recognizes that the pebble cause ripples underwater, disturbing different levels of life and the purpose of the pond.

An example of a code that integrates many random events may be the biopsychosocial concept. It may be represented visually as a butterfly with its center the biological aspect and the wings the psychological and social aspects. The butterfly flutters over the triaxial framework and is refracted and seen differently at different points. The refractions usually only allow one or another of its parts to be seen at any one time. If these seem fanciful explorations, they are nevertheless analogous to thought experiments in quantum physics.

Triaxial Framework for Stress and Trauma Illnesses

Although metaphors such as the above condense reality and allow otherwise disparate events to be held simultaneously in mind, the triaxial framework may be a closer representation of reality. For instance, by following the process axis and constantly adding the other two axes, the following summary of stress and trauma illnesses may emerge.

Stressors lead to a state of stress within which polymorphous, fluctuating biological, psychological, and social stress responses comprise the diagnosis of acute stress disorder. Emphases on particular stress responses provide names to a variety of adjustment disorder diagnoses in the *DSM*. The parameter and depth axes add their respective dimensions here and may include, for example, group processes, moral conflicts, and dilemmas of meaning.

Events may be resolved adaptively and lead to fulfillment. Otherwise, their three axes may be condensed in traumas, to be refracted and molded by defenses through traumatic memories to illnesses. Taking PTSD as an example of such illnesses, the parameter axis defines its manifestations according to the cultures of traumatic situations, their different phases, in different age groups, and in different social systems. The depth axis includes traumatic disruptions at different function levels manifested, for instance, in unresolved moral dilemmas, collapse of sense of identity, and spirituality.

Comorbid symptoms and illnesses may develop in parallel triaxial threads, falling into biopsychosocial clusters from related events. For instance, in Case 3, Anne's (chapter 1) PTSD, constipation and stomach pains, depressions, headaches, propensity to infections, period and genital pains, self-blame and shame, phobias, paranoia, and hallucinations were different aspects of her childhood abuse, each with its triaxial development.

Resolution of Conceptual Conundrums It is suggested that the triaxial framework resolves some scientific paradoxes. For instance, mind–body dualism is subsumed in the biopsychosocial view. Within it is acknowledged that biological, psychological, and social responses and their derivative illnesses "froze out" from the same energy ferment, difficult to view simultaneously, yet most usefully integrated as different faces of a common event. (Actually, it may be useful to think of all components on all axes biopsychosocially.)

The triaxial framework may help to bridge the science–humanism rift by introducing the parameter and depth axes. This acknowledges the importance to victims of social and depth axis aspects, and of helper views on treatment. Perhaps bedside manner and placebo effects are undetected fits and misfits of triaxial frameworks of victims and helpers.

Because in the triaxial framework symptoms and illnesses may be viewed from unidimensional points through linear to multidimensional nonlinear systems, distinctions such as biological and psychological, phenomenological and dynamic, linear and nonlinear, and scientific and humanist simply indicate choices of views within a unified whole. The reductionist–whole dichotomy then indicates a range of reductionist and whole possibilities. Koestler (1983) described the possibilities as the holonic principle, where *hol* stood for the whole and *on* (such as in electron, proton) for smallest parts. It is suggested that the triaxial framework represents a holonic view. Applied to illnesses, it involves understanding of which parts are observed in which theories and consciously choosing observations and interventions according to needs and possibilities, at the same time being aware of what is not dealt with.

Orientation and Enrichment Within the Triaxial Framework Within the triaxial framework and according to the holonic principle, any symptom, illness, or concept may be pinpointed accurately by the triaxial radar and be potentially expanded to varying degrees along the three axes. PTSD and angina are two examples that have been located and enriched in such a way (see also chapter 16).

It is suggested that each concept may be located and be enriched similarly.

For instance, the concept of memory may be enriched by considering biological, psychological, and social memories at different ages and system levels, affected by reigning values and philosophical beliefs. Repressed psychological memories may be usefully compared with unexpressed genetic and cultural memories. Another interesting thought experiment may involve time. Symptoms and illnesses may contain different time frames that may be traced back to recent and distant dynamically significant milestones along each axis. Trauma symptoms may manifest them all in a frozen time warp where past and present are indistinguishable to variable degrees.

Planning and Research Applications of the Triaxial Framework   In disaster and medical planning, the triaxial view may ensure that a biopsychosocial view is used across all ages and that social groups, including helpers, are catered for throughout all disaster phases. Disruptions in moral principles, dignity, values, and existential meanings are also considered. At the end of each formulation and intervention, the triaxial framework may be rechecked to see that all components have been considered.

Any factor being researched can be checked for influences from each axis. For instance, levels of a stress compound may be affected by a variety of adaptive and maladaptive biopsychosocial influences, disaster phase, time of life, social supports, and states of self, dignity, and spirituality.

In summary, perhaps the phenomenological and dynamic and the linear and nonlinear trends in conceptualizing illnesses present since the ancient Greeks reflect natural biases (such as left and right brain awareness). Perhaps in practice they are both used, and triaxial diagnoses are made almost automatically, with helpers using their own triaxial processing. Conceptualizing such processing may require new scientific paradigms and language where both measurements and metaphors have a place.

The triaxial framework appears to be a simple three-dimensional model, yet it provides a superordinate schema incorporating and adding to previous simple and complex views of illnesses.

The triaxial framework comprises one ingredient of the wholist perspective, the other being survival strategies. The latter add rich content to the triaxial coordinate points. It is to them that the following section turns its attention.

Part Three

Survival Strategies: An Octave for the Symphony of Traumatic Stress and Fulfillment

Although the triaxial framework provides an orientation for concepts, symptoms, and illnesses, survival strategies help to provide a rationale for, and enable categorizations of, their very variable, fluctuating, and at times contradictory contents. In terms of earlier speculations, the eight survival strategies are akin to a code, like an octave in the music of nature, whose different notes and harmonics give specific sense to points on the triaxial framework.

Survival strategies not only help to provide a rationale for stress and traumatic responses, but also serve as a counterpoint for adaptive, life-enhancing ones. The adaptive and maladaptive aspects of survival strategies may then be visualized as amino acid codes on a double DNA helix, with manifestations being the result of both the adaptive and maladaptive helices.

Survival strategies, then, are an added dimension to the three axes. Applications of survival strategies include tracing and elucidating origins and meanings of specific conceptual contents, symptoms, and illnesses prospectively and retrospectively as they ramify along the three axes. In other words, they enable meaningful recognition and categorization of the wide variety of manifestations of triaxial components such as traumas, illnesses, morals, meanings, values, and principles.

Because survival strategies are conceptually evolutionary survival templates shared with other animals, their place in evolution is briefly examined in chapter 7. That chapter examines previous searches for specific strategies of survival and ends with the introduction of a proposal for eight survival strategies. The next eight chapters examine each survival strategy in detail as they ramify throughout the triaxial framework. Applications of survival strategies together with the triaxial framework in the wholist perspective are examined in chapter 16.

Chapter 7

Introduction to Survival Strategies

Since Darwin, strategies such as fight and flight that favor survival and evolution have underpinned much of the philosophy of human behavior. They have also been more or less explicitly at the foundation of traumatic stress thinking. However, fight and flight are insufficient to explain the variety of means of survival. An updated evolution theory and the finding of other survival strategies has allowed a more comprehensive survival strategies framework. This chapter describes the historical development that has allowed the formulation of eight survival strategies.

EVOLUTION AND STRATEGIES OF SURVIVAL

Human Evolution

Human evolution shows a relatively recent divergence from other animals with whom humans have shared common means of surviving very harsh conditions. For instance, 99% of human genetic makeup is shared with chimpanzees (Koepping, 1989). Similarly, for 99% of its evolution (up to 10,000 years ago), human existence was closely bound to hunting (Lee & DeVore, 1977) and defense against predators. Thus, the unprecedented evolution of the human brain in the past half million years carried forward strategies of survival such as defense and hunting that humans shared with other animals (Koestler, 1974; Laughlin, 1977).

Human mentation and language probably developed only over the past 50,000 years or so (Maxwell, 1984) and helped otherwise vulnerable humans to hone their evolutionary survival skills in the wild. Indeed, it is only in the past 10,000 years, an evolutionary blink, that human civilization started, with production of surplus food, domestication of animals, and building of cities. It is only in the past few thousand years that bands and clans developed societies, and the old evolutionary templates were applied to economy, politics, and the higher function levels of the depth axis. For instance, myths gave rise to modern religions with single principles to explain the world only about 2,500 years ago. Concepts of moral rightness and goodness and of self-awareness also emerged at about this time.

On the whole, however, world views remained narrow, marked by ethnocentricity, territory, religion, and local economy. Only 500 years ago was the world's central place in the universe first lost. Only in this century did religion, ideologies, and the human mind blossom into scientific targets of study.

It is important to note the long evolutionary heritage of responses to current threats to survival, as well as of human fulfillment.

Theories of Evolution and Discoveries of Strategies of Survival

Darwin   Before Charles Darwin (1859/1974) published *The Origin of Species* in 1859, it was commonly believed that each species was immutably created by God. However, Darwin noted that species evolved through differential propagation of favorable variations, which Darwin called natural selection. Favorable variations could enhance life through a competitive edge in struggles with predators, environmental conditions, members of the same species, and struggle for progeny. Thus, various functions including instincts and emotions could evolve if they favored survival. In *The Expressions of the Emotions in Man and Animals,* Darwin (1872/1965) described rage and terror with accompanying fight and flight as strategies serving survival. He included cooperation as a means of enhancing life, too.

Darwin (1872/1965) hypothesized that many gestures and emotions were evolutionary throwbacks to earlier survival activities. For instance, males in rage expose their teeth across species. Increased pulse rate and dilatation of the pupils when in terror and flight are also seen across species. Similarly, human sneers could derive from animal snarls of defiance. In summary, Darwin saw biopsychosocial functions evolve because they served survival. Such functions included fight and flight.

Modern Evolutionary Theory and Expansion of Possible Strategies of Survival   The path to discovery of more strategies of survival was blocked first because of misinterpretation of Darwin's (1859/1974) natural selection as survival of the fittest. This view allowed only struggle for survival, or competition, as a survival strategy. The view was politicized to justify on evolutionary grounds entrenched power groups and racist, even genocidal theories. Neither survival of the fittest nor natural selection could explain altruism, or the fact that it was often the fittest who sacrificed themselves for the group. Last, it was unclear how natural selection worked.

Modern evolutionary theory holds that it is genetic mutations that produce the variations that are then naturally selected according to Darwin's theory. Mutations can be spread fairly rapidly through sexual reproduction in small populations. This so-called inbreeding, present in humans, too, during their evolution, made groups of a few hundred rather than individuals the units of evolution (Scott, 1989).

This means that altruism and sacrifice could potentially further evolution if more genes (albeit in kin) could be saved through it than would have happened if the fittest preserved only themselves. This "inclusive fitness" came to be seen as a vehicle of evolution (Scott, 1989). It opened up possibilities of means of survival beyond competition to behaviors such as protection, caretaking, and cooperation.

PRECURSORS TO SURVIVAL STRATEGIES

The survival strategies to be described already had historical precedents in the steps to their recognition as important means of survival. What follows brings them together as survival strategies.

Fight and Flight

Darwin's (1872/1965) descriptions of rage and terror were extended by Cannon in 1915 (Cannon, 1963), who added sympathetic nervous system arousal during their activity. Cannon clearly associated rage and fear with fight and flight, which served survival by alternately seizing prey and killing enemies and escaping enemies and danger. Cannon speculated that fight and flight were reciprocal, much depending on how events were perceived. To the present day, fight and flight are recognized underpinnings of traumatic responses and the arousal criterion of PTSD. Accompanying them are elevated epinephrine and norepinephrine secretions.

General Adaptation Syndrome, Conservation-Withdrawal Syndrome, and Loss and Grief

These three concepts are examined together because it is suggested that they are part of the same survival strategy.

General Adaptation Syndrome   Selye (1936) described a syndrome consisting of an enlarged adrenal cortex secreting high levels of cortisol; severe involution of the thymus, spleen, and lymph nodes; and deep bleeding ulcers in the stomach and duodenum. Because a variety of noxious agents produced this syndrome, Selye called it the general adaptation syndrome. Selye promoted the generalist view of illness (chapter 2), maintaining that a variety of illnesses such as peptic ulcers and immune diseases resulted from various derailments of the general adaptation syndrome, together with host vulnerabilities (Selye, 1946).

However, though Selye (1936, 1946) used a variety of chemically different stressors, they all overwhelmed animals to the point of shock and potential death. Thus, the responses were all strategically similar, even though the stressors varied. However, Selye did add to fight and flight a stress response of adaptation or surrender to overwhelming conditions.

Conservation-Withdrawal Syndrome   This syndrome was described by Engel and Schmale (1972) as a basic survival mechanism opposite to fight and flight. Its symptoms were weakness, tiredness, fatigue, hypotonia, emptiness, and depressive-type symptoms. The syndrome seems to be the psychobehavioral equivalent of general adaptation syndrome (see also chapter 11).

Loss and Grief   Loss and bereavement are stressors requiring adaptation. Freud (1917/1975k) in *Mourning and Melancholia* differentiated grief and depression. In grief, there is a clear reason for the condition, and there is a piecemeal painful detachment of the bonds to the dead. In depression, there is no clear view of what has been lost, and there is no detaching process from the lost person. Though not usually conceptualized as a strategy for survival, grief and mourning allow adaptation by relinquishing love bonds and turning to new ones Grief may be part of the adaptive psychic aspect of the general adaptation syndrome (chapter 11).

Attachment

Bowlby (1971) described attachment as a core biobehavioral phenomenon in all mammals. It involves bonding to a particular caretaker for the function of protection from predators and the teaching of survival skills. It is more basic than feeding, though it facilitates it and provision generally, as well as psychophysiological regulation. Until Bowlby, it was thought that infants attached secondarily to other physiological satisfactions.

Caretaking

Caretaking is also a core phenomenon found in all mammals and is reciprocal to attachment (Bowlby, 1971, 1975). Caretaking involves a psychobiological bond that facilitates retrieval, protection, and rescue as well as nurturance, home building, and psychophysiological regulation.

Search for Other Survival Biobehaviors

As it became clear that evolution favored a small number of basic biobehaviors on which to build many variations, some workers attempted to define the basic types of survival behaviors.

Scott (1989) specified 11 such behaviors, which included ingestion, elimination, shelter seeking, and fertilization, as well as defense, conflict, calling for and giving care, and flocking and cooperating.

Plutchik (1980, 1993; chapters 3 and 6) described eight primary emotions, each linked with a survival function. Fear was linked with escaping danger, anger with attacking enemies, joy with possessing a sexual mate, sadness with reintegration, acceptance with grooming and friendship, disgust with rejecting poison, expectation with exploration, and surprise with orientation.

Panksepp (1989a) described five executive emotive (or command) circuits of the brain linked to specific functions. The foraging-expectancy system motivates goal-directed survival activities such as hunting and obtaining food. The anger–rage system involves defensive aggression. The fear–anxiety system motivates flight and possibly freezing. The separation–distress–panic system includes separation-induced distress vocalizations. Sadness, sorrow, and grief are included in this system. Finally, the social–play system serves play.

It is suggested that some of these biobehaviors such as play and orientation are relatively nonspecific. Others, again, such as ingestion, elimination, and disgust, belong to lower levels of function. However, most above biobehaviors correspond overlap with, or are subsumed by the survival strategies described below. One challenge is to isolate specific discrete survival strategies at a consistent function level.

SURVIVAL STRATEGIES

Strategies of survival were previously suggested to explain diverse stress responses (Valent, 1984). Survival strategies were introduced and applied to secondary traumatic stress disorder or compassion fatigue (Valent, 1995b). Here, survival strategies are examined in more detail.

Definition and Description of Survival Strategies

The following is a brief definition of survival strategies: *Survival strategies are specific stress responses that include specific adaptive and maladaptive, biological, psychological, and social constituents.*

The replacement of stress responses in Figures 2 and 3 (chapter 3) by survival strategies is illustrated in Figures 4 and 5.

Characteristics of Survival Strategies   The following are suggested characteristics of survival strategies.

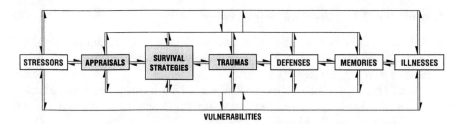

Figure 4 The place of survival strategies on the process axis.

Evolutionary Adaptedness   Survival strategies are evolutionary templates whose function is to enhance survival of evolutionary social units.

Finite Number with Multitude Potential Combinations   There is a small number (eight) of discrete survival strategy templates. They may function individually or in a wide range of combinations.

Level of Operation   Survival strategies function on a level between reflexes and instincts and abstract functioning, having rich, two-way connections with both. Like stress responses, anatomically they are intimately associated with MacLean's (1973; chapter 3) old mammalian brain, that is, the midbrain, limbic system, and primitive cortex, whose role is to "guide behavior with respect to the two basic life principles of self-preservation and preservation of the species" (MacLean, 1973, p. 12).

Biopsychosocial Nature   Each survival strategy has integrated biological, psychological, and social aspects that act as functional units.

Adaptiveness and Maladaptiveness   Survival strategies may be adaptive or maladaptive, according to circumstances. Adaptive survival strategies contribute to fulfillment, whereas maladaptive survival strategies contribute to strain, traumas, symptoms, and illnesses (Figure 6).

Modulation   Complex biological, psychological, and social feedbacks modulate survival strategies from each axis of the triaxial framework.

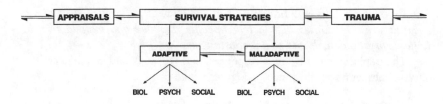

Figure 5 Survival strategies.

Figure 6 Survival strategies in fulfillment and trauma.

Ramification in the Triaxial Framework In traumatic situations, survival strategies intersect the depth axis at the level of physiological and security (survival) needs. On the parameters axis, survival strategies evoke, complement, or antagonize others' survival strategies in a reciprocal manner and manifest differently in different social systems and at different developmental levels. However, survival strategies ramify into components of each axis both adaptive and maladaptive and are represented at every point of the framework.

THE EIGHT SURVIVAL STRATEGIES AND APPRAISALS THAT EVOKE THEM

The eight suggested survival strategies and the appraisals of means of survival that evoke them are shown in Table 1.

It is suggested that these eight survival strategies include the survival biobehaviors described above. Inconsistencies with others' nomenclature is sometimes semantic, but at other times because it was considered that the suggested biobehavior was not specific enough, or it was subsumed at a lower function level within one of the survival strategies. The survival strategies examined here will be seen to reflect survival biobehaviors consistent with the literature from a number of disciplines.

Table 1 Survival Strategies and the Appraisals that Evoke Them

Appraisals	Survival strategies
1. Must rescue others	1. Rescuing
2. Must be rescued by others	2. Attaching
3. Must achieve goals	3. Asserting
4. Must surrender goals	4. Adapting
5. Must remove danger	5. Fighting
6. Must move from danger	6. Fleeing
7. Must obtain scarce essentials	7. Competing
8. Must create scarce essentials	8. Cooperating

Specifics of the Survival Strategies

The specifics of Figure 5 and Table 1 are brought together in more detail in Table 2. This shows the specific appraisals of means of survival, the survival strategies they evoke, and their adaptive and maladaptive biological, psychological, and social constituents. Two judgment columns denoting worth (chapter 5) are added to give a sense of where survival strategies may lead when used in higher functions. In the following chapters, hierarchical morality and justice are also detailed. (For their categorizations, see chapter 16.) Table 2 is centrally important to the coming chapters in which survival strategies are examined in detail.

It may be noticed that the first line under each survival strategy in the second column refers to physical or bodily survival and the second refers to resources. The first two lines in the psychological and social boxes of each adaptive and maladaptive survival strategy also reflect body and resources aspects, respectively. The third line in each box combines both body and resource aspects.

Many columns in the table are in a way artificial in that they separate concepts rather than objective functions. For instance, the lines separating biological, psychological, and social responses belie their unitary biopsychosocial functions. The double line between adaptive and maladaptive survival strategies should also not be seen to strictly separate the two, as survival strategies may alternate or straddle the two. In fact, it should be remembered that the table is part of a dynamic system (Figures 4 and 5).

Horizontal double lines separate opposing or complementary pairs of survival strategies, such as fight and flight and competition and cooperation. In life there may be frequent prevarication or switching within survival strategy pairs. Alternately, pairs of survival strategies may subserve complementary roles among interacting people. For instance, one may rescue while the other attaches to the rescuer, or one may attack (fight) while the other flees (flight). The first of each pair of survival strategies tends to be more active, the latter being relatively passive. However, survival strategies may be used very flexibly outside of pairs, in various combinations.

It may be noted that there are semantic difficulties in the descriptions of the ingredients of survival strategies. For instance, the word *care* may have nuances of meaning, which overlap survival strategies. Perhaps our language is not yet honed to distinguish survival strategies and their various ingredients.

In summary, survival strategies are discrete phylogenetic templates that have evolved as specific stress responses to aid survival. The eight suggested survival strategies are rescuing, attaching, asserting, adapting, fighting, fleeing, competing, and cooperating. Each act as biopsychosocial functional units and may be adaptive or maladaptive.

The next eight chapters examine each survival strategy in turn. Singly, they help to describe and find the source for specific manifestations of symptoms, illnesses, moralities, principles, and other components of the triaxial framework. Together, survival strategies help to explain the source and meaning of the great variety of fulfillment and stress and trauma responses. It is suggested that the reader refer to Table 2, and Introduction to Part 2 while reading the descriptions of the survival strategies.

Table 2 Survival Strategy Components

APPRAISAL OF MEANS OF SURVIVAL	SURVIVAL STRATEGIES	SUCCESSFUL/ADAPTIVE RESPONSES				UNSUCCESSFUL/MALADAPTIVE RESPONSES				TRAUMA RESPONSES
		BIOLOGICAL	PSYCHOLOGICAL	SOCIAL	JUDGMENTS	BIOLOGICAL	PSYCHOLOGICAL	SOCIAL	JUDGMENTS	
MUST SAVE OTHERS	RESCUING PROTECT PROVIDE	↑ESTROGEN ↑OXYTOCIN ↑OPIOIDS	CARE EMPATHY DEVOTION	RESPONSIBILITY NURTURE PRESERVATION	RESPONSIBLE GIVING ALTRUISTIC	SYMPATHETIC & PARASYMP AROUSAL	BURDEN DEPLETION SELF-CONCERN	RESENTMENT NEGLECT REJECTION	IRRESPONSIBLE NEGLECTFUL EGOTISTIC	ANGUISH COMPASS FATIGUE CAUSED DEATH
MUST BE SAVED BY OTHERS	ATTACHING PROTECTED PROVIDED	↑OPIOIDS	HELD, CARED FOR NURTURED LOOKED AFTER	CLOSE SECURE CONTENT UNION	WORTHY DESERVING LOVABLE	↓OPIOIDS	YEARNING NEED CRAVE ABANDONMENT	CRY INSECURE DEPRIVED SEPARATION	UNWORTHY ENCUMBRANCE REJECTABLE	HELPLESSNESS CAST OUT LEFT TO DIE
MUST ACHIEVE GOAL	ASSERTING COMBAT WORK	↑E, NE ↓CORTISOL ↑IMMUNOCOMP	STRENGTH CONTROL POTENCY	WILL HIGH MORALE SUCCESS	STRONG CAPABLE SUCCESSFUL	↑↑E, NE DEPLETION E, NE ↑BP, ?CHD	FRUSTRATION LOSS OF CONTROL IMPOTENCE	WILLFULNESS LOW MORALE FAILURE	INADEQUATE INCOMPETENT FAILURE	EXHAUSTION "BURN-OUT" POWERLESSNESS
MUST SURRENDER GOAL	ADAPTING ACCEPT GRIEVE	PARASYMP AROUSAL ↑CORTISOL	ACCEPTANCE SADNESS GRIEF HOPE	YIELDING MOURNING TURN TO NEW	PITIFUL SYMPATHY TRIBUTE	↑CORTISOL ↓IMMUNOCOMP ↑INFECTION, ?↑CA	OVERWHELMED DEPRESSION DESPAIR	COLLAPSED WITHDRAWAL GIVING UP	WEAK PATHETIC DESPICABLE	DAMAGED GIVEN IN SUCCUMBING
MUST REMOVE DANGER	FIGHTING DEFEND RID	SYMP AROUSAL ↑N, NE ↑BP	THREAT REVENGE FRIGHTEN	DETERRENCE WOUNDING RIDDANCE	BRAVE NOBLE HEROIC	↑↑SYMP AROUSAL ↓CORTISOL	HATRED PERSECUTION KILLING	ATTACK ERADICATION DESTRUCTION	VIOLENT WICKED MURDERER	HORROR EVIL MURDER
MUST REMOVE ONESELF FROM DANGER	FLEEING RUN, HIDE SAVE ONESELF	SYMPATHETIC & PARASYMP AROUSAL	FEAR TERROR DELIVERANCE	RETREAT FLIGHT ESCAPE	PITIABLE VULNERABLE REFUGEE	NE DEPLETION ↑E & CORTISOL	PHOBIA PARANOIA ENGULFMENT	AVOIDANCE PANIC ANNIHILATION	TIMID PANICKY COWARD	"INESCAPABLE SHOCK," BEING HUNTED, KILLED
MUST OBTAIN SCARCE ESSENTIALS	COMPETING POWER ACQUISITION	↑TESTOSTERONE SYMP AROUSAL	WINNING STATUS DOMINANCE	CONTEST HIERARCHY POSSESSION	SUPERIOR RESPECTED HONORED	↓TESTOSTERONE ↓FEMALE HORMS ↑CORTISOL	DEFEAT GREED, ENVY EXPLOITATION	OPPRESSION STRUGGLE PLUNDER	INFERIOR CONTEMPTIBLE HUMILIATED	TERRORIZATION MARGINALIZATION ELIMINATION
MUST CREATE MORE ESSENTIALS	COOPERATING TRUST MUTUAL GAIN	↑OPIATES ↓BP, E, NE	MUTUALITY GENEROSITY LOVE	INTEGRATION RECIPROCITY CREATIVITY	TENDER POIGNANT BEAUTIFUL	↓OPIATES ↑↑PARASYMP AROUSAL	BETRAYAL SELFISHNESS ABUSE	DISCONNECTION CHEATING DISINTEGRATION	DECEIVER ROBBER PERVERSE, UGLY	FRAGMENTATION ALIENATION DECAY

Chapter 8

Rescue–Caretaking

This survival strategy is deeply involved with the aspect of life's purpose that enables others to survive and fulfill themselves (chapter 5). Contrary to what one may think, in disasters as much as saving themselves people try to save others. Once safe, they feel much anguish for what they had not done to help (e.g., Case 1, chapter 1).

In rescue, life is preserved by saving another. The paradigmatic pictures are a man carrying another person to safety and a mother holding a baby to her breast. Maternal care is a mark of the evolutionary watershed between reptiles and mammals (MacLean, 1985). Parental and wider social protection and provision for the young evolved in species with increasing brain size, fewer number of progeny, and prolonged infancy caretaking (Goodall, 1988; E. O. Wilson, 1975). Caretaking also depended on the calculus of survival (E. O. Wilson, 1975). In times of scarcity, adults could look to their own survival ahead of that of their progeny.

Rescuing and caretaking may be most developed in humans because of their species vulnerability and prolonged early dependency. A new evolutionary step may be instant bonding akin to bonding to infants but generalized to strangers whose cues of helplessness can become imperative motivators to help (Siporin, 1976; Zahn-Waxler, Cummings, & Iannotti, 1986).

MacLean (1985) saw the altruism of jumping into a river to rescue a drowning person an extension of family behavior. According to Trivers (1971), this was governed by an evolutionary survival calculus. Thus, if the risk to rescuers was significantly smaller than the certainty of death to the victims, the evolutionary community gained from such rescues. Natural selection favored communities whose members had the capacity to act in this manner. (If the victim was from a different evolutionary breeding community, reciprocity of altruism favored both communities; see chapter 15.) Yet victims and children could be sacrificed when the survival calculus dictated this. For instance, in times of drought Australian aborigines killed one of newborn twins.

AXIS 1: THE PROCESS AXIS

Appraisal of the Means of Survival

Appraisal is that another person's life is at risk and that one can save them. Although even heroic rescuers may say in retrospect "It just seemed the only thing to do" or "I just did it instinctively," astute survival calculations are included in the appraisals.

> At a debrief I conducted of the staff of a television station after the 1989 San Francisco earthquake, a worker related how she had been totally preoccupied with finding her daughter and ensuring her safety. Later, she was shocked to realize that she had not thought of her workmates at all. Another woman was similarly shocked for not thinking of her family on the other side of the bay while she felt driven to transmit information to the public from the station's helicopter. Yet each woman had made astute calculations of how they could best help others.

The Holocaust threw up cruel "Sophie's choices" (Styron, 1979). In the Lodz Ghetto, the Germans demanded 20,000 souls, otherwise all would be killed. Rumkovsky, the ghetto leader, asked for the community to hand over its old and children, pleading that he had to cut off limbs in order to save the body (Campbell, 1994). Though appraisals have been noted to be influenced by past experience, roles, and values, in traumatic situations the pragmatics of group survival tend to dominate appraisals.

Stress Responses

Adaptive–Successful Responses
Biological Aspects   The thalamocingulate division of the limbic system is involved in especially maternal but also paternal activities. The areas have high receptor sites for the female hormones estrogen, progesterone, prolactin, and oxytocin, all of which activate maternal behavior (Rosenblatt, 1989) including

maternal aggression (Troisi, D'Amato, Carnera, & Trinca, 1988). Opioid activity may also facilitate caregiving behavior (Panksepp, Siviy, & Normansell, 1985), and high cortisol levels seem to facilitate human bonding.

However, helicopter ambulance medics secreted less than the expected amounts of 17-hydroxycorticosteroids during rescue missions (Bourne, Rose, & Mason, 1967). It is likely that different hormones are used in different rescue and caretaking aspects. Further research is required on their physiological profiles.

Psychological Aspects   Evolutionary investment in genes may be translated into emotional investment in others. It is suggested that care, possibly tinged with pity, is an intense outgoing protective emotion welling in the chest toward a helpless baby or a person in danger. The care is provided along an exclusive mental bond pulling to the person and is reflected in a propulsion toward the person with extended arms that ache to embrace and hold for maximum security. The desire to provide overlaps with the welling and is described as a convex fullness in the chest, requiring one to fill the other person's concavity or emptiness.

Empathy is the means of understanding the soul of the pain and injury from within the crucible of trauma (J. P. Wilson & Lindy, 1994). In the absence of verbal communication, empathy may be the only means of recognizing another's vital needs. It is a translation of *Einfühlung*, meaning approximately feeling at one with (Batson, Darley, & Coke, 1978). It may be called psychological altruism where one devotes one's emotional and cognitive resources to the understanding of another person.

Projective identification is the psychodynamic term for the means of conveying empathic information, and its reception is called countertransference. To be cognitively and emotionally open to the pain of others makes one vulnerable and oneself needing support (Valent, 1995b; Winnicott, 1963).

Care and empathy are part of devotion to protect and provide for another. It includes compassion, dedication, investment, and sacrifice for the other.

Social Aspects   People have a sense of responsibility for those they rescue and care for, and this is translated into social roles and duties of emergency workers and parents. Nurture, like paradigmatic breastfeeding, reflects the desire to give of oneself and one's resources to the other person. Resources include food, shelter, warmth, understanding, and oneself. Long-term nurture involves making others grow and prosper to their full potential. The final outcome is indeed preservation and nurturing of others' lives.

Maladaptive–Unsuccessful Responses
Biological Aspects   The literature on physiological concomitants of maladaptive rescue and caretaking is sparse. One may speculate that female sex hormones and opioids may show a variety of imbalances and that autonomic

nervous system and other physiological responses are aroused during difficult rescuing and caretaking.

Psychological Aspects   Strained rescuers and caretakers may feel the other person to be a burden, literally or psychologically too great a weight to carry— "He is really weighing me down." One may feel a weight on one's shoulders or back under which one is collapsing, being dragged down to one's doom. Empathic demands and social responsibilities may be similarly sensed as burdens.

Associated depletion of one's resources may feel like being drained of energy. One feels scooped, consumed, sucked dry, used up, and emptied (Segal, 1975). This leads to self-concern, caring for oneself, and replenishing one's resources.

Social Aspects   People in need may now be pushed away with resentment, marked by irritable gestures and words, or through passive withdrawal. Roles of responsibility are similarly resented. Neglect is the result of ignoring others' needs. The mental umbilicus of bonding is shut off. It may even merge into reversal of roles such as when mothers demand empathy from their children. An extreme example was adults taking milk away from children in Auschwitz (Valent, 1994, p. 26). Rejection is the final outcome. Rebuffing and repelling may be accompanied by stiffening and straightening of the body and placing the arms out stiffly with extended hands and fingers. Spitz (1965) described these features in a mother who rejected her newborn. The needy other person may seem to be dangerous, an undesired alien who may evoke aggression and contempt.

Though the situation may be severely strained, it may still make survival sense for caregivers to be cared for first in situations of scarcity, as without them no one survives.

Trauma

Anguish for another's life (possibly most intense for one's children) is one of the greatest agonies humans have to endure. Together with guilt, the anguish may be interminable. Anguish results from intense worry and preoccupation that death or injury may result or have resulted from one's failure to rescue or care. It may be described like the welling feeling in the chest being wrung and distorted, reflected in wringing of hands that cannot care. If the person dies, the anguish continues unabated or even intensified, with continuous worry about how one could have prevented the event or somehow undo it now.

Compassion fatigue is the ever present striving to give that which cannot be given. The desire to do something for the other is blocked and no effort succeeds. Compassion fatigue as an illness is described below. The ultimate trauma is the conviction that one caused the death of another whom one should and could have helped.

Illnesses

The ill effects on rescuers of caring for victims became obvious soon after establishment of outreach projects to disaster sites. Kliman (1976) noted that rescuers were secondary victims. A wide variety of physical and social stress symptoms was noted early (Berah, Jones, & Valent, 1984), as also in Case 1 (chapter 1). They included shock, confusion, depression, anxiety, helplessness, fatigue, sleep disturbances, restlessness, colds and flus, changes in drinking and smoking habits, and minor illnesses and accidents.

Similar symptoms were experienced by senior doctors of a hospital that was closing down as a cost-cutting measure (Valent, unpublished). However, the doctors also suffered anger, emotional outbursts alternating with emotional blunting, a variety of psychophysiological symptoms, and marital difficulties. These were related to loss of role, status, identity, and morale, but, worst, inability to provide proper care to patients. Long-term responsibility for life and death may contribute to doctors' relatively high morbidity and mortality rates.

Psychological Aspects   Reviews on psychological traumatic stress effects on emergency personnel (Beaton & Murphy, 1995; Figley, 1995a; Mitchell & Dyregrov, 1993; Raphael, 1986; R. C. Robinson & Mitchell, 1993) were consistent with the above findings. They further noted that effects were particularly severe on helpers when they were confronted with danger of death themselves or witnessed death, especially multiple, grotesque, and child deaths and deaths of people similar to themselves. These factors were noted to make for primary victim vulnerability, too (chapter 3). Helpers were also vulnerable when unsupported during sequential disasters, when pressed into service, when not being trained, and when not receiving resources and support from their organizations. Badly affected helpers were likely to suffer not only stress symptoms, but also traumatic flashbacks, intrusive and constricted thoughts, memory and attention disturbances, anxiety, anger, guilt, and self-doubt. Symptoms could start in the traumatic situation or be delayed for even years.

Figley (1995a, 1995b) coined two terms: secondary traumatic stress disorder and compassion fatigue. The former phenomenological diagnosis paralleled *DSM–IV* PTSD criteria and symptoms, except that the stressor was victims' traumas. The latter diagnosis referred to the cost of caring, empathy, deep sympathy, and sorrow for another (Figley, 1995b). This reflected a dynamic approach. The latter approach was also taken by Pearlman and Saakavitne (1995), who referred to vicarious traumatization as an almost inevitable result of dealing in depth with severely traumatized victims. Its features included blurring of therapists' sense of boundaries, self-esteem, and spirituality.

Valent (1995b) suggested that specific features, strain and trauma, occur in therapists when particular maladaptive survival strategies are evoked in them through inability to process or complement victims' survival strategies and traumas.

AXIS 2: PARAMETERS AXIS

Traumatic Situations and Disaster Phases

Help varies according to the needs of each disaster phase. Rescue usually occurs in the impact phase of disasters, whereas caretaking is a longer rehabilitating process. Help in different disaster phases is explored more fully elsewhere (Valent, in press, a).

Rescue–Caretaking at Different Social Levels

Traditionally, fathers give protection and provide food and shelter, and mothers provide their bodies, sustenance, and comfort. In modern societies, specific emergency organizations such as police and firefighters help with specific dangers. The medical system cares for the ill. On a wider scale, national and international relief organizations deal with major disasters. Different organizations have their own ideals, skills, and literature.

Rescue–Caretaking Across the Life Cycle

From a very early age, children play at parenting dolls, pets, and other children; help each other when in trouble; and attempt to do the same for their parents when the latter are helpless. Batson et al. (1978) noted that by the age of 2, empathy has developed to the stage where children can imagine how it would feel in the other's situation. Between 6 and 9, another person's plight can be responded to appropriately, including role reversals with parents (Valent, 1984, 1994).

Ability to rescue and nurture reach their peak in early adulthood, though aspects of them mellow and ripen with age. Selective bonding to their babies occurs in mothers in a crucial period within hours to days after birth and solidifies over years (Fleming & Anderson, 1987). This may be paralleled with the needy in traumatic situations. Inability to establish satisfactory bonding with babies may cause much distress, and this is possibly reflected in anguish and guilt toward those one did not help properly.

With maturity, help is less biological and more psychological, such as giving of knowledge and wisdom.

AXIS 3: FULFILLMENT AND TRAUMA
ALONG THE DEPTH AXIS

Preservation of life and its nurture is deeply purposeful, and failure of this process causes deep suffering.

Fulfillment

Rescue, care, nurture, and preservation carry deep pleasures and joys. Saving lives is supremely good, and caretaking is associated with virtues of kindness, patience, pity, and charity. Altruism and self-sacrifice are admired as very worthy, and there is a sense of having done the right thing looking after the weak. Meanings include that one is capable and highly moral in saving and perpetuating lives of others.

Parents; those in the medical profession; and rescuers such as police, firefighters, and charities have particular ideals, and all place high value on the worth of preservation and facilitation of others' lives. Principles include care for the ill and the weak and provision of circumstances where they can pursue their potentials and happiness. The right to life, care, and dignity may be codified. For instance, medical ethics includes respect for the body, proper boundaries, confidentiality, and, if all fails, death with dignity. Right to life and pursuit of happiness may be enshrined in constitutions.

Magical rituals and sacrifice may be practiced as in witch-doctoring to augment one's natural capacities. In modern religion, churches may provide pity, charity, and comfort, but one may also identify one's task with God's. Alternately, one may carry out socialist ideologies such as taxing the rich and providing social welfare for the needy. Symbols of care are mother breastfeeding baby or Jesus sacrificing so others can live. Rescue agencies have specific symbols, such as the Red Cross.

Successful rescuing is incorporated in one's identity as a good firefighter, doctor, or mother; a life giver; or empathic nurturer. Creativity and esthetics may be added now in delightful ways of providing food, clothes, shelter, and even entertainment. Firefighters may delight in uniforms, shiny red fire engines, and brass bands.

Rescue and caretaking make one part of the sacred gift of life in the universe. Mary feeding Jesus represents this sacred universality. Knowledge of this gift and its process provides a deep existential truth and fulfills the purpose of life itself. Wisdom understands the balance between loss and preservation of life and propagates knowledge that saves and fulfills ever more lives.

Trauma

Feeling burdened and depleted are very unpleasant, whereas having allowed or caused death is a special traumatic agony. In particular, survivor guilt for having survived instead of the other racks one's conscience, associated with a sense of unworthiness and shame for having been neglectful and self-concerned. One caused undeserved, unjust death and suffering. This means that one is irresponsible and cannot be trusted with others' lives.

Ideals of rescuer and parental roles crumble, and it appears that others' lives and happiness are devalued. People seem to work according to the "me-first" principle and "human selfishness coming out in bad times." Human dignity and entitlements of the needy are rebuffed, and the usual codes and ethics are abandoned. Religion and ideology seem sadly unpractical in times of burden and depletion, though further guilt ensues for being uncharitable and callous. So to one's identity as a bad firefighter, doctor, or mother is added the self-image of a selfish sponge who feeds off others' lives. Symbols of one's dereliction and guilt are sensed to be everywhere. Whatever one still manages to provide is uncreative and aesthetically crude and drab.

The sacred giving of life is replaced by arid barrenness in the space vacated by the dead. Initially, martyrdom of giving beyond one's resources may be attempted. But unlike with saints, masochistic and even sadistic manifestations may result. In extreme situations, letting or even making someone suffer or die may be associated with relief.

Knowledge of failure to help, or as may be felt, having prevented others to survive and to prosper disrupts one's existential meaning and purpose.

In summary, giving life gives purpose to life; to not preserve or nurture it takes away life's purpose.

Chapter 9

Attachment

Attachment is the complementary force to bonding in rescuing–caretaking and is the vehicle whereby the young and weakened have others supply their needs. In attachment, one's life is saved by another. The paradigmatic picture is being carried to safety or an infant being held securely while being breastfed.

Attachment evolved along with parental care about 180 million years ago (MacLean, 1985). It is present in all mammals and birds and is the infant's contribution to the proximity needed for rescuing and caretaking. The separation call of the young may be the earliest mammalian vocalization (MacLean, 1985).

Attachment is important and prolonged in humans, as they are the most dependent and vulnerable species. It occurs in relation to mother through a complex type of imprinting process. It may generalize to other caring and dominant group members. Akin to bonding, intense attachment may form in the pressure cookers of traumatic situations.

AXIS 1: THE PROCESS AXIS

Appraisal of the Means of Survival

The appraisal is that one needs other(s) to save and provide. There is little appraisal of the survival calculus in attachment in infants, but in extreme situations such as the Holocaust, children as young as 4 could let go of their parents without protest under authoritative direction (Valent, 1994), and older children could stay silent while alone in hiding for long times.

Stress Responses

Adaptive–Successful Responses

Biological Aspects   The thalamocingulate division of the limbic system and hormones similar to those in bonding are probably involved here, too, as are opioids that facilitate social comforting generally. However, more exploration of the biological aspects of adaptive attachment is needed.

Psychological Aspects   Adaptive attachment includes some of the most intense human pleasures. Being held and cared for against the chest with maximum body contact by a familiar attachment figure stills distress and provides a warm sense of security. The curled position may hark back to safe envelopment in the womb. Psychological holding includes being seen, recognized, and held in the other's gaze and mind (Winnicott, 1960a). Physical and psychological holding are associated with minute-by-minute handling and ministration, as well as long-term consistency, reliability, and predictability.

Being nurtured involves satisfaction of physical needs such as hunger, sleep, and warmth, each with its own physiological pleasures. Analogous to food filling the stomach and promoting physical growth, empathy fills the psychological holes and provides psychological pleasures and growth (Winnicott, 1963). Being looked after and cared for by a very special, powerful, abundant, and benevolent person specially devoted to oneself provides blissful physical and emotional satiety.

Social Aspects   From the first days of life, a baby is pacified by being picked up, caressed, and talked to (Bowlby, 1971, p. 265). Similar pacification through closeness and security may be provided by rescuers in disasters.

> Looking back on his resuscitation after a heart attack, a patient reported to me, "I just concentrated on that nurse's hand. She was like an angel, I knew that she would carry me through. I still think I owe my life to her."

The secure closeness and nurture lead to contentment. This is not a passive Nirvana state where all desire is extinguished (Freud, 1920/1975c). Rather, the abundant investments are assimilated and then zestfully used to fulfill life. Union with an attachment figure is like being in a psychosocial envelope that harks back to the secure, nurturing, life-augmenting womb.

Maladaptive–Unsuccessful Responses

Biological Aspects   Separation calls (distress vocalizations) are associated with the cingulate gyrus, in areas rich in opioid receptors (MacLean, 1985).

Indeed, morphine and endogenous opioids sharply reduce separation cries, whereas their antagonist naloxone increases them (Panksepp, Meeker, & Bean, 1980). Opiate withdrawal may be associated with the perception of social isolation (Panksepp, 1989a; Panksepp et al., 1985).

The sympathetic nervous system is active in separation distress, with high norepinephrine secretion. In the later passive phase, heart rate and temperature are decreased, ACTH and adrenal cortical secretions are elevated, and the immune system is depressed (Field & Reite, 1985; Panksepp et al., 1985). Because mothers are important instruments in setting points for physiological functions (Coe et al., 1985) and normal integrated development (Reite & Capitano, 1985), separations may adversely affect psychobiological synchrony and biopsychosocial attunements (chapter 3). For instance, immune system function in monkeys is compromised in short- and long-term separations (Coe et al., 1985), and this adversely affects their later resistance to cancer (Panksepp et al., 1985). Premature weaning can diminish lymphocyte proliferation to a cancerogenic agent for over a year. Prolonged separation experiments on humans cannot be performed. However, the immune system is extremely sensitive to even minor stressors and emotions (Editorial, 1992; Knapp et al., 1992). It is possible that child and adult separations may contribute to later vulnerabilities such as to cancer (Grossarth-Maticek et al., 1982) through immune system dysregulation.

Psychological Aspects   Maladaptive attachment is associated with some of the most intense unpleasures. It is suggested that yearning is a specific emotion directed to retrieval and is felt in the chest as an intense pull and longing toward the absent person. Raphael (1984) described yearning as separation pain. The intensity of this mental pain rivals the most intense physical pain.

> A 38-year-old man reported to me that he had been visited by his mother after being burnt in a fire. "I just wanted her to touch me, to show she cared, to make me feel I mattered." As she left without having touched him, a yearning pain developed in his chest. He said, "That pain was worse than the pain of being burnt."

Like grief, yearning appears within hours of separation, comes in waves, and stays for weeks (Parkes, 1972). It may be confused with pangs of grief and missing an irretrievably lost object (chapter 11).

Absence of caretakers leads to need and craving. Each lack evokes its specific unpleasure, such as hunger. Analogous psychological or person hunger may be confused with physical hunger. However, it is suggested that it is a specific craving, a painful emptiness centered in the chest, relieved by being held.

> A 24-year-old woman seen in the emergency department had taken an overdose when her abusive boyfriend on whom she depended threatened to leave her. Worse than any abuse, the threat produced an intolerable pain, a huge chasm in her chest demanding to be filled. A hug from her boyfriend filled the space and relieved the pain instantly. In the past, only heroin had eased it.

Absence of a desperately needed attachment person is felt as aloneness and abandonment. The cognitive counterparts of the inner emptiness are reflected in terms of extreme isolation such as "being on a raft in the middle of an ocean" or "in a space capsule alone in the universe." Lifton (1967, p. 43) quoted an atom bomb victim: "Even stronger than thoughts about life and death was this feeling of loneliness . . . of having no home and no family." The soldier who feels he is dying cries out for his mother (Appel & Beebe, 1946; Dasberg, 1976; M. M. Stern, 1966). The hospital patient described below linked his current disaster with childhood abandonment. Contrast him with the with the held patient (chapter 9).

> I realized that I might die in the coronary care unit. I felt terribly alone, no one helped me. It was really the same loneliness I always felt at the core of my soul. In my childhood, everybody lived around me, not with me. No one ever looked at me. No gaze, no bond, no touch. I was alone in the universe. It gave me a painful emptiness [indicating his chest], a never-ending hole. I have carried it all my life, but I felt it in a naked form in the coronary care unit.

Social Aspects   The distressed insecure person cries out (the separation call) and reaches out arms in order to be picked up and to cling. This plaintive posture is usually extremely evocative, though in maladaptive situations it may be perceived as burdensome. If mobile, the whole person is like the arms, searching, trying to match an intense mental image with the tangible person. Calming or offering substitutes may increase agitation. When the found person rejects the supplicant, the above behavior may become more insistent, which in turn may be sensed as demanding, and a vicious spiral may develop.

Deprivation due to lack of care and neglect lead to a variety of particular deficiency states such as malnutrition, exposure, and lack of thriving. Spitz (1965) noted that severe emotional deprivation in infants was also akin to having been deprived of some vital element of survival. Separation is like being cast out of a belonging psychosocial envelope, a physical and psychological rejection into a hostile environment.

Trauma

Attachment trauma has been designated at times as the main human trauma, with helplessness as its hallmark (Allen, 1995; Freud, 1926/1975h; Holloway & Fullerton, 1994; van der Kolk, 1987). Freud (1927/1975e) likened it to a newborn alone in the face of cruel nature.

> A psychotherapy patient of mine, while reliving childhood physical abuse, described her helplessness as being in a vacuum yet surrounded by danger. Her drawing of the experience depicted a small child in its cot surrounded by monsters. In a corner of the drawing was an angel looking the other way.

Helpless isolation is sensed as being cast out into "bondlessness," without roots or connectedness, in an alien realm dominated by threat. Psychological casting out may be like falling into a mental vacuum, unrelatedness, and nonentity (Guntrip, 1973). Like the Australian aborigine who has the bone pointed at him as a symbol of ostracism and dies, the traumatized, totally isolated (Wolfenstein, 1977) person feels he or she is left to die. "Nobody cares whether I live or die" may be the last tragic thought before death, or a traumatic imprint carried deep inside for many years.

Illnesses

For convenience, biopsychosocial symptoms and illnesses are noted separately.

Biological Aspects

Psychophysiological Symptoms   It is suggested that suppressed separation screams may present as breathing difficulties. Next, because person hunger may be symbolized as food hunger (chapter 9), attachment difficulties may present with a variety of digestive difficulties, from "3-month colic" in infants (G. J. Taylor, 1987) to later nausea, indigestion, hunger, obesity, and a variety of esophageal, stomach, and bowel symptoms.

Some of these symptoms may progress to psychosomatic illnesses such as esophagitis and peptic ulcer. Dunn (1942) noted that dyspepsia was the single most prevalent symptom in British soldiers in the Second World War, and radiologically diagnosed peptic ulcer followed not far behind. Alexander (1950) suggested that the latter was prone to develop in situations of suppressed need to be dependent and cared for. Weiner et al. (1959) confirmed this in army inductees, especially those who also had high pepsinogen levels. Hostility and impaired coping ability may be aspects of maladaptive attachment quoted to be associated with ulcers (Folks & Kinney, 1995). However, Folks and Kinney pointed to the need for more refined research.

Urticaria, neurodermatitis, eczema, and angioneurotic edema have been suggested to be associated with separation trauma and deficits in holding (touching) needs (Alexander, 1950; G. J. Taylor, 1987). Alexander (1950) suggested that asthma was associated with repressed dependence on mother as a protector. Relative preponderance of parasympathetic activity may be one method of transmitting emotional factors to the lungs (Moran, 1995). Weiner (1977) noted that as well as allergic predispositions, in half the patients the threat or actuality of separation could mobilize an unexpressed cry for the mother and an asthma attack.

> A 2-year-old boy seen in the emergency department developed his first asthma attack just as his father was abandoning the family. His asthma subsided when his parents took him to bed with them. Subsequent arguments also led to asthma attacks, calmed by the original maneuver.

Total emotional deprivation of infants, even if they are physically cared for, led to failure to thrive and a variety of physical illnesses and even death (Kraemer, 1985; Spitz, 1965).

Suggestions have been noted earlier (G. J. Taylor, 1987; chapter 3; chapter 11) that separation trauma could contribute to illness indirectly through early interference with biopsychosocial attunements leading to later vulnerabilities such as compromised immune system responses. Susceptibility to infections, allergies, autoimmune diseases, diabetes, and cancers may result (Coe et al., 1989). Coe et al. noted that research in this whole area is only beginning.

Psychological Aspects   When Freud (1926/1975h) came to see separation as the core trauma, he also came to see it as the root of neuroses. He thus saw separation anxiety, phobias of the dark, being alone, or being with strangers as symbolic reenactments of early abandonment experiences. Specific defenses were postulated to mold different clinical pictures. For instance, avoidance of outside spaces led to agoraphobia, obsessional defenses to obsessional neuroses.

Object relations pioneers such as Winnicott (1960b), Kohut (1971), and Kernberg (1975) suggested that childhood deficiencies of empathy, holding, recognition, and psychological attunement could lead to psychological deadness manifested as a false self and illnesses such as anorexia nervosa and borderline personalities. Though, as noted, the latter can result from early sexual abuse, they may also arise from other contexts.

> Jim, a psychotherapy patient with a borderline diagnosis, had a chronically depressed mother who rejected him emotionally from birth. He developed a state of "anxious attachment." Whenever he attempted to genuinely progress in life, he suffered severe anxiety, agitation, loneliness, and a sense of alienation.

Social Aspects   In children, acute stress responses may include crying, clinging, dependence, and school refusal. In adults, symbolic comforting may manifest through food, cigarettes, alcohol, drugs, sexual demands, and doctor visits. These responses may become entrenched under the diagnostic umbrella of dependent personality disorders. Early social dysregulation may predispose to fragile modulation of behavioral impulses and social interactions. Extreme manifestations include antisocial actions, accidents, overdoses, and self-mutilation.

AXIS 2: PARAMETERS AXIS

Traumatic Situations and Disaster Phases

Children separated from parents cry and scream variably for days, refusing comfort from nurses (Bowlby, 1975; Robertson & Robertson, 1967–1973). They cling to familiar objects, yearn and search for mothers, and may develop hostile and regressive behavior. If parents do not return, despair and later detachment develop (Bowlby, 1975). On reunion, children may be hostile, but anxious and clinging if further separation is threatened—anxious attachment.

In the impact phase of disasters, bodily attachment can be important for security. Nurture and being cared for may be important later. Mental representations of bonds may hold and comfort people in long-term life-threatening situations (Dimsdale, 1974; Henderson & Bostock, 1977).

Attachment at Different Social Levels

Individual attachment is first to another person, though it can spread to family, group, community, and nation in ever-increasing circles. Substitutes may be attempted for any of them, with variable success. There is a tendency to regress to more intense and central attachment figures when vulnerable or to see rescuers as omnipotent, according to early childhood thinking.

Families, groups, and societies may themselves attach to ever bigger social units for protection and provision. Communities beseech and pay homage to their earthly and religious attachment figures through beautiful buildings, rituals, and pageants.

Attachment Across the Life Cycle

Attachment is most literal in the womb. From birth, discriminate biological bias starts through smell, voice, face, and touch (D. N. Stern, 1984). Attachment to a specific person is clear by 2 months, fully established by 6 months, and most intense between 3 and 12 months and remains intense till 3 years of age. Psychologically, the infant can initially attach only to fragments of mother. At 6–8 months, the infant can perceive her as a whole and to remember her (Mahler, Pine, & Bergman, 1975). At this stage, anxiety to strangers appears. Autonomy develops slowly, by means of transitional objects and greater abilities to care for oneself. Earlier separation experiences are cued by later separation challenges such as school entry, adolescence, leaving home, or a parent's death. Attachment to parents and the concept of powerful protectors and providers remains to some extent throughout life. Analogous attachment imprinting and adaptive and maladaptive responses occur in traumatic stress, but telescope into a much shorter time.

AXIS 3: FULFILLMENT AND TRAUMA ALONG THE DEPTH AXIS

Fulfillment

The survival pleasures of attachment are variable and intense and may appear to be fulfillment in themselves, especially when absent. However, they are foundations for further fulfillment, such as judgments that include that one is lovable and worthy and justly deserving because one was good and pleasing. Derived meanings include "I am good, valuable, lovable," "The world is safe and good to me," and "My requirements are always met somehow."

Ideals include notions of perfect protection and care, reciprocated by perfect obedience and virtue. One's life and satisfaction of its needs are a supreme value not only to oneself but to caretakers, the principle being that all should be done to make one happy. There may be a sense of right and entitlement to being specially loved and cared for and to develop to maximum potential. This may be codified in children's rights in law and constitutions. Though weak and small, victims' and children's dignity is protected and designated by their potentials.

When attachment figures are absent, they may be remembered, imagined, or manufactured. The early magical power of being cared for may be transferred to amulets, rituals, rites, and religion where God answers prayers and good deeds. In heaven, all attachment needs are eternally satisfied. Ideology may promise heaven on earth. For instance, communism promised to give to all according to people's needs.

Attachment symbols may have historical connections to past attachment aspects. Because sucking the breast was associated with both secure contact and feeding, it may be a compound symbol for both protection and provision. Sucking or eating may serve as retrograde symbolic evocators of maternal security. So may softness, warmth, and skin contact. Whole attachment figures may be symbolized in transitional objects, authority figures, and religious figures that resemble parents.

Secure attachment is thought to lay the foundation for a coherent identity that includes cognitive, emotional, and moral maturity and a happy and respected sense of self, with a deep sense of group and spiritual belonging. There is an aesthetic delight in oneself and one's burgeoning potentials and individual creativity.

The breastfed child like Jesus at the breast is a symbol of the miracle of receiving life from another through a universal principle. The sacred stream of life and those who are its instruments are viewed with awe and reverence. Knowledge of one's vulnerability and dependence on benevolent others who lovingly pass to one the stream of life for the purpose of one's own life's fulfillment provide a deep existential meaning or truth. Wisdom appreciates its value and tenuousness.

Trauma

The trauma of disrupted attachment not only threatens survival but is accompanied by some of the worst human suffering. Judgments of this happening include hierarchical morality and guilt for having been bad, reflected in the age-old explanation of calamities as being punishment for sin (chapter 1). One may feel shame for being small, needy, and dependent and feel worthless, an unlovable, rejectable encumbrance. Self-blame can maintain a semblance of justice and control in the world, but awareness of innocence evokes the plaintive cry "Why?!" frequently heard in disasters, along with a collapse of a sense of justice in the universe. Derived meanings include either that one is not worth caring for or that in a callous world one has to look after oneself. One is of no value to others; there is no principle of being cared for. There are no ideal caretakers, and one has no right to ask for one; there is only indignity of ostracism, being nothing. No magic helps, and even God has abandoned one. No symbols satisfy. For instance, opiate drugs only transiently simulate attachment comforts and are followed by more adverse effects.

One's identity has no secure boundaries, coherence, or controlled modulation. One is alienated from the world and self. Creativity and aesthetics are replaced by nothingness, boredom, and dilapidation. There is no sacred connection across the generations, with a universe helping to create and nurture its parts. Knowledge and truth are avoided, for they may reveal that with no one to love and care for one, life has no purpose.

In summary, fulfilled attachment contains the vision of paradise, but its traumatic equivalent is being cast out into most purposeless insignificance.

Chapter 10

Assertiveness: Goal Achievement

Goals of obtaining food, shelter, and secure territory and to fulfill roles toward these ends occupy much everyday effort.

In assertiveness, life is preserved by achieving essential goals. The paradigmatic picture is of an individual hunting, working, or soldiering. Foraging is present in all animals from amoebae on. Because foraging occurs in territories that also provide a secure space to shelter and reproduce (Ardrey, 1967; Lorenz, 1968), territorial combat may supersede sexual, and even foraging, activities (Esser & Deutsch, 1977). Hunting is usually of other species, though cannibalism occurs in many species, especially in times of scarcity (E. O. Wilson, 1975). In mammals, hunting and combat usually involve male groups.

Humans also forage and carve out territories and combat for these resources. It has been contended that hunting has been the master behavior pattern of the human species for 99% of its existence, directing its recent huge evolutionary spurt (Isaac, 1977; Laughlin, 1977; Lee, 1977; chapter 7) and thus underlying more recent human achievements. Hunting resulted in a durable and flexible creature, with an intelligence that could learn intricate habits of hunted animals, seasonal cycles, geography, and calculation of odds. Social groups evolved around hunting, influencing size of breeding populations, gender roles, and male groupings. For instance, 10 or more males was the ideal group to hunt large animals (Ardrey, 1976; Canetti, 1973). Similarly sized male groups comprise core combat units, sanctums of power, committees, and even sports teams.

Combat can resemble hunting (Scott, 1981), with other humans being the game (Washburn & Lancaster, 1977). Cannibalism has indeed been present throughout the world till recent times (Kroeber, 1948). However, goal-oriented combat these days usually occurs for territory and other resources, other humans being fortuitous hindrances to these goals.

Gathering food, preparing for the hunt, and butchering were early type work. Work today is usually for money, which then buys food, territory, and resources.

AXIS 1: THE PROCESS AXIS

Appraisal of the Means of Survival

The appraisal is that in order to survive, essential goals must be achieved. The survival calculus may prioritize and organize multiple and complex goals, roles, and boundaries.

Stress Responses

Adaptive–Successful Responses

Biological Aspects   Predatory or "instrumental" aggression that includes stalking and quiet, biting attack is associated with the lateral perifornical hypothalamus, ventral aspect of the midbrain periaqueductal gray, and ventral and lateral tegmental areas (Shaikh, Brutus, Siegel, & Siegel, 1985).

The little research on human hunting has only indicated that it is not associated with elevated male hormones (Worthman & Konner, 1987). On the other hand physiological responses in combat, hazardous sports, and work have long shown decreased secretion of 17-hydroxycorticosteroids and cortisol (Bourne et al., 1967; Bourne, Rose, & Mason, 1968; Hoch, Werle, & Weicker, 1988; Ursin, Baade, & Levine, 1978) and of male sex hormones (Rose, 1969). However, activation of the sympathetic nervous system results in increased levels of epinephrine and norepinephrine, glucose, cholesterol, fatty acids, and to a lesser extent thyroxin and growth hormone and in a decrease in blood coagulation time. Endogenous opioids may facilitate motivational behavior and suppress pain (Panksepp, 1993; Smith, 1991).

Repeated assertiveness arousal may lead to physiological and psychological toughness (Dienstbier, 1989) associated with low arousal, strong sympathetic response, resistance to brain epinephrine and norepinephrine depletion, enhanced immune system competence, and suppressed pituitary–adrenal cortical responses.

Psychological Aspects   Pursuit of goals is accompanied by alertness, anticipation, concentration, ready absorption of new information, and mustering of past learning. Psychological and physical strength and energy emanate from deep within, radiating into muscles whose actions may be harnessed into brute effort, stamina, and perseverance, according to need.

One has a sense of control, a confidence in one's command of mind and body, environment, life, and destiny. Potency includes a sense of vigor, energy, mastery, and effectiveness; and a sense of autonomy and capacity to have impact (McClelland, 1975).

Social Aspects Assertion of will channels strength to its target. It is associated with clarity, decisiveness, authority, determination, and forcefulness. Group will involves high morale (chapter 2), which itself includes smooth coordination of roles and skills within groups, esprit de corps with a high degree of devotion and faith in success, and conviction that the goal must be achieved. Ultimately, the goal is indeed successfully achieved and savored.

Maladaptive–Unsuccessful Responses

Biological Aspects With sustained effort, excessive and chronic sympathetic hyperactivity is accompanied by raised levels of the adaptive psychophysiological responses (Frankenhauser, 1980; Friedman, 1991; Steptoe, 1981). States of exhaustion may be reflected in depletions, such as opioids (Friedman, 1991) and norepinephrine (van der Kolk & Greenberg, 1987).

Psychological Aspects Thwarted effort leads to frustration. Associated tension and exhaustion in both muscles and mind is accompanied by an irritable hostility that Dollard and Miller (1950) cited as the cause of anger. Though certainly a cause, other struggling survival strategies also have their particular angers. Also distressing is the sense of loss of control, which may involve the environment, others, or oneself. Loss of control over cognitive processes may be referred to as a nervous breakdown and loss of control over emotions as "going over the top" or "cracking up." Finally, ineffectiveness of one's will, strength, and capacity leads to a sense of impotence.

Social Aspects Frustration and inability to accept reality may lead to willfulness. Further waste of resources and energy may then manifest as wantonness and folly. Because of their magnitude, they are especially noticeable in wars (Tuchman, 1983). Lifton (1973) described the huge cost of American willfulness in Vietnam. Inevitably demoralization (chapter 2) sets in, with loss of spirit, confidence, and devotion to the task. There is failure to achieve goals.

Trauma

When one's effort meets unyielding resistance, something gives. Burn-out is an intuitive concept akin to giving out, like a flame that has run out of fuel. Exhaustion and fatigue indicate that physical and mental energy have run out.

The term *burn-out* is often applied to workers and rescuers (to be distinguished from *compassion fatigue*; see chapter 8). Combat exhaustion is applied to soldiers (chapter 2). Each state is characterized by a sense of powerlessness, the incapacity of one's efforts to achieve life goals. In exhaustion, there may be a deep coming apart of one's capable being. If effort continues for long times, as it may also in civilian life, the taut muscle in one's core may give in or tear. This is the state in which heart attacks occur (chapter 10). The following includes both burn-out and exhaustion.

> A 53-year-old man's company had been taken over. Group morale was low. The new boss demanded more productivity, which led to lower standards. The man felt trapped because he was too old to find a new job. He was constantly tense and frustrated, work became mental torture, and his functioning deteriorated. He was exhausted but could not sleep. He was constantly alert but was impotent to channel his energy usefully. He felt his life was a failure. He expended much effort to not go over the top. He developed severe chest pain that this time was diagnosed in the emergency department as due to muscle tension.

Illnesses

Assertiveness illnesses are given more space as they contribute to major causes of morbidity and mortality.

Biological Aspects

Psychophysiological Symptoms   Psychophysiological symptoms from intense sympathetic nervous activity can affect all organs of the body (chapter 3) and produce tension headaches and pains in the neck, chest, and back; palpitations; sweating; breathlessness; restlessness; and arousal symptoms of PTSD. Muscular chest pain may have contributed to what in the army has been variably called da Costa's syndrome, effort syndromes, or cardiac neurosis (chapter 2) and in civilian life may mimic angina and heart attack (see previous case). Depletion of the sympathetic nervous system, especially of norepinephrine, has been postulated to be associated with the exhaustion states.

Psychosomatic Illnesses   Though sympathetic activation in fight, competition, and possibly flight may also contribute, maladaptive assertiveness fits best research into the following illnesses.

Sudden death. Fatal arrhythmias (especially ventricular fibrillation) are adversely influenced by sympathetic inputs. Though stress-induced sudden death is more frequent in the already compromised, this is not always so (Niaura & Goldstein, 1992; Steptoe, 1981).

Hypertension. Blood pressure increases immediately and very sensitively in response to arousal stressors and has been shown to be able to stay elevated for months in combat soldiers and disaster victims (Steptoe, 1981). In work situations, work pressure, excessive responsibility, lack of control, and role conflict all contributed to unsuccessful assertiveness of active coping styles and hostile frustration, potent precursors to hypertension (Niaura & Goldstein, 1992, 1995; Perini, Müller, Rauchfleisch, Battegay, & Bühler, 1986; Steptoe, 1981). Such factors may be behind the high prevalence of hypertension in modernizing Third World populations where aspirations are often discordant with possibilities.

Coronary artery disease. The following typical (in my experience) case illustrates frustration and powerlessness, this time ending in a heart attack.

A 58-year-old factory owner had channeled early anger with his abusive father into working 10–14 hours a day up to 7 days a week. He exhibited a typical Type A behavior pattern. With the recession, he worked even harder. When he discovered that his factory was on the brink because his partner had stolen money, he developed chest pain. Soon after, the man's mother, his prime emotional support, had a sudden stroke. The chest pain became worse, and angina was diagnosed. Three days later his mother died, and he developed a myocardial infarct. Throughout this process, the man worked ever harder, to no avail.

Many epidemiological studies have confirmed such clinical findings. Civilian bombing (Janis, 1951) and disasters have already been noted to be followed by raised frequencies of myocardial infarctions. Boman (1982a) found that U.S. Second World War veterans suffered coronary artery disease in excess of controls in each postwar decade in proportion to the severity of their combat and prisoner of war experience.

In work situations, the same factors that contribute to hypertension do so for coronary artery disease, too (Boman, 1982a; Goldstein & Niaura, 1992, 1995; Steptoe, 1981). Appels and Mulder (1989) described "vital exhaustion," a syndrome similar to burn-out and combat exhaustion, as predictive of coronary artery disease.

Last, since Friedman and Rosenman (1959) first described the type A behavior pattern of the alert, intense, harassed, frustrated, and sympathetically aroused personality as predictive of coronary artery disease, many studies have confirmed this, especially when a hostility component was added (Goldstein & Niaura, 1992).

In conclusion, there is a congruence between statistical and dynamic approaches indicating that assertiveness trauma predisposes one to hypertension and coronary artery disease. This is enhanced by the physiological components of sympathetic arousal, such as raised levels of cholesterol and fatty acids known to predispose to these illnesses (e.g., van Doornen & van Blokland, 1989).

Strokes. Physiological predispositions, psychosocial contributions, and pathology are similar to those of coronary artery disease (Boman, 1982b; Steptoe, 1981). However, though common, apart from its association with depression

(McNamara, 1995) stroke has not captured the psychosomatic imagination as has coronary artery disease.

A 65-year-old man seen by me felt increasing frustration because he was prevented from doing his usual work as he was about to retire. His frustration increased when he saw that his successor, whom he had to train, was incompetent. It now seemed that his life's achievements were nothing. A week before retirement, he had a stroke.

Psychological Aspects   Failure to achieve developmental tasks such as reading and writing are labeled under a variety of developmental disorders. Burn-out is becoming recognized as an illness. Powerlessness when others control one's destiny (external locus of control) may predispose one to PTSD and other illnesses (Flannery, 1987; Garber & Seligman, 1980; Joseph, Yule, & Williams, 1993). Even a modicum of control such as communicating against orders with fellow prisoners may contribute to more favorable outcomes (Hunter, 1993).

Social Aspects   Tensions, frustrations, and failures may lead to drug taking, temper outbursts, and antisocial attempts at assertiveness. Fear of failure may lead to work addiction and type A behavior pattern. Needs to relieve tension and do something may lead to folly, and failure may breed failure.

AXIS 2: PARAMETERS AXIS

Traumatic Situations and Disaster Phases

Hunting, combat, and work situations have different challenges and breakdowns at different times. For instance, combat demoralization manifests differently at induction, in combat, and in postwar readjustments (chapter 2). Cardiovascular symptoms in the military were already present among the 40% rejected soldiers in the Second World War (Craighill, 1954). They too tended to progress from psychophysiological symptoms to coronary artery disease over time.

Assertiveness at Different Social Levels

Different goals require different social groups. Individuals have developmental and role goals. Families work toward common shelter, sharing food, warmth, and maturation goals. Work and combat occur in social groups. National aims may involve securing territories and resources.

The hunting and combat group templates are recognizable in different assertiveness settings. For instance, President John F. Kennedy's cabinet during the Cuban missile crisis (Janis, 1972) and the Israeli cabinet during the Entebbe hostage crisis (Maoz, 1981) showed psychosocial responses of combat units.

Gangs (Thrasher, 1927) and sports teams also manifest similarities to hunt and combat groups, often using their symbols and vocabulary.

Assertiveness Across the Life Cycle

The breast may be seen as the first hunting ground, battlefield, and workplace. Each developmental goal such as weaning and learning can be a field for increasing skills, potency and confidence, or demoralization, impotence, and failure.

Learning (the work of children), combat, and work morale can be motivated by survival and discipline threats but are much enhanced with love and complementary fulfillment goals (Cass & Zimmer, 1975; De Board, 1978; McGregor, 1960; Mintzberg, 1973; Robbins, 1991). Each phase of life has its learning curve and goals. The last one is a good death.

AXIS 3: FULFILLMENT AND TRAUMA ALONG THE DEPTH AXIS

Fulfillment

Although in attachment heaven seems provided, in assertiveness one provides it for oneself. Potency, control, and success in achieving important goals are among the sweetest pleasures. They are accompanied by intense moral satisfaction, for success is praised and rewarded as good, and the person is esteemed and is in turn filled with pride. In fairness to the achievement, the person is offered medals, fame, and honor. Meanings of success include "If I want to I can do it" and "Success goes to the strong, and I am strong."

Ideals may include always succeeding, never needing to seek help, and strength to do anything. Independence, wealth, and making a mark are cherished values. Principles maintain that people should have the opportunity to pursue essential goals, interests, and values.

Hunt, combat, and work have codes of behavior and marks of regard, reflected in a sense of dignity that includes eminence and distinction. Rights of ownership of territory and pursuit of survival goals may be codified in law.

Hunting and wars have been surrounded by magic, myths, and rituals, serving both to receive supernatural support and reconciliation with the souls of the killed. God is enlisted in both hunts and wars. Religion may lift morale, and religious wars can be particularly fierce. Religion also provides an inner reward for the Puritan work ethic, and consolation to the unsuccessful in that rewards will come in an afterlife, in happy hunting grounds, or in a land of eternal goal fulfillment. Ideologies such as socialism promise fair reward for effort on earth.

Natural disasters may be symbolized as big animals one needs to combat. Emergency teams often resemble hunting and combat teams. Females have been symbolized as objects of the hunt in many cultures, the penis representing the hunting weapon and the female sex organs the heart of the animal (Roheim,

1968). Weapons, from spears to atomic bombs, have symbolized control, power, and potency and, one may say, an erect phallus. Territory has been symbolized as mother, as in *motherland,* and could be represented in removed symbols such as flags. Money has come to symbolize resources. Business may be like a jungle where traders calculate, gamble, stalk, and pounce with a killer instinct and the same surge of adrenaline as hunters (Tiger & Fox, 1971).

Identity crystallizes the above into a coherent self-image of one having achieved security, career, wealth, and procreation as a result of one's respected capabilities. This is extended in creativity and inventiveness and in use of new skills and technology. Aesthetic delight is derived from adorning and artistically fashioning and representing all sources of strength from body, tools and weapons to political and religious symbols.

Whereas in attachment one received the sacred stream of life, in assertiveness the sacred stems from appropriating it within a chain of life. Rites of passage to becoming hunters and warriors had sacred elements, but ultimately hunters and warriors took life to give life as part of a universal cycle. Eating life can still be sensed as sacred.

Knowledge includes the capacities and potentials of human life that one carries within. Actualization of these potentials (Maslow, 1970) is joyful and existentially meaningful. Truth is that the energy for one's life comes from other life. Wisdom appreciates the joys in the context of their dependence on the chain of life, to which one will one day contribute one's own life.

Trauma

Powerlessness and impotence are most terrible feelings, aggravated by guilt at failure and one's worth being judged as inadequate. Specific incapacities are judged as stupid, clumsy, or lazy. As part of justice, one receives poor grades, loses stripes, or is dismissed from a job. This comes to mean that one is inadequate and doomed to stay a failure. Ideals and dreams of achievement crumble. The values of self-sufficiency and being somebody are lost, as is the principle of opportunity. One's dignity is stripped, reputation is low, and entitlements are irrelevant.

Neither God nor ideology help. Identity shows poor development, few achievements, or respect. Creativity is impaired, potentials are unfulfilled, and there is little delight in a dilapidated life. There is little sacred connection with life and the universe. Hunting and killing have become mechanical and profane (Keegan, 1985), as ultimately in concentration camps. Thrills of mechanical power may give temporary sense of potency and connection, but one has lost the knowledge of inner human potential, as well as the truth and wisdom of one's place in the chain of life.

In summary, although achieving life's goals is associated with greatest human satisfactions, not achieving them is associated with a sense of a failed human being.

Chapter 11

Adaptation: Goal Surrender

Adaptation as used here implies a need to change oneself to fit new realities rather than making new realities. In adaptation, life is preserved by surrendering unachievable goals so that one may turn to new ones. Paradigmatic pictures are surrendering soldiers and the grief of bereavement.

Perhaps the most extreme manifestation of surrender is shock. It is suggested that lesser degrees have been called *animal hypnosis* (Gilman & Marcuse, 1942; Kaufman & Rosenblum, 1967) and general adaptation syndrome (Selye, 1936, p. 178). They are found in living things from insects on when they are potentially overwhelmed by predators or enemies. The associated flaccid immobility that Darwin noted made animals less likely to be seen and attacked and could stimulate predators to release their grip. It has have been found to facilitate scooping up and carrying to safety (chapter 1), and it may help in refinding lost animals.

Physical and psychic shock and general adaptation syndrome are well known in humans. The flaccid state, it has been suggested, has been described the *conservation-withdrawal syndrome* (Engel & Reichsman, 1956; Engel & Schmale, 1972), which these authors saw as a basic survival mechanism when people were overwhelmed (chapter 7). Lesser stunned states have been described as the *disaster syndrome* (Glass, 1959; Wallace, 1957).

Grief seems to be a recent evolutionary phenomenon, though aspects of it have been found in elephants, birds, and primates. Grief and mourning rituals occur in all cultures (Stearns, 1993), though understanding and tolerance for sadness varies. In Anglo-Saxon culture, pride in grief for indicating love and depth of personality has been replaced over the past 200 years with relative disdain. Understanding of depression as related to loss is quite recent and sporadic, and appreciation of death altogether seems to be only partial.

The evolutionary survival value of grief and weeping may be puzzling. Weeping as protection of the eyes does not explain its function in grief. One may speculate that perhaps tears evolved as signals to evoke support without the need for collapse. Otherwise, one may join the poets in the use of an evolutionary metaphor where weeping promotes healing of psychological wounds akin to weeping in physical wounds.

AXIS 1: THE PROCESS AXIS

Appraisal of the Means of Survival

Appraisal includes the need to surrender something important in order to preserve something more important. Though prioritization may be made almost instinctively, at some time processing involves agonizing and grief. Unambiguity such as viewing the dead facilitates prioritization and processing.

Stress Responses

Adaptive–Successful Responses
Biological Aspects   Responses to loss and depression appear to be associated with the limbic system, including the hippocampus and septum (Panksepp, 1986a). Shock, general adaptation syndrome, grief, and depression sensitively activate the parasympathetic system, the hypothalamic-pituitary-adrenal (HPA) axis, increased cortisol secretion, and suppression of the immune system. Even just recalling sadness can evoke these responses, with decline in mitogenic (cancer) lymphocyte reactivity (Knapp et al., 1992). Though Selye called this adaptation syndrome *general*, it is specific (Henry, 1986). Selye (1973) himself came to see it as only part of a "rolling with the punches" strategy.

Psychological Aspects   Unambiguous appraisal, shock, and outcry acknowledge at least cognitive acceptance that the loss has occurred. This is followed by grief and sadness. They may be feedback mechanisms indicating not having attained one's goals and eliciting others' compassion (Stearns, 1993), but the pangs of grief and missing resulting from severance of love bonds (Parkes, 1972) are among the greatest pains humans have to suffer (Bowlby, 1981). They are often described as the heart being wrenched and torn.

A 50-year-old widow seen in the emergency department described the loss of her husband. "It was an excruciating pain, a severe crushing agony, as if my heart was rent in two. It was like a blow to the heart, a severe wound, a bruising, my heart was bleeding, leaving a pain. A part of me died."

And yet, as Ovid said, "It is a relief to weep; grief is satisfied" (as cited in Sadoff, 1977, p. 381). Tears soothe the inner pain of sorrow, and grief allows both renunciation and retention of love across the chasm to the new.

Though the image of grief may be eternal pain, its pangs, accompanied by the tears, deep sobs, and wails of sorrow like other pangs, last in the order of minutes and ease slowly over weeks (Parkes, 1972). The phases of grief are described below, but eventually its gray veil lifts and hope of life and love return.

Social Aspects   Though adaptive adaptation involves yielding, it is but a tactical surrender in the process of adapting and adjusting to unavoidable circumstances. It is suggested too that, parallel to grief, which provides a psychological milieu for healing, mourning provides a social one. The bereaved are supported and comforted by others like the physically wounded and ill whom they resemble (Engel, 1961; Parkes & Weiss, 1983). They are allowed to go over their loss in detail, to express their feelings. Funerals and mourning ceremonies provide further framework for the process (Raphael, 1984), but they are increasingly spaced out to encourage new life too. Society helps its wounded members to find personal hopes, provide answers and meanings, reintegrate, and steer a new course. The mourning process has a clear goal of piece by piece withdrawing emotional and social investment from the old and turning to the new (Bowlby, 1981; Freud, 1917/1975k; Stearns, 1993).

Maladaptive–Unsuccessful Responses

Biological Aspects   Depression shares with grief its anatomical and physiological substrates. Thus, in depression too are found increased levels of corticotrophin-releasing factor, ACTH, and cortisol (Panksepp, 1993; Sachar, 1975b), as well as features of diminished immunocompetence. The latter involve T and B cells, natural killer cells, and humoral parts of the immune system (Bartrop et al., 1977; Calabrese et al., 1987; Irwin et al., 1987). These responses can be quite prolonged and variable according to the use of defenses.

Because antidepressants block the reuptake of monoamines such as epinephrine and norepinephrine, it has been postulated that depression is associated with amine depletion (Baldessarini, 1975). However, low epinephrine and norepinephrine may only be correlates (Smith, 1991).

Psychological Aspects   Being overwhelmed has at times been used generically as the hallmark response to trauma (e.g., Figley, 1985; Freud, 1920/1975c). However, as Parkes and Weiss (1983) noted for the initial responses to bereavement, being overwhelmed may not be indicative of later responses. It may be seen as an extremely intense stress response that may or may not lead to trauma. Here the state refers to a situation that is at the time too intense to accommodate.

However, without space for acceptance and grief, depression may ensue. Depression as an illness is considered below. As an emotion or mood, it is often confused with sadness. However, although the latter is like the pain of a wounded heart that is clearly caused by loss, depression is like a heaviness in the chest or heart that may contain compressed hurt and tears but whose cause may be obscure. Even so, there may be a sense that tears and sobs would offer release. Bowlby (1981) suggested that a depressive mood replaces sadness when a person loses emotional interchange with the outside world and loses hope. As a corollary, I have repeatedly found, as in Case 1 with the depressed bush fire victim (chapter 1), that reassuring contact and generation of hope can facilitate reversion of depression to grief.

However, if this does not happen, hopelessness and despair may supervene. Yet even despair is only a feeling, often a phase in grief (Bowlby, 1971, 1981). Macy (1981) has compared it with grief, but cold, heavy, and almost breaking the chest and body. A patient of mine described it as "a set of skyscrapers in the chest, but instead of concrete they were made of solid tears." Later, crying moved the skyscrapers.

Social Aspects   Disaster syndrome, conservation-withdrawal syndrome, and psychic shock manifest a range of states from being stunned to collapsing like a physical felling. Most commonly, people stand, sit, or lie mute and relatively motionless for minutes to hours. At the more severe end of the range, people describe extreme fatigue, as if even lifting a little finger was impossible. Yet they can oblige and stand up without apparent trouble. There is an associated absence of thoughts, different to dissociation. Rather, the mind is flaccid, suggestible, and people are docile. This may allow one person to direct many others to safety. The above states are frequently overlooked when victims or patients are quiet and obedient, yet it is suggested that these states are as common as arousal responses.

Depression and conservation-withdrawal are associated with withdrawal, ranging from retreat and seclusion to a cocoonlike state in bed. The stage of giving up includes an attitude of despair and hopelessness of effecting change by self or others (Engel & Schmale, 1972; Schmale, 1972; Sweeney, Tinling, Schmale, & Rochester, 1970).

Trauma

Sometimes the loss is so overwhelming, intense, cumulative, or prolonged that the heart is torn asunder with permanent damage. At the least, scars remain, causing major distortion. A man who saw his family murdered in the Holocaust described his heart rending: "Something . . . tore loose within me as I sank to the floor. The small childish sobs did not come, instead my chest felt crushed" (Kestenberg & Brenner, 1986, p. 311).

In unremittingly overwhelming situations, people may give in. Of new prisoners in concentration camps, 20%–50% succumbed just due to a loss of desire to live (Bettelheim, (1943, 1960). They included especially the old (Kral, 1951) and those who lost existential meaning. Frankl (1959, p. 75) said, "The sudden loss of hope and courage can have a deadly effect." In civilian life, one also hears of people dying after giving in. Spitz (1965) described children in institutions without regular caretakers who, despite being well fed, failed to thrive, looked beyond despair, became marasmic (akin to Mussulmen, chapter 2), ill, and sometimes died.

Illnesses

Biological Aspects

Psychophysiological Symptoms   These include tiredness, fatigue, and dizziness. Psychic shock and collapse may be accompanied by cold and nausea. Excess vagal activity may facilitate arrhythmias, and even sudden death (Steptoe, 1981). Suppressed sobbing may be felt as a lump in the throat (globus hystericus).

Psychosomatic Illnesses   Death of a spouse has been shown to be the most potent civilian life stressor (chapter 2), leading to a variety of illnesses in the year after bereavement. The bereaved showed a sevenfold increase in incidence of more severe illnesses over controls (Parkes & Weiss, 1983), and the same was found for increased mortality (Rees & Lutkins, 1967). Schmale (1972) noted that giving up preceded hospitalization in 80% of patients with a variety of diagnoses.

Although a number of survival strategies may have been active in these nonspecific correlations, infections ranging from influenza to tuberculosis and autoimmune diseases such as systemic lupus erythematosus and myasthenia gravis (Stein, 1981) seem specifically related to ungrieved losses and diminished immunocompetence. The same may be said of cancers. Hopelessness (Schmale & Iker, 1966) and loneliness (West, Kellner, & Moore-West, 1986) were predictive of cancer development, and two thirds of cancer patients developed their illness in a state of despair evoked by current losses tied to unresolved griefs (Vachon, 1987). It appears that though many variables need to be taken into account, these research findings still have validity (Levinson & Bemis, 1995).

Last, physical symptoms may be identifications with the dead (see below).

Psychological Aspects   Grief and mourning may not proceed in so-called *traumatic grief* in both adults (Bowlby, 1981; Parkes, 1972; Parkes & Weiss, 1983; Raphael, 1984) and children (Eth & Pynoos, 1985). It is suggested that

traumatic griefs may involve traumas of other survival strategies such as in death of a child (rescue–caretaking), in ambivalent relationships and little social support (attachment), and in horrible and multiple deaths (fight–flight). These traumas need some resolution before grief can proceed.

Unresolved or pathological grief. If grief cannot proceed, one of three overlapping pathological grief syndromes may develop (e.g., Parkes & Weiss, 1983). In chronic mourning, the lost person is maintained in quasi-life. For instance, their belongings are maintained as on the day of death. This is thought to indicate unabated yearning in a dependent (attachment) relationship. Delayed, inhibited, or absent mourning may manifest prolonged features of being over-whelmed. Aspects of grief such as unexplained crying may emerge unexpectedly with variable awareness of the reasons. Such a picture used to be called neurotic depression and uses a variety of defenses. Conflicted or distorted mourning continues conflictual relationships in life. Anger and guilt toward the dead may persist as continued attachment and caretaking conflicts. Identification with the dead may occur in these syndromes through physical symptoms, possibly symbolically being with them or appeasing guilt toward them. Symptoms may intensify at anniversary and other symbolically significant times.

Depression. Depressed mood of understandable origin may be called adjustment disorder with depressed mood or dysthymia. In major depressive disorder, or simply depression, the same symptoms intensify and are more prolonged and understanding of their origins is frequently lost. Symptoms of depression include maladaptive and traumatic features described above, such as tiredness, withdrawal, despair and hopelessness; and aspects of pathological grief syndromes such as anger, guilt, or dependence (Bowlby, 1981; Deutsch, 1937; Parkes & Weiss, 1983). Admixtures of attachment (Burnett et al., 1994) may include psychomotor agitation, representing the impulse to search, and suicidal thoughts with desires for union.

Depression is one of the most important clinical diagnoses in psychiatry. It is also the most frequent comorbidity diagnosis with PTSD (e.g., Sutker et al., 1994), and indeed the most common condition following catastrophic events (Yehuda & McFarlane, 1995). It is therefore important to consider its potential trauma dynamics.

Social Aspects Excessive need for support manifests as dependency and is a factor in much increased doctor visits after bereavement (Parkes & Weiss, 1983). Delinquency in children (Raphael, 1984), shoplifting in women, accidents (chapter 2), and suicidal gestures occur after losses. Promiscuity, pregnancy, and premature marriages may be results of seeking substitutes. Psychic pain may be appeased by alcohol and drug taking. Suicide may be the final way out.

AXIS 2: PARAMETERS AXIS

Traumatic Situations and Disaster Phases

Similar phases of grief are described for bereavement (Raphael, 1984), loss of body parts (Krueger, 1984), and dying (Kübler-Ross, 1969). Denial and shock are followed by anger, bargaining, sadness, and depression, then followed by final acceptance and hope.

The poignancy of grief work has long been known. As Parkes (1972, p. 55) quoted C. S. Lewis, "So many roads once; now so many *culs-de-sac*." So many threads of the knot to untie. It may take years to achieve full acceptance and its bittersweet nostalgia (Kleiner, 1970; Parkes, 1972), and even then resurgences of grief may occur at poignant times. Eventually, the person looks forward to new bonds and revised goals, still united with the old bonds but now in a richer narrative.

Clinically, the phases have no such fixed progression (Vargas, Loya, & Hodde-Vargas, 1989). Rather, the phases overlap and are influenced by tendencies to healing and other circumstances. For instance, grief may be inhibited and delayed, crying suppressed because it imperils survival or the needs of others (Valent, 1994).

Adaptation at Different Social Levels

Many griefs are individual, but others are shared in family and group contexts. Natural disasters, war, and uprooting may be grieved in community contexts. Parkes and Weiss (1983) noted that a whole people can share the loss of a leader or major religious or ideological symbols. Macy (1981) suggested that world despair over nuclear and environmental threats needs to be faced and grieved in order to do something new about them.

Helpers experience secondary grief, and concentric circles of diminishing grief may reverberate with those more distantly affected.

Adaptation Across the Life Cycle

The first expression of grief and weeping occurs at 6 months (Darwin, 1872/1965), when the infant can appreciate mother as a whole and can experience precursors of depression (Segal, 1975). Between 7 and 16 months, if allowed, children manifest progressively more adult type grieving (Bowlby, 1981), depression, and despair (Robertson & Robertson, 1967 ["John"]). This may be obscured to a degree by young children's concentration and attention spans being shorter, their living more in the present, their larger anxieties about their survival, and their adult attitudes.

Developmental stages influence the deeper meanings of death (Lonetto, 1980). Children under 5 may see death as living under different circumstances;

between 5 and 9, death may be personified; and older children can see death as final and lawful. Adults often harken back to these childlike concepts. The life cycle brings inevitable losses, of the breast, parents, youth, and life itself.

AXIS 3: FULFILLMENT AND TRAUMA
ALONG THE DEPTH AXIS

Fulfillment

Grief and sorrow may be among the sweetest and most poignant affirmations of love. Grief releases despair and the grip of giving in as well as frozen traumas and meanings. It allows regret and reparation and loving anew. Morally, grieving lost loves and finding new hope is approved. Pity, sympathy, and tribute affirm the worth of the person and the wound as well as capacity to adapt. Justice often draws on love and life being transient or lent and the borrower taking back his loan.

Meaning is made of every aspect of the lost relationship, and it is redefined in new, more inclusive meanings or schemas. One's relationship now includes the meaning of its beginning, middle, end, and thereafter. Values of surrender and grief include stoicism, humility, and fortitude, the capacity to cry but not lose hope. Ideals include cheerfulness in adversity and being able to adapt to anything Fate dishes out. One accepts the principle that it is better to have loved and lost than not to have loved at all. Surrender in both mourning and combat is codified in rituals. They ensure the safety and dignity of the vulnerable person. Dying patients and even executed prisoners are accorded rank and last wishes. They have rights to not lose more than necessary or to have salt rubbed in their wounds.

Magic, myths, and religion attempt to explain and mitigate loss and death by denying their finality. Through God and heaven, every loss is retrieved, and there are no more surrenders and losses. Earthly cults and ideologies promise eternal life through belief and faith, even if not today through future generations. Many symbols represent grief, such as black clothes, prayers, gravestones, and commemorations. Monuments such as the pyramids may symbolize continued life, though memories, rituals, and memorials may also be transitional objects in the parting process.

One's identity changes with surrender and bereavement. Thus, one may no longer be a husband or wife. However, a new identity may incorporate the old and carry it forward. For instance, one may help future bereaved people through one's own experience. Lost love can be fertile for ground creative outlets in poetry, drama, and architecture. Death and love are often counterpoints in art and are presented with aesthetic eloquence.

Being part of the divine lending and taking back of life with ultimate eternal heavenly life has provided a religious sacred sense to loss and death. Acceptance of death into life provides this deeper connection in a secular sense (Becker, 1973; Brown, 1968; Lifton, 1980). Life and its connections with natural rhythms of extinction and regeneration are present within this life. As noted, death itself may be chosen as meaningful, part of generation or regeneration (chapter 2). Knowledge includes that of death in life, that love is essential to life, and that the cost of commitment and love is the pain of its loss. Truth is that all life's loves and fulfillments may be lost, often in senseless circumstances, but that through pain one may reach love again. Wisdom accepts the vicissitudes of loves and losses. It may include judgment of when to cross the mythical river (of real tears) not to the other world, but to a different real world in which meanings and life's goals must be readjusted.

Trauma

There is a sense of too much loss, irretrievable damage. Tears and grief would only accentuate the pain and reinforce hopelessness and despair. There is no virtue in the losses, and one's grief when not tolerated may seem weak and despicable, and one may be blamed and stigmatized for one's sorrows. The moral world collapses, and one asks why the injustice of the good dying young and the innocent having to bear the pain. There is no meaning in the event, and it takes away what meaning there was in past and future. All that is valuable is lost, and one's self feels devalued. Ideals of stoicism have no meaning in a world that runs on the principle that it is foolish to love, for it only brings pain. Whether in surrender or loss, one is stripped of dignity and rights. No ideology, magic, or religion helps, for God himself cruelly allowed or caused one's misfortunes. Many cues symbolize one's losses and sorry state. One's identity, such as prisoner or widow, incorporates one's depression and hopelessness. If creativity survives, it depicts misery without any delight. Sacred connections are lost, though as in psychotic depression one may take on the blame for all the world's ills. Knowledge holds that all is lost and irretrievable. Truth of grief is frozen in overwhelming pain, and wisdom of regenerative grief is absent.

In summary, grief is like a weeping wound, without which loss rips life apart.

Chapter 12

Fight: Defense

This is a very important survival strategy as its maladaptive aspects have been instrumental in much of the violence and atrocities in human history. It is suggested that the survival strategy approach may help to understand such tragic human aberrations.

In fight, life is preserved by removal of danger. The paradigmatic picture is readiness to defend, to "kill or be killed." White blood and immune cells already form armies to defend against foreigners and territorial intruders (the xenophobic principle; E. O. Wilson, 1975), killing viruses, bacteria, and deviant cancer cells. Such aggression, called *defensive* or *affective,* has been documented in all social animals from ants to humans. Typically, males engage in defense across the species, though females are also capable of the survival strategy.

Humans also fight when threatened and manifest xenophobic and territorial tendencies (Ardrey, 1967). In addition to external aggression, humans are peculiar in having evolved the emotions disgust and revulsion. They accompany riddance of internal poisons through excreta such as vomit, but they may also be felt toward human invaders who in turn may be associated with their body wastes (Rozin, Haidt, & McCauley, 1993). Threatening foreigners are often labeled *dirty* and *stinking.* Body wastes are used in sorcery as alternative means of fighting malevolent wars (Evans-Pritchard, 1967; LaBarre, 1979).

AXIS 1: THE PROCESS AXIS

Appraisal of the Means of Survival

Appraisals of others' postures, vocalizations, insults, and territorial intrusions alert one to the need to defend (Dengerink, 1976). One's own aggressive postures may deter attackers, tilting the fear–aggression balance (Shalit, 1994) to them withdrawing. The crossing of the line from riddance to killing occurs with the conviction that it is now kill or be killed. This may occur when one of a group of soldiers (Lidz, 1946; Sobel, 1949), especially a buddy (Brende, 1983; Fox, 1974) is killed. Renner (1973, p. 173) quoted a soldier, "Before these two friends were hit, I had a sort of lukewarm feeling against the enemy. But after seeing them hurt so bad, I had a true hatred for all VC, and . . . I wanted to kill as many of them as I could."

Stress Responses

Adaptive–Successful Responses

Biological Aspects   Fight is served by the hippocampus, medial amygdala and stria terminalis, medial tegmentum, medial hypothalamus, and the periaqueductal gray (Blanchard & Blanchard, 1988; Heath, 1992; Kling, 1986; Shaikh et al., 1985). Some of these areas are also involved in sympathetic nervous system activity and testosterone uptake (Blanchard & Blanchard, 1988). Androgens increase aggression and territory across species (Yahr, 1983) and are associated with human violence (Dabbs, Frady, Carr, & Besch 1987; Knol & Egbering-Alink, 1989; Olweus, Mattsson, Schalling, & Low, 1988). The sympathetic system is very active (Cannon, 1939; Panksepp, 1986b). The HPA axis is not activated or may be even inhibited (Henry, 1986), and raised immunocompetence may occur (Dienstbier, 1989).

Psychological Aspects   The purpose of adaptive fight is to frighten off the source of danger. To be credible, threats must be delivered with genuine determination to fight if necessary. This includes physiological arousal, attack postures, and emotions of anger akin to a glowing red furnace in the chest radiating energy into muscles of attack.

The situation intensifies when blood is drawn or a wound occurs, though in humans it may be a psychological wound (Dengerink, 1976). As Aristotle (1988) noted in *Nicomachean Ethics*, revenge requires retaliation in kind, and when thus justifiable it can be deeply satisfying, very sweet, and lead to peaceful sleep. Even so, the purpose of revenge is still a signal to deter further attacks. Vengeance ranges from almost reflex retaliation (Scott, 1980) to an all-consuming passion (Socarides, 1966) that can smolder for years (Athens, 1989) and, in feuds, even across generations. Successful threats and revenge frighten off attackers.

Social Aspects   Successful arousal of fear in potential attackers eventuates in successful deterrence. Retaliatory wounding is a second line of defense. Physical and mental scars leave deterrent reminders of dangers of attack. Riddance, with a permanent lesson not to return, may have been effected. Body fluids and disgust may be used to rid attackers.

> While reliving a sexual attack, a patient of mine felt nausea and a need to defecate as she coughed up phlegm accumulating in her lungs.

Maladaptive–Unsuccessful Responses

Biological Aspects   The physiology of maladaptive fight seems to be similar to though more intense than its adaptive counterpart. When arousal to fight is suppressed, physiological responses may be sustained at high levels. Suppressed aggression contributed to higher heart rates, diastolic blood pressures, and hyperadrenegic reactivity (Perini et al., 1986; Quanty, 1976).

Psychological Aspects   Aristotle (*Rhetoric,* Book 2:4) distinguished anger, which could be appeased by required behavior, such as withdrawal, and hatred, which demands final destruction. In the latter, ritualized constraints are gone, fear is no longer a prevaricating factor, and gestures of appeasement now incite more intense attacks (Athens, 1989). Hatred may be felt as a great turmoil in the chest or a twisting of the gut that massively demands elimination of both the feelings and those who evoke them. Persecutory desires involve relentless hatred and desire to attack, ultimately to kill the enemy and feel secure again.

Social Aspects   Attack with intention to kill may result in flight of the enemies. However, if the latter have already caused deaths and could pose a danger in the future, they must be pursued and eradicated. Fear of counterattack and revenge may require elimination in ever wider circles. The result is destruction—of life, but also of everything that belonged to that life: forests and cities, property, culture, values, dignity, purpose, and meaning.

Killing of the mind and soul may be achieved by selective killing, terrorism and torture (Simpson, 1993), and attacks on dignity, fabric, and sacred institutions.

Trauma

It may not be clear a priori that killing is traumatic. In clear kill-or-be-killed situations it may indeed not be, but most situations have some ambiguity at the time or in retrospect. The killer experiences horror, dismay, numbness, unreality, nausea, and severe headaches (Browning, 1992; Lifton, 1973). Policemen in serious shooting incidents almost always suffer PTSD symptoms (Gersons, 1989), especially if shootings turn out to be unnecessary (Manolias & Hyatt-Williams,

1993). Many Nazis suffered PTSD after massacres. Horror may only set in later when killings previously rationalized as necessary for survival are seen as wanton.

> A religious professional man seen by me was commanded to take part in the shooting of prisoner soldiers. He could assimilate having to kill in combat, and even obeying the above orders. But he was horrified that he had taken money and photos from the dead men. This apparently volitional act made him feel that he had intentionally and unnecessarily killed. He could not reconcile this with his self-image as a religious, tolerant, civilized man.

The horror involves having trespassed the greatest taboo and through murder having become evil.

Illnesses

Biological Aspects
Psychophysiological Symptoms associated with sympathetic arousal are similar to those in assertiveness. Parasympathetic disgust-related symptoms include nausea and vomiting.

Psychosomatic Illnesses   Though the literature does not distinguish the hostility of frustration in assertiveness from that of hatred in fight, the latter may be quite significant in hypertension and coronary artery disease. For instance, early conflictual relationships predispose one to essential and malignant hypertension, whereas acute conflicts precipitate them. As well, many hypertensive people are especially sensitive to danger, scorn, and malevolence in others, while prone to explosions of rage themselves (Weiner, 1977). Similarly, high hostility tests have predicted premature mortality and coronary heart disease over 30 years (Barefoot, Dodge, Peterson, Dahlstrom, & Williams, 1989; Kubany, Gino, Denny, & Torigoe, 1994).

Psychological Aspects   The *DSM* does not apportion diagnoses to rage and hatred as it does to emotions of depression and anxiety, though anger is implied in antisocial, paranoid/aggressive, and borderline personalities. However, with Freud (1915/1975j, 1917/1975k, 1920/1975c), aggression formed a dialectic with the sexual and life instincts at different times. Freud visualized aggression as channeled to a variety of illnesses, depending on defenses. For instance, projection led to paranoid aggression. Later, aggression came to be seen as the death instinct turned outward. Fused with sexuality, it led to sadism and masochism.

Social Aspects   Much social violence results from displacements in time and social systems and is considered below. Aggression can also be turned on oneself in order to avoid conflict.

AXIS 2: PARAMETERS AXIS

Traumatic Situations and Disaster Phases

In the preimpact phase, there is splitting of "the enemy" and "us." Stories of danger and treachery of the outsiders are coupled with preparation and training to be rid of them. In situations where the others are objectively benign, one's own enmity is projected on the enemy. When the other side is obliged to become hostile and retaliate, the self-fulfilling prophecy of their role is through projective identification.

Obedience to leaders and conformity to the group are established. The tendency to yield judgments to authority and peer pressure (Asch, 1952; Crutchfield, 1955) to the extent of performing dangerous acts (S. Milgram, 1963; Orne & Evans, 1965; Zimbardo, 1972) has been demonstrated in laboratory studies. This is much enhanced where ideology, group survival, and personal survival (disobedience possibly being lethal) enter the equation, as they did when Germans massacred Jews (Browning, 1992). Conformity is further enhanced with rewards of safety, loot, women, and even heaven (Gibbon, 1978).

Arousal to fight may be facilitated by oratory, martial music, and creation of tension needing discharge (Futterman & Pumpian-Mindlin, 1951; Grinker & Spiegel, 1945). Incitement can turn an aroused crowd into a violent mob (Canetti, 1973). TV violence may tip susceptible people into action (Geen, 1976), as may arousal in sports. In the impact phase, conflict and violence may occur. Postimpact there is triumph and relief if danger is gone. In the reconstructive phase, destroyed objects and defenses are rebuilt.

Fight at Different Social Levels

All group configurations from individual to nations may use fight. Its psychological concomitants such as splitting, projection, apportioning of roles, and conformity occur in small groups (Bion, 1961), large groups (E. J. Miller, 1976), boys' groups (Sherif, 1966/1970), gangs (Thrasher, 1927), and ethnic and political groups (Fornari, 1975; Valent, 1982).

Many atrocities occur through scapegoating when the source of danger is unclear. There is a tendency to find someone to blame for adversities (Raphael, 1986). It may be the nearest person or stranger(s) (Scott, 1977) or malign neighbors (Wright, 1965/1967). A soldier who had suffered a near miss, then learned that his father had cancer, and soon after that learned that his wife had been unfaithful began to shoot and mutilate Vietnamese civilians (Yager, 1975). In My Lai, a U.S. company that had suffered deaths from guerrillas raped and killed 405 men, women, and children in an action conceptualized as revenge (Lifton, 1973). Social targets may be influenced by traditional enmities and scapegoats (Harkness, 1993; *The Longest Hatred* [Documentary], 1993) or by recently found or designated scapegoats (Fornari, 1975; Staub, 1989; Valent, 1982, 1987).

Fight Across the Life Cycle

The above mechanisms are established early in life and can be carried over the life cycle. Infants already have available murderous rage and psychological mechanisms of splitting, projection, projective identification, and displacement (Segal, 1975). By 4–7 months of life, anger may be directed at the source of discomfort. Parts of parents, then parents, and later strangers are attacked physically, with body fluids, and in fantasies. Feared and hated parents are atavistically dehumanized into objects or demonized as predators, monsters, giants, and witches.

Suppressed hatred and revenge can smolder for many years and then be displaced at a time of crisis. Childhood abuse and trauma can lead to adolescent (Burton, Foy, Bwanausi, Johnson, & Moore, 1994) and adult (e.g., Collins & Bailey, 1990) violence. Such abuse was a contributing factor to committing atrocities in Vietnam (Bey & Zecchinelli, 1974; Haley, 1974; Yager, 1975; Zaidi & Foy, 1994).

Dissection of childhood trauma and abuse include two frequently overlapping pictures: brutalization and love deprivation. The former includes terror, humiliation, subjugation, and traumatization by a male authority figure who later coaches the adolescent in masculine violence and displacement ("It's a kill-or-be-killed world out there"). Suppressed hatred and desire for revenge are displaced from the abuser to outside, along with identification with the abuser (Athens, 1989). The process resembles military bastardization and training of torturers. Love deprivation is often part of abuse trauma and neglect and leads to underdeveloped capacities and searing resentment, which at times of stress can explode in violence (Walsh, 1991). Past abuse, trauma, and love deprivation are more important predictors of violence than the oft-quoted social (subculture of the young, male, non-White, and low socioeconomic status), physiological (inability to inhibit aggressive impulse), and genetic (e.g. separated identical twins being concordant for criminality) factors (Athens, 1989; Walsh, 1991).

And yet although brutalized and loveless antisocial persons may commit atrocities more readily, and ruthless leaders with a paranoid vision such as Hitler and Stalin (Tucker, 1986) do it on a wider scale, current situations are very important in producing atrocities. On the one hand, though many high-level Nazi mass killers came from love-deprived and at least authoritarian if not brutalizing environments, in other times the likes of Himmler (Fromm, 1973), Eichmann (Arendt, 1963), and the Nuremberg criminals (Kelley, 1947) could have been innocuous clerks or neurotics with anxieties, suicidality, and tendencies to explosive outbursts (Dicks, 1972). On the other hand, few even normal people have the strength to resist committing atrocities in "atrocity-making" situations such as in My Lai (Lifton, 1973; see above).

AXIS 3: FULFILLMENT AND TRAUMA
ALONG THE DEPTH AXIS

Fulfillment

Riddance of enemies and defending life provide a deep sense of satisfaction. It is a supreme good to risk one's own life in the line of duty for the just cause of self-defense. Soldiers are further judged as brave, noble, and heroic. Defense is highly meaningful in terms of preservation of not only the values of life and property, but also territorial integrity (of motherland), sovereignty, independence, and way of life. Fighters are ideally resolute, formidable, brave, deadly, and invincible. They work on principles such as "Attack is the best form of defense"; the talion principle of eye for an eye, life for life (Leviticus 24:19–22); and "kill or be killed."

Warrior codes and war conventions describe when it is right to go to war (*jus ad bello*) and when it is right to kill (*jus in bello*). For instance, there may be rights to claim ransom, but no entitlement to kill prisoners and civilians (Walzer, 1984). Warriors' dignity stems from their power, but one exercised for a higher cause.

Magical rituals connect warriors with higher powers. Ancestors, God, and religion support the just cause of which the warrior is a part, and if he should die, rewards await him in heaven. The enemy may be depicted as anti-God, especially in holy wars. Ideological defense is akin to a secular religion. Fascist and Hegelian ideology include war as a tool for the ancestrally connected nation (master race) to expand and fulfill itself.

Symbols of the warrior might include ferocious animals and masculine size and shape. Though the identity of "us" includes legends of common ancestry harking back to primitive breeding populations, it is in fact defined by symbols of territory, language, and culture (Kasfir, 1979; Wright, 1965/1967). Similar symbols are used to xenophobically demonize or dehumanize the enemy. Reminiscent of childlike atavistic fantasies, the former denotes enemies as predators and monsters, the latter as disgusting small animals or objects. The Nazis caricatured Jews as both predators and parasites (Lifton, 1986). Vietnamese were dehumanized as "slopes," "gooks," and "slime" (DeFazio, 1978).

Creativity and aesthetics are used in chivalric martial arts and diplomatic politeness and courtesy. Gallantry allows withdrawal without humiliation. Pageantry, rhythm, music, and art decorate weapons of war and can incite to fight. Through their liberty to inflict death for the sake of life and eternal values and staking their own lives on their beliefs, warriors have enjoyed awe and sacred status. Their knowledge is that of taking of life. Wisdom weighs up the necessities of true defense against empathy for people on the other side who are like oneself and who are often killed for wrong reasons. With elimination of predators and sufficient world resources and boundaries becoming ever more symbolic, killing for the purpose of life is an ever more misguided survival strategy.

Since Plato (*Laws,* Book 1) through Hobbes (1651) to Freud (1921/1975f), conventional wisdom has held that humans are natural murderers. Yet observations of children (Lemerise & Dodge, 1993; Scott, 1980), histories of violent people (Athens, 1989), soldiers (Lifton, 1973), nations at war (White, 1986), rising empires (Gibbon, 1978), and genocides (Staub, 1989) consistently show that at the source it is fear of extinction and inability to exercise adaptive fight, together with displacements on to symbols and scapegoats in certain circumstances, that lead to maladaptive derailments. Together with mechanization and greater destructiveness of weapons, these factors have led to major calamities and danger of eradication of civilization itself.

Trauma

Hatred and killing may still save life against a malevolent enemy. However, the realization that one killed innocent people evokes traumatic horror and dismay. Morally, one is wicked, a violent, evil murderer who perpetrated the greatest wrong. The meaninglessness of innocent murders is extreme.

Ideals, values, and principles such as "Shoot first and ask questions later" are abhorrent when misapplied. So is the absence of law and order, where anything goes. Neither killer nor killed retain dignity; dehumanized victims are especially humiliated. Enemies have no rights and are often stripped of their entitlements before they are stripped of life.

Violence may be fueled by rabid religious and ideological fanaticism that may give encouragement even to the point of genocide (e.g., Deuteronomy 32). People may even kill for ideological or religious symbols such as flags or words such as *communist* or *Catholic.* A minority of new killers, whether criminal (Athens, 1989) or war atrocity perpetrators (Browning, 1992) come to like killing, its rush and ecstasy (Athens, 1989).

A Vietnam veteran described killing to me. "It is the ultimate feeling, one you can never have in ordinary life. You have the power to kill and you do. It gives you a surge in the chest, a rush, that no adrenaline or drug can give you. You control the world. The world is in your hands. You can do anything. You have an erection and you have a mighty orgasm."

Such so-called virulent killers become addicted to the exultation of power they derive from killing. They may become identified with killing (Shatan, 1973) and through their sense of omnipotence may sense a perverted sacred transcendence, being elevated to the role of God (Fromm, 1973), deciding on human existence. Yet killing may become routine and profane (Keegan & Holmes, 1985). It lacks creativity and aesthetics, being crass, savage, noisy, and messy. The addiction requires greater heaps of dead (Canetti, 1973), even if only to reassure of the capacity to kill. In Vietnam, body counts (no matter of whom) demonstrated this capacity. The ultimate profanity was perhaps in Auschwitz where mealtime management topics included whether mothers should go with or without their children to gas chambers (Lifton, 1986).

Knowledge involves that of power over life and death, of evil and one's potential for abrogating the purpose of life. With no wisdom, killers become dehumanized and lose connection to life. They may rationalize their actions in terms of self-defense (Valent, 1964, unpublished) and continue to use wartime defenses such as conspiracy of silence, split morality, and doubling (Bar-On, 1990; Lifton, 1986). At times, Nazis' children carried awareness of the guilt and horror of their fathers' actions (Sichrovsky, 1988; Posner, 1991).

However, many Vietnam atrocity perpetrators who faced horror, guilt, and remorse themselves came to understand their own victimization and betrayal of their humanity (Haley, 1974; Silver & Iacono, 1986; Parson, 1993). Some then exposed the truth and helped to bring the war to a close.

In summary, the scientific and empathic approach of this survival strategy allows understanding of violent killings as having roots in a combination of earlier suffering of perpetrators, atrocity-making situations, and human capacities to fear, defend desperately, symbolize, and displace.

Chapter 13

Flight: Escape

Flight is the reciprocal strategy to fight, with which it may alternate. In early societies, death from wild animals contributed to a life expectancy of 25 (Laughlin, 1977). Perhaps this vulnerable history underlies human propensity to this survival strategy. Eradication of predators may have led to fear and paranoia being mainly directed toward other humans (Valent, 1987).

In flight, life is preserved by removing oneself from danger. The paradigmatic picture is of an animal running to escape a predator. Other means of flight are avoidance, retreat, freezing, and hiding. Amoebae already avoid physical stimuli, light, and chemicals. Most animals have developed ingenious means of distancing, hiding, and camouflaging.

Humans also use running, hiding, freezing, and camouflaging to escape. Flight may be to the center of one's territory and group, though at times it needs to be into exile. Psychosocial elaborations of flight include physical and psychological fortresses, avoidance, subterfuges, and dissimulations to put others off the track. Flight may be into oneself (Dixon & Kaesermann, 1987) or one's mind (Roth & Cohen, 1986), or even from one's mind.

AXIS 1: THE PROCESS AXIS

Appraisal of the Means of Survival

One appraises that to survive one must escape danger.

Stress Responses

Adaptive–Successful Responses

Biological Aspects   Flight is associated with the anterior hypothalamic, medial preoptic regions and dorsomedial hypothalamus, with strong rostral connections to bed nucleus of stria terminalis and amygdalar basal nucleus and descending connections to centrum mediastinum–parafascicular complex, down through the dorsal part of midbrain central gray (Henry, 1986; Panksepp, 1989a).

Activation of the sympathetic nervous system is similar to that in fight (Cannon, 1939). However, increase in pulse rate, blood pressure, and norepinephrine are not as sustained as in fight, and epinephrine is relatively more elevated to norepinephrine. There may also be some cholinergic activity and mild elevation of cortisol (Henry, 1986).

Dopaminergic activity, b-endorphin, serotonin, curare, carbachol, and excitatory amino acids may facilitate flight and freezing behavior. Alcohol, benzodiazapines, and GABA ameliorate its fear and anxiety (Dixon & Kaesermann, 1987; Panksepp, 1989a).

Psychological Aspects   Although fight is red and hot, fear is yellow and cold: "My teeth chattered with fear." Attack is replaced by trembling and weakness: "My muscles went to jelly" or "my knees gave way." Fear includes butterflies in the stomach, need to defecate and void, palpitations, hard breathing, and other psychophysiological symptoms (see below). Displays to defuse others' attacks include pallor, making the body small and still, casting eyes down, and speaking with a squealing voice (Darwin, 1872/1965; Panksepp, 1986b).

Whereas fear leads to appeasing behavior, terror is accompanied by an imperative desire to escape as overpowering attack or engulfment are seen to be unavoidable. Bernadette described the Gestapo arresting her family:

> The very first bit is my father's face. . . . A gun at his head. . . . My father's face was the image of terror. . . . I just wanted to be out of there. . . . I remember running in terror. All I knew was that I was so terrified that I ran and ran and ran. . . . Terror is the only word to describe it." (Valent, 1994, p 54)

The following is suggested to differentiate some terms referring to terror. *Frozen terror* is the intense fear that Bernadette's father may have felt, associated with total stillness yet readiness for to escape. *Fright* refers to short-term surges of frozen terror, and *startle* is fright that arises unexpectedly, such as in sleep. *Anxiety* in this survival strategy (each survival strategy has its anxiety) refers to fear from an uncertain source. *Arousal* is also a general alerting signal but is commonly "fitted" with fight and flight (Öhman, 1993).

Deliverance is the feeling of having escaped to security. It is associated with a sense of salvation, liberation, and bodily relaxation.

Social Aspects   Retreat is prudent withdrawal in the face of superior threatening forces. Once in a place of relative security, regrouping or realignment can occur. Flight associated with terror has every sinew working to its capacity to run to safety. Even when vehicles replace limbs, the sympathetic nervous system may pump as if one was running. When physical flight is impossible, freezing, hiding, and camouflage are used. For instance, many Jews lived as Christians in Nazi-occupied Europe. They also hid their various fears (Valent, 1994, 1995b). Successful escape means reaching long-term safety from dangers and enemies.

Maladaptive–Unsuccessful Responses

Biological Aspects Maladaptive flight has the same but more sustained physiology as its adaptive counterpart. For instance, Friedman (1991) noted raised sympathetic nervous system response in combat veterans with PTSD in basal conditions and intense elevation when exposed to combat stimuli evoking intense flight impulses.

The traumatic state of inescapable shock may be associated with norepinephrine depletion, and subsequent sensitivity of parts of the brain to norepinephrine stimulation. Associated analgesia seems to be mediated by endogenous opioids (van der Kolk & Greenberg, 1987).

Inability to escape may evoke cortisol secretion and lower imunocompetence (Knapp et al., 1992).

Psychological Aspects Arousal, fear, terror, freezing, fright, startle, and anxiety may become protracted or entrenched if escape is impossible. When no longer adaptive, disproportionate fear of objects wrongly assumed to be threats to life may be called phobias. Öhman (1993) noted that four types of evolutionary fear-relevant stimuli were prone to being conditioned into phobias. Fear of predators (and enemies) is associated with phobias of snakes, insects, and other animals (as well as humans). Fears related to death and injury are associated with phobias about illness, blood, contamination, and disability. Claustrophobia can be linked to engulfment, choking, and drowning. Fear of losing status and dignity lead to phobias of conflict and risk of humiliation. Finally, fears increase when away from home territory and security figures, hence agoraphobia, school phobia, and fear of the dark.

Paranoia is an excessive fear that one is hated, attacked, humiliated, or persecuted. As with hatred and persecution, such feelings are often displaced from other times and places (see below). Engulfment is the sense of being caught and about to be destroyed.

Social Aspects Avoidance is a maintained retreat associated with vigilance against constantly lurking danger, especially phobic objects. Psychological avoidance puts distance from dangerous thoughts and emotions.

Though the term *panic* is often used synonymously with *terror*, here it refers to social situations where all curbs on the impulse to flee collapse. Quarantelli (1954) noted that this occurs on the rare occasions when flight is about to be blocked and entrapment threatened, as when there is only one exit in a fire (Valent, 1984; Veltfort & Lee, 1943). Then crowds may trample over each other in a wild stampede.

Annihilation is destruction by attacking forces. It is often conceptualized in atavistic predators, poison, and malevolent sorcery terms. This is especially evident in children's nightmares and fairy tales. Psychological fragmentation can be sensed as annihilation of one's sanity.

Trauma

The term *inescapable shock* denotes a situation of no escape from danger. It is borrowed from animal studies of electrically shocked animals, whose responses of learned helplessness have been suggested as models of human trauma (Abramson, Garber, & Seligman, 1980; Maier & Seligman, 1976; van der Kolk et al., 1984). Although it is suggested that the responses generated in the experiments more conform to powerlessness (chapter 10), there is no doubt that inability to escape what seems impending death is highly traumatic. It was commonly described by Vietnam veterans.

> "I fell. A guy yelled 'booby trap!' The commanding officer said, 'he's dead meat.' Numerous close calls. 'You can be hit and never know it. . . . Oh, he's going to shoot me! You're never safe!" Vince felt the terror that he would inevitably "get his." (Lindy, 1988, p. 68)

There is a sense that like a hunted animal one will be killed. Survivors of mass and mock executions and other near-death experiences describe an intense cognitive appreciation that nothing can be done; "This is it!" Emotionally, there may intense frozen terror, mixed with dissociation and emotional numbness, as well as resignation and bewilderment. Some remnant of hope may remain, which allows last-minute quick thinking.

Illnesses

Biological Aspects

Psychophysiological Symptoms   These are associated with anxiety and panic and are very common and widespread. They include palpitations, the feeling that one's heart is ready to burst or is in one's throat, chest pain, pressure in the chest, inability to get breath, and hyperventilation. The latter may lead to dizziness and tingling, but, more important, it can reproduce a wide array of psychophysiological symptoms (Lum, 1975) related to any survival strategy. Hence, anxiety is a common differential diagnosis for many somatic symptoms and is a recognized factor in the amplification of symptoms in many organic illnesses.

Psychosomatic Illnesses Too little is known to confirm the lay concept of dying of fright in previously healthy people, though Saul (1966) described fresh myocardial infarctions in two situations of no escape. However, anxiety may predispose one to arrhythmias, including ventricular tachycardias and sudden death in predisposed individuals (Niaura & Goldstein, 1992). As the physiology of flight overlaps with those of assertiveness and fight, it may contribute to hypertension and coronary artery disease, but more research is needed to elucidate the specific role of flight in these illnesses.

Psychological Aspects Arousal, fear, terror, freezing, fright, startle, and anxiety are central features of PTSD. The *DSM–IV* also differentiated panic, phobic, and generalized anxiety disorders, though these diagnoses overlap clinically, and close examination uncovers similar fearful events in their development (Öhman, 1993).

The dynamic stream also sees irrational anxiety based on earlier understandable fears and frights to be central. Freud (1893/1975p, 1921/1975f) noted that fear of real events later returned as anxiety or a variety of symptoms, depending on the defenses used against the anxiety. To expand on Freud, it is suggested that in hysteria the terror is symbolically displaced onto the body; conversion in phobias, onto objects and places; in obsessive–compulsive neuroses, onto thoughts and compulsive actions; in paranoia, onto people.

At times, even paranoid schizophrenia may appear more understandable with this approach. In Case 3, Anne (chapter 1) developed persecutory visual and auditory hallucinations when she defied the threats of her early abusers that they would kill her if she ever told.

A patient of mine had developed paranoid schizophrenia with delusions and hallucinations of police making sexual insinuations and the devil attacking her body. A recent stress cued reliving terrors of her father's earlier sexual abuse, which was displaced on the devil and other father figures.

Social Aspects Fearful and avoidant responses may become entrenched as timid, paranoid, or schizoid traits. Psychosocial escapes may be to television, music, sex, alcohol, and drugs.

AXIS 2: PARAMETERS AXIS

Traumatic Situations and Disaster Phases

The danger may be defined in the preimpact phase and avoided by withdrawal or evacuation. Flight in the impact phase has been described above. Postimpact, there may be avoidance of the previously dangerous situation and any cues reminiscent of it. Current anxiety and paranoia may be due to generalizations or displacements from past experience.

Flight at Different Social Levels

Depending on circumstances, flight may occur at individual, family, or group levels. Aspects of flight such as paranoia and engulfment may also range from individual to national levels. As in fight, social displacement may occur in which sources of paranoia parallel scapegoat targets. As with hatred (chapter 12, chapter 16), splitting and displacement may offer compromises to untenable situations.

Flight Across the Life Cycle

Infants withdraw their gazes, heads, and limbs from unpleasant stimuli, and they move away from fearful situations as soon as they are mobile. With historical high infant mortality rates and with infants having been prime prey to predators, it may not be surprising that atavistic fears and paranoia are present from infancy. Klein (Segal, 1975) described graphically the terrors of infant persecution and perceived threat of annihilation, which only slowly subside to "normal" proportions.

Flight may initially be from a persecuting engulfing breast, later mother as a whole, then father, strangers, and strange groups, becoming ever more akin to adult flight. However, earlier fears may be projected on later objects.

AXIS 3: FULFILLMENT AND TRAUMA ALONG THE DEPTH AXIS

Fulfillment

Deliverance from danger provides great relief. Although refugees are given pity for their vulnerable states, they are also commended and admired for their often hair-raising, ingenious escapes. It is just to give the persecuted the refuge and liberty that they deserve. Meanings gleaned from flight may include the need to be prepared to leave places, not to hang on to possessions, and having suitcases packed in a dangerous world. Ideally, one is always able to discern and avoid danger, and it is best to live by the principles of "It's a dangerous world" and "Be prepared" to run, have your passport ready. Swift-footedness, cunning, and deftness are valued qualities that facilitate flight, as are pity, safe passage, and offers of haven, sanctuary, and permanent welcome in host communities.

The latter are included in codes of behavior toward refugees. They include giving them the dignity of fellow human beings who are currently in trouble but who still have human rights and entitlements to have their basic needs met.

Magical potions, amulets, obsessional rituals, prayers, and thoughts may provide comfort that one can escape poisons, ill wishes, and bullets "Only a bullet with my name on it can harm me." "If it is meant to happen, it will; if not, not." Churches, religious sites, and embassies may be designated sanctuaries. Joining a religion or ideology may provide havens or promises of future havens. Heaven is the ultimate haven.

Religious and ideological symbols such as the Statue of Liberty indicate sanctuary. Many symbols may signify past dangers that may evoke flight responses. Such symbols define identity as "them" and "us," as in fight. Refugees may have conflicts of belonging to old and new cultures.

Flight is commonly depicted creatively in drama, and along with violence is daily fare on television. Tom-and-Jerry–type escapes are reflected in more mature heroes who maybe escape even more than they kill. Chases and hide-and-seek are the most common games of children. Aesthetic qualities of timidity, mildness, heedfulness, and circumspectness may evoke gallantry. Sanctuaries such as churches may be sacred, as may be ancestral lands sanctioned by God, such as Israel. Death may be sacred as connection with a universal sanctuary.

Knowledge may include different types of escapes suitable for different circumstances. Truth is that all are vulnerable and will eventually be caught by death. Wisdom includes heedfulness and prudence, so as to avoid later necessity to flee. When necessary, it enables one to leave well and in good time. It values and maintains continuous sanctuary while aware of the need to leave it in certain circumstances.

Trauma

Although from the fleeing person's point of view flight in panic is the only means of survival, it may be condemned as cowardice and lack of moral fiber. Cowards should not be given refuge but punished. From the person's point of view, this means that the world is a persecutory place of inescapable danger ready to engulf one at any moment. Ideally, one should be constantly vigilant, on the principle that something is always ready to pounce, valuing capacities of hiding, avoiding, and fleeing. One's identity as a victim in this case carries no dignity; rather, it carries stigma, blame, and abhorrence. One may be identified with a persecuted group, such as traditional scapegoats. There is no pity, codes of behavior are abrogated, and victims have no right or entitlement to refuge and life. No magic seems to work, and there are no religious or ideological sanctuaries, only demonic persecutors. God himself seems to have turned them loose. Everything threatens and may be a symbol of danger. Everything beautiful and creative is gone, though senseless killing has a fascination for the media. There may have been some overall connection to the universe as a hunted prey in the evolutionary past, but being a senseless victim ruptures all sacred connections to the universe. It brings home knowledge of the truth that life is dangerous. Wisdom sees the possibility of being killed at any time.

In summary, although flight fulfills needs of sanctuary from danger, its traumatic aspects are the stuff of paranoid nightmares.

Chapter 14

Competition: Struggle

Struggle of all against all is a common misconception of human nature and evolution. Yet as with fight, survival strategies may shed light on the source of some of the most maladaptive and ugliest human characteristics.

In competition, life is preserved by obtaining scarce essentials. The paradigmatic picture is of two individuals fighting for a single prize. However, what may be lost in the pessimistic view of struggle is that adaptive competition is for status in dominance hierarchies (pecking orders) and that once established they avoid further struggle. Further, unlike in fight, there is no desire to wound badly or be rid of the opponent. Hierarchies in their adaptive states are ubiquitous utilities present already in the cells of animals that ensure maximum survival for the population through prioritization and lines of distribution and communication (Halliday, 1981; Scott, 1977; E. O. Wilson, 1975).

Dominant individuals obtain preferentially scarce resources of food, shelter, territory, sex partners, and comforts. In return, they ensure distribution of resources so that even the weakest get some, maintain internal order, and defend the group. If altruistic survival strategies do not overtake them, dominant animals reproduce more, perhaps due to higher testosterone levels. For instance, dominant baboons have harems and offspring, whereas peripheral baboons, even if they copulate, have low fertility rates. So competition serves to maintain as many and as superior group genes as possible.

There are clear parallels between animal and human hierarchies and advantages. Hierarchical dominance gave tribal chiefs more food, wives, children, attention, and comforts (Laughlin, 1977; Tiger & Fox, 1971).

Without hierarchies, struggle is seen from lowliest species such as barnacles and worms (Scott, 1989; E. O. Wilson, 1975) to chimpanzees (Dunbar, 1985) and humans. The latter evolved greed, jealousy, and envy, perhaps to facilitate competition for peculiarly human resources, such as wealth, love, and higher level fulfillment requirements.

AXIS 1: THE PROCESS AXIS

Appraisal of the Means of Survival

Appraisals of hierarchical status determine whether to take the first and lion's share of resources or to wait in line for what is given. One may contest hierarchical position with relative equals or, in desperate situations, grab what one can.

Stress Responses

Adaptive–Successful Responses

Biological Aspects   Intermale social aggression is associated with the medial preoptic and medial anterior hypothalamic sites, which also selectively take up testosterone. Across species, those with higher hierarchical status have higher testosterone levels (Knol & Egbering-Alink, 1989; Mazur, 1983). Even having won or lost competitive tennis matches increases and decreases sensitively subsequent testosterone levels (Booth, Shelley, & Mazur, 1990). Testosterone levels in early life influence later testosterone levels and hierarchical status. Competition between females may be facilitated by estrogen and progesterone as well as by adrenal testosterone (Henry, 1986). Dominance may include high norepinephrine levels as well (Panksepp, 1986a).

Psychological Aspects   The desire to win includes both a covetousness felt in the chest that can only be satisfied by incorporating the prize and a need to diminish the opponent. Victory is associated with exhilaration, swelling of the chest, and feeling 10 feet tall. There may be an impulse to beat one's chest and let out a triumphant roar. The result of winning is status, accompanied by a sense of superiority and expectation of privileges, obedience, attention, and respect. High status confers a sense of dominance and power. Power gives a sense of control and comfort in the world, but it also carries a *noblesse oblige,* that is, responsibility even at personal sacrifice to those who are in one's charge.

Social Aspects   Contests establish superiority. Postures, gestures, and words similar to those in fight may be sufficient to extract appeasement, especially in those previously defeated. Physical contests are also ritualized to avoid permanent damage. Symbolic defeats such as drawing blood may end conflicts. Contests may be mixed with machismo both in animals and in humans. For instance, sword fights were mixed with peacocklike displays and the winning of ladies.

Although status is associated with privilege and power, hierarchy ensures lack of internal struggles and distribution of available resources. Advantages even on the lower rungs can be substantial. For instance, feudal peasants knew that they would be taken care of from birth to death, and in the main they accepted their low status.

Nevertheless, possession of scarce materials is the ultimate prize of competition. And even though it carries responsibilities and risks, it gives preferential advantages to survival, reproduction, and fulfillment and gives advantages in case struggle breaks out.

Maladaptive–Unsuccessful Responses

Biological Aspects   Defeat may be associated with the hippocampus and septum (Henry, 1986) and opioid-facilitated "defeat analgesia" with the arcuate nucleus and periaqueductal gray (Blanchard & Blanchard, 1988). Defeat, submission, and subordinate status are sensitively reflected in low levels of androgens and testosterone and are associated with high levels of glucocorticoids, corticosterone, and ACTH (Blanchard & Blanchard, 1988; Dixon & Kaesermann, 1987; Henry, 1986; Leshner, 1983). Further defeats are associated with surges of corticosterones.

Defeat leads to marked increases in the female luteinizing and follicle-stimulating hormones, though the same hormones may increase female status. Immunocompetence may be compromised with defeat (Fleshner et al., 1989) and enhanced with victory. Defeated animals may die of infections, whereas injecting them with testosterone can lead to recovery (E. O. Wilson, 1975).

Psychological Aspects   Defeat may be accompanied by bitter tears of disappointment, chagrin filling the collapsed chest where the coveted object was to be. The whole body may feel smaller and shorter, and this self-image may lead to a spiral of defeats. Excessive power may be used to crush the defeated, preventing any chance of a later contest. This may be felt as crushing of the chest. Gloating and "putting the boot in" may lead to psychological crushing.

Strains in the hierarchy and in the distribution of resources lead to greed, envy, and jealousy. Greed is an insatiable craving, a gnawing inner void, that no amount of grabbing, sucking, and devouring (Segal, 1975) can fill. Greed for food is called gluttony; for money, avarice and rapaciousness; for sex, lust. Envy is a torment of spite and vindictiveness in the chest or gut, likened to venom or an acid, which if not hurled at the envied person corrodes oneself. Jealousy may be special form of envy where a rival possesses a love object, and envious feelings are turned on the rival (M. Klein, 1952/1975a).

Though they may be destructive, it is suggested that these strained feelings have potentially adaptive potentials. In Case 1, for instance, envy redressed imbalances in distribution, and greedy accumulation enabled later exchanges.

However, the same feelings may fuel exploitation. Resources that should have been distributed flow to those in power in the form of tribute, labor, and taxes, as well as psychological homage and adulation.

Social Aspects   With the development of civilization, power itself could be accumulated like other resources and used to increase wealth through oppression and coercion (Maxwell, 1984). Patronage, work, and work and hierarchical status could be reinforced through intimidation by police and soldiers. Such situations invite hierarchical struggles. They may or may not overlap with general social disorganization and extreme insufficiencies. If they do, circumstances can arise (reminiscent of the atrocity-making situations of fight) that produce the jungle situation of each man for himself. For instance, in Case 1 people scrambled for exits and wet towels (chapter 1). In Auschwitz, women stole the little milk available for children, saying, "Look, you're not going to make it anyway, so give us a chance" (Valent, 1994, p. 26).

> A survivor of Hiroshima said, "Of course I thought much about my children, but egotism was so great that each person was alone. . . . I felt strongly that human beings were animals—even . . . parents and children . . . fought with one another to get their food. (Lifton, 1967, p. 45)

The end result of defeat, dispossession, and exploitation is a state of being plundered of physical and psychosocial resources.

Trauma

Terrorization crushes those lower in the hierarchy. In dictatorships (Bauer, Priebe, Häring, & Adamczak, 1993), hostage situations, and abusive families, the terrorized are stripped of possessions and privileges. They are marginalized to the lowest hierarchical status, including forced infantilization where even excretory functions are in the power of superiors (Chodoff, 1970).

Elimination may happen with sorrow as when communities have to let their very young or very old die. But elimination of dehumanized inferiors was exemplified in concentration camps: "The weak work for the strong, and if they have no strength or will to work—then . . . let them die" (Friedrich, 1981, p. 37). The totally exploited human commodities finally slip off the hierarchical ladder to oblivion.

Illnesses

Biological Aspects   Competition is seldom noted, especially as a contributor to illnesses. However, sympathetic nervous system arousal may produce the usual psychophysiological symptoms. Defeat may include tiredness and resemble burnout.

Psychosomatic Illnesses   Deprived cultures and lower socioeconomic classes suffer higher frequencies and mortality rates of many illnesses. They range from infections such as tuberculosis and rheumatic fever to diseases of the heart and immune system. Hypertension and coronary heart disease may be facilitated by the competitive component of Type A personalities and unwinnable hierarchical conflicts (Niaura & Goldstein, 1992). Aggression toward superiors raises blood pressure; expressing it to inferiors lowers it. Defeat may contribute to the state of vital exhaustion that precedes coronary heart disease (Appels & Mulder, 1989).

Psychological Aspects   There are no designated phenomenological illnesses relating to this survival strategy. However, envy and greed are recognized as important emotions in psychoanalysis. Father–son competition for mother in the Oedipus complex (and mother–daughter competition for father in the Electra complex) have been seen as central hierarchical organizers of families and later societies. Terrorization is in this case the castration anxiety, resolved by acquiescence to father.

Social Aspects   Social illnesses involve greed and corruption, envy, tyranny, exploitation, and struggle. They are considered further below.

AXIS 2: PARAMETERS AXIS

Traumatic Situations and Disaster Phases

Preparation and training for the contest or struggle take place in the preimpact phase. Much enterprise, seduction, and intimidation may go into preliminary jostling. The impact phase is marked by actual contest or struggle. Postimpact, there is assimilation of victory or defeat and new positions in the hierarchy. In the recovery and reconstruction phase, one adjusts to the new situation or makes preparations for subsequent contests.

Competition at Different Social Levels

Every social group can potentially have its members compete against each other. Family conflicts of needs and rivalries and jealousies occur between parents, parents and children (e.g., see above), and siblings.

Male–male competition has been studied most and was considered above. However, females also have hierarchies, like hens as well as roosters have pecking orders, and they also compete for partners through sexual attractiveness and enviously spoiling that of others. Females may compete for preferential survival of their offspring.

Intragroup power struggles are common in work and politics. Revolutions against oppression make up much of history. Those in power may preempt them by finding outside scapegoats and promising wars that will bring wealth. Intergroup competition for scarce resources has occurred for waterholes (Lienhardt, 1966). The Iroquois League fought for beaver. Wars can be waged for territory or for other resources such as oil. Colonization oppresses and exploits all local resources. Kings and nations may compete for status symbols and their vanities.

Competition for resources may be interspecific. Most vicious competition to the point of genocidal elimination occurs frequently among species ecologically and taxonomically closest to each other (E. O. Wilson, 1975). Ardrey (1976) speculated that our species eliminated the Neanderthals. This may fit with the frequent dehumanization of enemies as a subhuman species.

Competition Across the Life Cycle

Primitive greed and envy may be turned to parts of the mother such as the breast, then mother as a whole, followed by others.

Competition between peers is present by the age of 2 (Cummings, Hollenbeck, & Ianotti, 1986). It translates into academic, sports, and social competition at school and later in work and in a variety of social groups. Early experiences of high status or defeat, insufficiency, and envy may be displaced on to later objects.

AXIS 3: FULFILLMENT AND TRAUMA ALONG THE DEPTH AXIS

Fulfillment

There is joy in winning and enjoyment of superiority and its advantages. Worth is recognized through respect and deference and expressed in authority and confidence. It is just that ambition, enterprise, and excellence should be preferentially rewarded and the community benefit down the line. It is good that the best should rule and use their talents and powers for social order, and it is bad to be greedy and envious. The world has meaning in terms of hierarchical order, with oneself having an important role in it. Personal ideals include reaching the top, striving for excellence, achieving wealth, power, prestige and honor, and being a good ruler. One upholds values of law and order, tradition, and everyone receiving their dues. All accept their place. Principles include that the superior are the best to rule but are obliged to make sure that all have enough and to maintain social order.

Aristocracy and the middle class observe codes of courtly and bourgeois behavior, encompassing both respect and contest. Other codes exist for paying homage up the hierarchy and its graceful acknowledgment and patronage down the hierarchy. Rights and entitlements are enshrined in laws that protect power and property, though all members have their rights. Dignity is tied to shows of status, good name, and superior mien, though lower levels fiercely defend their own dignity, even if it is that of a good servant.

Hierarchical positions may be imbued with magical power, and aristocracies and clergy may claim mythical links to divinity. Rituals, pomp, and ceremony reinforce this. The ideology is conservative and includes hierarchical morality (chapter 5) and concepts of benevolent tyrannies drawing on models of family and God. Divine laws such as the Ten Commandments (Exodus 20) reinforce exclusivity, hierarchy, and avoidance of socially destabilizing greed and envy.

Symbols of status and power can become important in their own right. They include nonverbal communication such as postures and greetings; clothing such as feathers, crowns, and hats to make one taller; and symbols of wealth such as jewelry, bigger and higher houses, and these days slicker cars and modern gadgets. Psychological symbols of prestige and honor may be as important. Sporting contests can serve as social symbols of earlier contests of physical prowess and tribal competitions. Class and status, including all of the above, are important parts of identity.

High class is associated with the aesthetics of comfort and luxury. Emphasis is placed on good taste, elegance, decorum, and etiquette. Hierarchy may have a sacred dimension of universal order. For instance, the Pope ("Papa") is in direct line to God. Sacred buildings, monuments, rituals, and creative arts emphasize the sacredness.

Knowledge is that of power and privilege and that everything has a place in the universe. Truth is that the powerful are only humans like others, and power is a transient commodity of the temporarily superior. Wisdom prevents taking one's status too seriously, but rather as good fortune to be enjoyed and shared with the less fortunate as much as is prudently affordable.

Trauma

Defeat may mean not being able to obtain essential resources and to be ignominiously eliminated. Victors are felt to be oppressive and exploitative, abusing their power with avarice and lust. They inflate their worth through vanity and sycophancy and have contempt for the lowly. Their rule is unjust, as it is based on force, not on superior qualities that benefit the community. All this means that unless one struggles, one is a loser who stays at the bottom of the pile.

Hierarchical ideals are shattered. It is capacities for intrigue, ruthlessness, and elimination of rivals that become values in a world whose principles are those of the jungle, where dog eats dog, and "to those who have shall be given; from those who have not shall be taken." Codes of contest are abrogated, and unfair triumph is reinforced by gloating and "putting the boot in." Force backs oppressive laws that also demand obeisance and veneration and exact humiliation. For instance, insufficient prostrating has meant death. Dignity is traumatically stripped, and one feels leveled, degraded, and dishonored.

Religion and ideology are disillusioning tools used for extortion, adoration, and profligacy. Power and status symbols become desired ends in themselves acquired with greed and corruption and vaunted in depravity. Creative arts are harnessed into personal adornments, displays, and monuments, sometimes absorbing the wealth of a people. Aesthetics such as elegance and wit become self-indulgent parodies. Identities are polarized into superior and inferior classes. The sacred order is challenged when humans take on the mantle of God for profane gain and glorification.

Knowledge is directed toward greedy enlargement of power. Truth appears to be that power and wealth ensure survival in the struggles of the world and happiness. Lack of wisdom prevents seeing the seeds of revolution one is sowing, for eventually the oppressors are overthrown.

In summary, competition promises the advantages of power and wealth and hierarchical order. However, it may result in scramble and deadly struggle. When maladaptive fight is added, the worst human excesses can occur.

Chapter 15

Cooperation: Love

Love, creativity, and generativity are some of the greatest joys and fulfillments of mankind. Perversions of love are among the greatest destroyers of happiness.

In cooperation, life is preserved by pooling resources to create more essentials than the aggregate of the individual ones. Paradigmatic pictures are mutual help (saving life) and procreation (making life).

From insects to chimpanzees, animals help each other and give and reciprocate resources (E. O. Wilson, 1975). When reciprocity is apparently absent, giving appears to be altruistic. However, Trivers (1971) noted that reciprocity could be delayed and the favor returned to a group member of the initial altruist. In the end, this "reciprocal altruism" enhances the survival calculus of both populations.

Reciprocity including grooming, touching, scratching, and associated pleasures-enhanced bonds and affection. A special reciprocity is sexuality. Sex cells join to create new cells, and sexual intercourse facilitates this in mammals.

All human societies have been concerned with giving and taking (Eibl-Eibesfeldt, 1980), the social glue (Youniss, 1986) that results from this process, and problems of trust and cheating (Trivers, 1971). Benedict (1963) noted intricate patterns of endless reciprocal commercial transactions in early societies.

Such activity led Tiger and Fox (1971, p. 147) to say, "Economic behavior is as much a part of human nature as sexual behavior: to take away a man's right to exchange, to make deals, to be in debt and repay, is . . . to deny humanity."

Hugging, stroking, and kissing seem to be human equivalents of grooming and are parts of courtship and affectionate bonding. Love, like grief, may be a relatively recent evolutionary acquisition. Though already recognized in the ancient empires of China, India, and Egypt, some languages still do not have a word for it, especially for falling in love.

AXIS 1: THE PROCESS AXIS

Appraisal of the Means of Survival

It is appraised that one needs another's involvement to create more essentials and fulfillments. Giving and taking engage such involvement.

Stress Responses

Adaptive–Successful Responses

Biological Aspects   Affiliation and sexuality are associated with the amygdala, temporal pole, and orbital frontal cortex (Steklis & Kling, 1985). They have the highest concentration for mu-like opiate receptors, and opiates enhance social comfort and mutual bonding with affection and trust (Kimball, 1987). The opioid antagonist naloxone intensifies social need, grooming, and sexual activity. Sex hormones promote both sexual desire and social bonding in both sexes (Panksepp, 1993), and serotonergic systems contribute to grooming and affiliative behavior. Most activity is trophotropic (cholinergic) with decrease in pulse and blood pressure as well as epinephrine and norepinephrine secretion (Henry, 1986).

Psychological Aspects   Mutual bonds of trust are forged during sharing of dangerous situations and falling in love (the two may overlap). They are reinforced by cognitive concentration on the preciousness of the other, exclusiveness of the shared situation, and altruistic generosity.

Generosity is felt as a fullness in the heart needing to be shared through hands and body: "a centrifugal act of the soul in constant flux that goes toward the object" (Y Gasset, 1959, p. 20). Giving increases one's own wealth. As Juliet says, "My bounty is as boundless as the sea, my love as deep; The more I give to thee, the more I have"(Shakespeare, *Romeo and Juliet,* II:133).

Love is also felt as a fullness in the chest often referred to the heart. An ache reminiscent of an overfilled breast may carry the person to the beloved with a readiness to give them one's heart. Reciprocated love provides excitement, happiness, tenderness, pleasure, a sense of health, an inner and outer glow, and unbounded future (Christie, 1969, Liebowitz, 1983). It may also provide a sense of unity, safety, exultation, and transcendence (Hatfield & Rapson, 1993). The initial intense bonding or falling in love mellows to affection and companionate love (see below).

Social Aspects   Love bonds are forces of integration. Melding is characterized by unique contributions of partners in reciprocal giving and taking. It is nonhierarchical, even across usually hierarchical social systems. Thus, in their mutually creative process, a mother receives as much as a baby. "A cow needs to suckle as much as a calf needs to suck." Whereas in combat and disasters reciprocity is immediate, in courtship and friendships it may take time. When one cannot immediately repay an altruistic act or generous gift, gratitude and a sense of debt maintain the desire to reciprocate (M. Klein, 1952/1975b; Tiger & Fox, 1971; Trivers, 1971). Reciprocity need not be in kind, but in proportion to the value to the receiver and sacrifice and unselfish generosity of the giver. Giving leaves partners intact; only their creative parts meld. As Gibran (1972, p. 16) said, "Love one another, but make no bond [tie] of love; Let it rather be a moving sea between the shores of your souls."

From the mutual sea of gifts and love arises creativity. Y Gasset (1959, p. 11) said, "Nothing is so fertile in our private lives as the feeling of love. . . . Many things are born out of a person's love . . . like the harvest from a seed."

Maladaptive–Unsuccessful Responses

Biological Aspects   Perception of social isolation seems to be associated with the cingulate gyrus and decreased opiate levels (Panksepp et al., 1985). External opiate taking may attempt to compensate for this. Suppression of male sex hormones may diminish sexual desire and sexual crime, but no clear hormonal deviations have been found even in major sexual dysfunctions. Much research is needed on the physiology of maladaptive cooperation.

Psychological Aspects   Broken promises, nonrepayment of debt, abuse of trust, and cheating by a partner are felt as betrayal. It may be felt as being pierced in the heart or stabbed in the back. Selfishness replaces generosity and reciprocity, and the victim feels taken advantage of. At its worst, abuse is the coercive and destructive use of the trust, love, and creative resources of another. Perhaps the most extreme abuse is that of children, especially sexual abuse. Betrayal and perversion of a child's inevitable natural love by the very people who should be partners in the child's creative growth may be the ultimate betrayal, and is most soul destroying.

Social Aspects   Whereas love binds, betrayal and abuse disconnect. Feeling cheated accompanies every aspect of unraveling. Wounds of unreciprocated generosity, seduction, lying, and broken promises may lead to bitter quarrels over mutual products such as children and property and to festering hurts.

A woman told me how hurt and puzzled she was even after 50 years about why a woman with whom she had shared her bread in a concentration camp later refused to share her bread with her.

Perhaps because cheating, especially if undiscovered, may offer survival advantages, it may be quite subtle. People may mimic generosity and friendship and not even be consciously aware of their own deception (Trivers, 1971). Suspicion and mistrust require continued proof of loyalty and character, and when eventual trust is abused one feels particularly robbed.

Finally, disintegration replaces synthesis and creativity. With creativity, 1 plus 1 equals more than 2. Now 2 divided by 2 equals less than 1.

Trauma

Disintegration of family, friendship, community, and psychological bonds results in their fragmentation. A woman said, "I am in a thousand fragments." Splitting of hope and reality and fragmentations of knowledge have been described as defenses. However, here they denote the rupture of the mind as a creative psychosocial synthesizing organ.

Without psychosocial coherence and creativity, one experiences alienation. In *The Outsider,* Albert Camus (1961) described well its hallmarks, which include a world without significant emotional bonds, love, enjoyment, and creative thrust. Nothing is important or interesting; time drags in boredom. There may be a longing but not knowing for what (Greenson, 1953), accompanied by a paradoxical pain of being empty of oneself (Balint, 1963). Vain attempts to feel alive through drugs, sex, violence, pain (such as cutting one's wrists), and pretense lead only to counterfeit life (Lifton, 1967, 1980). Barrenness leads to stagnation and decay, a living death.

Illnesses

Biological Aspects
Psychophysiological Symptoms   Relationship difficulties underlie a wide variety of psychophysiological and sexual disorders. The latter include arousal difficulties, vaginismus and pain on intercourse, premature ejaculation, and impotence. Dissociated responses from abuse situations may present as gynecological and other body problems.

Psychosomatic Illnesses   Although loving relationships protect against illnesses possibly through soothing and better immunocompetence (Jemmott, 1987), relationship breakdowns precede a variety of illnesses in epidemiological studies (chapter 2).

Psychological Aspects   Epidemiological studies have also indicated that childhood physical or sexual abuse precedes 40%–60% of psychiatric diagnoses, ranging over depression, anxiety, somatization, paranoid, addiction, personality, borderline, multiple personality, and other disorders (Herman, 1992).

Psychodynamic thinking also holds that a variety of disorders stem from childhood sexual difficulties (chapter 2). They may result from reliving traumatic situations or their displacements to uncreative sexual satisfactions such as exhibitionism, fetishism, and other paraphilias (Freud, 1905/1975q, 1940/1975m). It is suggested that distortions may also occur from fragmentation of the biopsychosocial unity of love with overemphasis on sexuality, romantic love, or sterile social arrangements. Last, other maladaptive survival strategies may contribute distortions. For instance, fight contributes to sadism and attachment to love bonds being confused with earlier maternal comforts (Christie, 1969; Hatfield & Rapson, 1993).

Social Aspects   Relationship and sexual problems, alienation, and the drastic means of trying to alleviate them, present frequent social problems.

AXIS 2: PARAMETERS AXIS

Traumatic Situations and Disaster Phases

Reciprocal altruism may be most intense in the impact phase of disasters when people may give their lives for others. Mutuality and generosity of the postimpact phase is known as postdisaster utopia (Siporin, 1976, chapter 2). At this time, friendships are forged, and seeds are literally sown, with an increase in the birth rate. In the recovery phases, mutual help continues but may conflict with individual and other survival strategy needs. "The honeymoon is over."

One could say that the phases are paralleled in love. Preimpact courting tests commitment and loyalty. In the impact phase, foreplay recapitulates life's earlier exchanges of gifts, trust, and bodily exchanges, culminating in sexual intercourse. In the later, building phase, in which security and progeny require constructions of new fabrics of loves, so-called romantic or passionate love gives way to companionate love (Hatfield & Rapson, 1993; Lilar, 1965). It may be that passionate love is to form bonds for later companionate love. The latter provides the matrix for long-term reciprocity and creativity, and its features include tenderness, intimacy, mutual understanding, tolerance, compromise, and loyalty. Wholesome love may require both phases of love.

Cooperation at Different Social Levels

New combinations of unique ideas lead to individual creativity in business, art, humor, and thought. Male–female sexuality leads to progeny, and parent–child relationships provide mutual fulfillments and reciprocal caretaking over the life cycle. Families provide a matrix for help and loving exchanges. Same-sex friendships are often forged through shared trials and challenges and may be accelerated in soldiers, emergency workers, and victims. Intergroup bonds may similarly develop through giving and taking and trade and may be accelerated among allies in war. Each partnership has specific love and affection bonds, as well as measures of reciprocity and cheating.

Cooperation Across the Life Cycle

Mothers and babies exchange body products, smiles, and gazes and are finely attuned to each other's needs. Symbolized in the later reciprocal gaze of love, they are essential ingredients for mutual esteem and self-esteem, delight, and growth. Lack of what is sometimes called mirroring (Baker & Baker, 1987; Lacan, 1966; D. N. Stern, 1984) or to have one's love impulses rejected shatters trust and sense of one's self.

Gratitude and generosity occur in the first year of life (M. Klein, 1952/ 1975a), and giving and taking of food occurs in babies (Eibl-Eibesfeldt, 1980). In the second year, children share toys and define friendships by reciprocal giving (Youniss, 1986). By the age of 9, selected friendships occur in which fair and equal treatment is demanded.

There is some evidence that children experience passionate, peer "sex-love" from the age of 3½ (Hatfield & Rapson, 1993). Its manifestations have characteristic features at each developmental phase.

Traumatic distortions of any cooperation ingredients may be specifically reflected in later development.

AXIS 3: FULFILLMENT AND TRAUMA ALONG THE DEPTH AXIS

Fulfillment

Love, sex, creativity, and generativity are among the most poignant human pleasures. They also make one feel good and worthwhile. Mutual love, faith, and loyalty are admired and raise the self-esteem of the partners. Generosity and reciprocity in value are both virtuous and just. All this means that people are basically good hearted and are there when one needs them and that one's own generosity is productive. Idealization of the merit of every detail of the beloved occurs in love of a person, country, or God. Yet principles of reciprocity also require warm corroboration and fair give and take. Ensuring them are values of honesty, reliability, and decency. In turn, they are codified in traditions of trading goods and favors and in marriage and contract laws. Everyone is entitled to make deals with dignity and to expect fair trade and promises to be kept.

Magic and myths have abounded around love and fertility. For instance, magic potions and mythical third parties may be invoked to fulfill one's desires. In religion, God promises rewards in exchange for sacrifices, rites, prayers, and obedience. A sense of mutuality and love may develop toward God. St. John said,

> Beloved, let us love one another, for love is of God . . . for God is love. . . . God sent his only begotten Son into the world, that we might live through him . . . and he that dwelleth in love dwelleth in God, and God in him. (*1 John* 4:7-8)

Religious injunctions to generosity are contained in doing unto others as one would others do to oneself and loving one's neighbor as one would oneself (Leviticus 18:17-18). Overlapping with this, communist ideology held that each person give according to ability and take according to needs.

Aspects of cooperation such as smiles, handshakes, gifts, and marriage ceremonies symbolize trust and reciprocity in various bonds and alliances. Circumcision and the cross symbolize deals with God. Identity labels such as *wife, friend,* and *business partner* denote different aspects of bonds, morals, and symbols and what is mutually hoped for with whom.

Love and generativity have a sacred dimension as a creative force that draws things together and renews them in nature's eternal life cycle (Freud, 1921/ 1975f; Lilar, 1965). Sacred bonds and fertility may be biological or spiritual.

Perhaps because of their own relationship to creativity, love and sexual relationships have occupied a large segment of art, poetry, drama, music, and the electronic media. Loved objects are seen as aesthetically beautiful, charming, and delightful.

Knowledge is that of love and creation, sex and fertility. Lilar (1965, p. 241) wrote,

> [The meaning of sex for women] is only illuminated by love. She . . . is immersed in the night of sex. Out of the world of the Mothers, where the mystery is accomplished in the darkness propitious to all gestation, she emerges with a prodigious experience. If she . . . carries lucidity into the heart of this irrational thing, she will even attain—through the sublime play of sacral sexuality—to the great way of Knowledge.

Truth includes the apparent contradiction of sex as an act shared with animals being part of the physical and spiritual generativity of humans. Wisdom acknowledges the different aspects of love and sex such as in Plato's *Symposium*—ranging between mortal and divine, a union whose love spreads to both biological and spiritual offspring. Wisdom ensures that all love has its place.

Trauma

Disintegration of trust and what was or could have been whole is the source of much unhappiness. Lying, cheating, stealing, betrayal, and unfaithfulness are unfair wrongs and sins perpetrated by reviled worthless, sleazy cheats. Sex itself may be seen as bad, dirty, and sinful and being tainted with it, even as a victim, can evoke guilt and shame. This is particularly unfair for sexually abused children whose trust and love have been destroyed. Meanings crystallize that one's love is unworthy, it is foolish to trust and hope, and others just take without return. Ideals of love and principles of honesty and reciprocity are shattered and devalued. Love is seen cynically as "child of illusion, parent of disillusion." Codes and traditions regarding promises and contracts, the dignity and rights of victims, are abrogated. There is no magic in the pain of betrayal and abuse, and no magic or myth salves it. No human ideology or religion helps, for even God has let one down. No symbols of affection comfort. Anything symbolizing one's sexuality may make one ashamed and dirty. Identity such as being cuckolded, left, robbed, or abused carries negative stigmas. One's self-image is at an ebb.

Perhaps worst, connections between sex, love, soul, and the universe are broken, and each fragment is desecrated. Perpetrators may derive temporary thrills from forbidden sex or owning the sacred vessels of another. Through seduction and coercion, victims can be made to collaborate and cooperate. But perpetrators too are defiled and profane, disconnected from love and soul. Mind and body are barren, uncreative, decaying. The world is aesthetically ugly, vulgar, and scattered.

Knowledge is of the perversion of trust, sexuality, and spirit. Truth is that there may not be the appropriate resources to combine for mutual benefit. Rather, the combination may be destructive. Lack of wisdom allows bad to breed bad, even down the generations.

In summary, love and creativity have the potential to fulfill a major part of life's purpose by mutual giving of life and fulfillment (chapter 5). To not do so for others, and not have others do so for oneself, depletes a major part of that purpose.

This completes a survey of the eight survival strategies and their ramifications across the triaxial framework. The following chapter examines their applications within the wholist perspective.

Part Four

The Wholist Perspective:
An Integrated Framework
of Traumatic Stress and Fulfillment

This final section integrates the benefits of the wholist view or perspective, which includes the triaxial framework and survival strategies. In chapter 16, I show how the wholist perspective facilitates orientation of traumatic stress and fulfillment manifestations through the triaxial framework and explain through survival strategies the sources and reasons for the manifestations.

Perhaps at least as important, too, I show how the wholist perspective provides a framework for understanding and categorizing the range of biological, psychological, and social stress responses, traumas, defenses, and symptoms, as well as other features of the triaxial framework such as emotions, pleasures, unpleasures, anxieties, angers, guilts and loves, and spiritual depth axis components such as meanings, ideologies, the sacred, and the profane.

By enhancing diagnosis and making sense of manifestations, the wholist perspective has clinical, planning, and research applications in the field of traumatic stress. It also has applications for other areas, such as medicine, ethics, law, and linguistics

The concluding chapter summarizes the journey of this volume. It reiterates that trauma disrupts the journey of fulfillment of life. It can do so from the smallest physiological components to existential meanings. I hope that knowledge of when, where, how, and why this happens may tilt the dialectic from trauma to life.

Chapter 16

The Wholist View of Traumatic Stress—Making Sense Within the Life–Trauma Dialectic

In this chapter, the wholist perspective model with its triaxial framework and survival strategy constituents is described and conceptually integrated. This is followed by application of the perspective to enriching, categorizing, recognizing, and diagnosing traumatic stress and fulfillment phenomena.

AN ELEGANT MODEL
FOR THE LIFE–TRAUMA DIALECTIC

It is suggested that the wholist perspective contributes significantly to understanding the magnitude and complexity of traumatology and the life–trauma dialectic. To denote such complexities requires nonlinear codes and metaphors.

The tapestry of life is one such common metaphor. Applying the wholist perspective, it may be said that the damaging agent (stressor) puts stress on the tapestry. Depending on various factors, including the strengths and vulnerabilities of the tapestry, a tear or other damage (trauma) results in particular patterns (illnesses). Although this represents the process axis, the parameters axis includes the particular damaging agent, the backing and frame (social system levels), the age of the tapestry (developmental phase), and the phases of damage and rescue (disaster phases). The depth axis includes the proper or improper making of the tapestry (morals), and the picture with its meanings, values, art form, aesthetics and purpose of the creator. The fibers (survival strategies) are crucial and interweave within the three axes. Their elasticity represents adaptive responses. Excessive stretching represents stress or maladaptive responses. The physical features of the fibers represent biological features of survival strategies, their different hues the emotional features, and their arrangements the social aspects. The more one views the further reaches of the tapestry on the depth or social axes, the less one is aware of the nature of its fibers (corresponding to the area of lighter stippling in Figure 7). Though such ramifications are complex, people are programmed to often be able to quickly pick the place and type of damage in the tapestry. It is suggested that the wholist perspective is a useful model that can be applied to all tapestries and their infinite complexities. In another metaphor, the triaxial framework may be likened to a radar screen whose points of orientation are colored by survival strategies. Alternately (Part 3), the triaxial framework provides points in a symphony of survival and fulfillment made up of survival strategies, which are like notes of an octave with their harmonics and overtones. Counterpoints represent survival and fulfillment mani-festations. In each case, the three axes and eight survival strategies resemble the elegance and economy of nature, where a small number of basic ingredients are used to build up an infinite variety of matter and life.

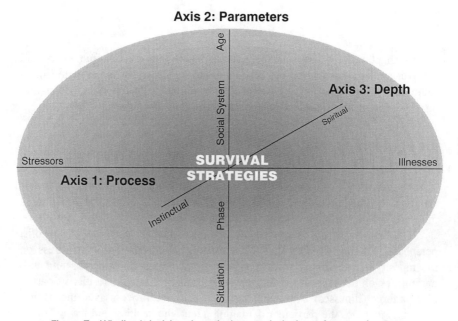

Figure 7 Wholist (triaxial and survival strategies) view of traumatic stress.

Although the three axes and survival strategies can, like notes and points in symphonies, ramify and intersect in an infinite number of ways that span the varieties of human responses, it is suggested that their limited number and typical organization can provide useful abstractions and categorizations. In other words, it may be said that although nuances are limitless, concepts and categorizations are limited and follow recognizable rules and patterns. Such patterns are starkest and least ambiguous in traumatic situations, whereas those ramified along the reaches of the triaxial framework are the most complex and have the most nuances. This is represented by differential stippling in Figure 7. Yet, last, wherever in the wholist view, its perspective integrates previous part–whole, mind–body, and humanist–scientific dichotomies.

APPLICATIONS OF THE WHOLIST PERSPECTIVE

The wholist perspective is applied to explain the great variety of often contradictory traumatic stress phenomena, followed by orientation and diagnosis of traumatic stress and fulfillment responses. Next, the framework is used to develop an enriched paradigm of trauma illnesses. It is then used to enrich and categorize other triaxial points, which include acute stress responses, trauma, moral judgments, meanings, ideologies, the sacred, and the profane. The wholist perspective is applied to examine defenses and language. Finally, contributions of the perspective to clinical and research implications are considered.

Framework for Great Variety of Traumatic Stress and Fulfillment Responses

The triaxial framework provides multiple points for orientation of the wealth of survival strategies' content. Although the triaxial framework provides the orientation, or where, of manifestations, survival strategies help in the dynamics of particular content and help to elucidate how it got there. Survival strategies thus contribute to understanding the what, how, and why of manifestations. In terms of PTSD, survival strategies help to tell what is relived and avoided and why.

Applying the wholist perspective to Case 1 (chapter 1), it may be seen how different survival strategies were used at the same triaxial points. For instance, people altruistically risked their safety for others when rescue was appraised to be the appropriate survival strategy, but they competed and struggled against each other for limited exits or wet towels when survival contingencies demanded this. Similarly, in Case 3, Anne tried to please her sexually demanding caretaker (attachment), whereas in another moment she wanted to disappear (flight). In both cases at later and deeper triaxial points, the victims tried to abstract principles and make universal judgments and existential meanings from these events. One can then see that survival strategies provided a great variety of responses throughout traumatic situations. Because circumstances in traumatic situations are often multiple and can fluctuate and be contradictory, manifestations of survival strategies and their ramifications are similarly varied, fluctuating, and contradictory.

Orientation and Diagnosis of Traumatic Stress and Fulfillment Responses

Being aware of the triaxial framework and its survival strategy contents provides the possibility of making sense of specific traumatic stress and fulfillment responses. By orienting them at particular triaxial points and qualifying the survival strategies at work, responses can be traced meaningfully back to their original contexts. For instance, yearning or separation anxiety may be dissociated fragments that may be diagnostically oriented as acute stress response emotions of maladaptive attachment. The responses may be traced back to contexts of unmet needs for attachment figures. Similarly, specific guilts, angers, shames, meanings, shattered values, desecrations, and loss of purpose may be oriented on the depth axis and be seen to belong to specific adaptive and maladaptive survival strategies. They in turn can be traced back to survival conflicts and contexts. For instance, in Case 3, Anne's identity as a sexual object could be traced back to her shame at being unworthy, a maladaptive attachment judgment resulting from her need to survive her sexual abuse.

The wholist view allows various degrees of orientation and diagnosis, as was already noted when considering the triaxial framework (chapter 6). Point diagnoses involve orienting and classifying a symptom such as an emotion. Linear models may trace symptoms along their specific survival strategy ramifications between two points, for instance, high blood pressure from suppressed rage. More complex diagnoses involve ranges of more complex nonlinear views involving dynamic interactions of survival strategies along multiple axes. And yet the most complex orientations and interactions in the web of Figure 7, just like in the ripples of the pond, lead back to a relatively small number of basic survival possibilities. This explains in part the paradox of infinite possibilities of trauma and fulfillment responses, yet a small number of discernible patterns.

Orientation and Diagnosis of Fulfillment Responses   What has been said of orienting and diagnosing traumatic stress responses is equally true for fulfillment responses, but this time they can be traced back to adaptive survival strategy responses to stressors and challenges of life. In practice, adaptive and maladaptive responses and their ramifications exist in a dynamic system. Thus, even in the presence of traumatic forms of survival strategies some degree of their adaptive forms may be present (even if only in some split-off fantasy). Other survival strategies may be present in mainly adaptive forms. Yet even fulfilled persons are aware in some part of their minds of opposite traumatic possibilities.

A Wholist Paradigm of Stress and Trauma Illnesses

A wholist paradigm of stress and trauma illnesses can now extend the triaxial framework one in chapter 6. It incorporates the dynamics of the triaxial framework, and the range of survival strategies, which ramify across it and its intersections. The paradigm of trauma illnesses may be the following.

In traumatic situations, various appraisals of stressors evoke various stress responses, which at the level of survival are the survival strategies represented in Table 2. Because survival strategies frequently fluctuate rapidly according to circumstances, their biological, psychological, and social features result in the frequently described polymorphous nature of acute stress responses.

Each survival strategy has specific hopes and anxieties associated with visions of fulfillments and traumas. If things go well, adaptive survival strategies feed back specific pleasures. If stress results, maladaptive survival strategies feed back specific unpleasures. Now anxieties of trauma increase unless defenses intervene. Survival strategies also have two-way feedback connections with the other axes (Figure 1). For instance, survival strategies may influence and be influenced by morality and value considerations on the depth axis, whereas who evokes or is the target of survival strategies and their moral ramifications is determined by the parameter axis.

Adaptively resolved stresses may again lead to triaxial fulfillments. Otherwise, specific maladaptive survival strategies; their biological, psychological, and social components; and feedback from other axes may be condensed in specific traumas, to be refracted and molded by defenses through traumatic memories to illnesses. To reiterate, trauma illnesses include maladaptive biological, psychological, and social manifestations of specific survival strategies and their triaxial feedbacks, refracted by defenses and memories and added to by current triaxial interactions. PTSD contains the reliving and avoidance of this rich amalgam.

Comorbid diagnoses develop in similar triaxial ways, with specific survival strategies contributing to their particular biological, psychological, and social contents. For instance, in Case 3 (chapter 1), Anne's phobias related to flight responses from dangerous situations in the past. Her paranoia also related to flight responses, this time from dangerous people. Her headaches related to rage associated with a fight response she felt when told of her parents' deaths. Her depressions and propensity to infections related to unresolved grief and possible immune system suppression in maladaptive adaptation. Her low self-esteem included self-blame and shame, reflecting her maladaptive attachment judgments of being unlovable. The wholist perspective enables various symptoms and phenomenological diagnoses to be seen concurrently as refractions from different facets of the same situation. This enhances a unified approach to treatment rather than fragmented symptomatic approaches to the various symptoms.

To summarize, the triaxial framework orientates traumatic stress manifestations, and survival strategies provide their contents. Recognizing the two ingredients can help to make sense of symptoms and illnesses as they arise in vivo, as well as retrospectively.

Enrichment of Concepts on the Triaxial Framework and Categorization of their Contents

Because there exist "only" eight survival strategies and three axes, it is possible to categorize survival strategy manifestations at different triaxial points. In previous chapters, survival strategies were described individually across the triaxial framework, but it is possible to collate them at analogous points. Categorizations are then cross-sectional collations of observations of survival strategies at particular axial points.

A particularly important axial point is acute stress responses on the process axis. Collations of survival strategies at this point, as well as traumas, appraisals, and judgments of worth serve as their categorizations in Table 2.

It is theoretically possible to take any axial point and categorize its contents according to the variety of survival strategies. Examples of categorizations follow for acute stress responses, emotions, morals, meanings, ideologies, and the sacred.

Categorization of Acute Stress Responses   In Table 2, survival strategies categorize acute stress responses according to their adaptive and maladaptive biological, psychological, and social characteristics. It is suggested that this provides an initial framework for the polymorphous acute stress responses in different traumatic situations (chapter 2), which then ramify along the axes. This answers part of the challenge formulated by McFarlane and Yehuda (1995), Solomon et al. (1996), and Brett (1996; chapter 6), who suggested that the primary task for traumatology was to understand and specify the uniqueness and variability of acute traumatic stress responses because they influence later trauma and illnesses. It may be added that adaptive responses also influence later fulfillments.

Vertical columns in Table 2 categorize basic survival emotions and social actions. Their adaptive and maladaptive aspects can be meaningfully contrasted (horizontally) and further honed according to whether they pertain mainly to the body (first line), resources (second line), or their combination (third line). For instance, attachment emotions of being held and cared for, nurtured, and looked after contrast respectively with yearning, need and craving, and abandonment.

It may be possible to also categorize physiological responses according to survival strategies. It stands to reason, for instance, that the physiology of adaptation grief is different from that of fight. However, more refined categorizations of physiological patterns than shown have been hampered because much research has assumed single physiological trauma responses as global markers of trauma, and because such individual markers (such as norepinephrine or cortisol) are used in the patterns of different survival strategies.

Categorization of Acute Stress Responses According to Axes   If the acute stress response point is kept constant, and is allowed to intersect with different points on the other axes, the categorizations in Table 2 may take on different qualities and nuances. For instance, categories of emotions and actions may have different slants at different disaster phases, at different social system levels, or at different developmental phases. Crossed with the latter, stress responses give modulated pleasure and unpleasure feedbacks in adults, but in the earliest developmental phases such naked and intense feedbacks may categorize childhood heavens and hells.

Categorization of Traumas   Categorization of traumatic states is repre-sented in the Trauma responses column in Table 2. Each state has been sepa-rately postulated to be central to trauma, but now they can be seen as specific traumatic states according to which survival strategies have failed. As noted, each traumatic state contains in a condensed manner contributions from each component of the process axis as well as components from the other two axes, all in two-way interactions with each other.

It is suggested that as well as specific unpleasures of maladaptive survival strategy responses, each traumatic state evokes a specific anxiety. They are, respectively, anguish and anxieties of separation, failure, being overwhelmed or giving in, aggression, annihilation, defeat, and disintegration. Like each trau-matic state, each anxiety has at different times been seen as "the" anxiety.

Categorization of Moral Responses   It is suggested that survival strate-gies can be used to categorize the variety and often conflicting nature of depth axis moral judgments of good and bad, worth, and justice (chapter 5). Categori-zations of worth (self-esteem and shame) have already been listed in Table 2 in the Judgments columns. The other moral responses have been collated from previous survival strategy chapters.

Virtues and guilts in the order of survival strategy chapters and Table 2 may be, respectively, self-sacrifice–survivor guilt; obedience–wrongdoing or sin; achievement–failure; adapting–giving in; defense of life–murder; escaping danger–cowardice; taking prize–priority guilt; and generosity–exploitation.

Justice and injustice include, respectively, reaching out to the weak or with-holding life and care; good rewarded and bad punished or good rewarded with bad and bad with good; fulfillment of roles and their promises or failure to fulfill roles and their promises; yield to superior forces or collaboration with the enemy; self-defense or killing of innocents; escape circumstances of annihila-tion or desertion of others; privilege of first access or expropriation of more than one's due; fair share and exchange or abuse of trust.

Survival strategies can help to hone and label different types of moral re-sponses, such as with the term survivor guilt. Survival strategies can also pro-vide a broader categorization of emotions by including moral responses.

Categorization of Basic Meanings   In the survival strategy chapters, basic meanings were described for individuals. Here meanings are categorized according to quips or proverbs applicable to wider social systems.

- Hard times bring out the best in people.
- In hard times, everyone looks after his own.
- If you do the right thing, things go well.
- Bad things happen to good people. (The good die young.)
- One can achieve anything if one sets one's mind to it. (Just do it.)
- There is no point breaking your head against a brick wall.
- It is better to have loved and lost than not to have loved at all.
- Love is dangerous because you only get hurt.
- You have to show strength to not be attacked.
- To be safe, you have to kill them all.
- Stay safe in your zone of security.
- There is no safety in the world.
- One needs to accept one's place in the world.
- The world is a jungle where dog eats dog.
- To love and be loved is the most precious thing in the world.
- To love is to get exploited.

Ideologies   Akin to meanings, philosophers may generalize their individual survival experiences into national or world ideologies. Macchiavelli returned to Caesarism (a contemporary fascism) when the Swiss blitzkrieg ended the dreams of the Renaissance. Hobbes emphasized the need for hierarchy (conservatism) after experiencing the instability of the English Civil Wars. Alternatively, Locke, who had experienced the terrors under the Stuarts, advocated human rights above all. It is suggested that ideologies too may be categorized according to survival strategies. The following are not in the usual order of survival strategies, for ideologies often subsume more than one survival strategy and some survival strategies such as rescue and cooperation are infrequent political ideologies. Nor are ideologies divided into adaptive and maladaptive. The assumption from within ideologies is that they are adaptive, for they are seen to solve prevailing fears of danger and need. However, they easily become maladaptive and traumatic in their simplistic executions.

Caesarism and fascism extol the virtues of assertiveness (strength, will, potency), fight (nationalism, expansion of territories, destruction of enemies), and competition (struggle to superior destiny). Conservatism favors competition, with hierarchy as maintainer of peace. Liberalism and democracy favor free and equal opportunity of contest in trade and contract between rulers and the ruled (competition and cooperation). Communist ideology holds cooperation as its model, where all eventually belongs to the same class and is given and taken generously. The welfare state uses rescue and attachment concepts. Nationalism incorporates fight and flight concepts of defense and safety within one's territory. Zionism heralded Israel as a sanctuary from persecution for Jews.

The Sacred and the Sacrilegious   Even sacredness and sacrilegiousness or perversity may be categorized tentatively. The order of survival strategies in Table 2 is followed again.

The sacred gift of life may be passed on through the generations or from the strong to the weak. However, life may be replaced by barrenness and life feeding on itself. One may be a valued part of the universe through revered providers of life and growth. One may also be cast out by them from the stream of life. One may pass sacred rites of passage and achieve challenges throughout the cycle of one's life. One may also be thwarted, mechanized, or dehumanized. One may be part of the natural rhythms of life, death, and regeneration. But hope and faith may be replaced by despair, desecration, and absurdity. Sacred defense of life may become perverted into its senseless torture and massacre. Sacred territories and sanctuaries are breached for senseless debaucheries. Divine and semidivine hierarchical arrangements with all having a place in the scheme of things may collapse into chaos through corruption and venality of priests, kings, and their delegates. Finally, the creative force of love may be betrayed and defiled by exploitation of its vulnerability and innocence.

It is suggested that categorizations of other depth components such as principles, values, and dignity may be similarly achieved by abstracting their survival strategy contents.

The Language of Traumatic Stress and Fulfillment Phenomena

In addition to subsuming point and linear concepts, the wholist perspective gives trauma and fulfillment responses much increased conceptual scope. Every point on the triaxial framework can potentially carry one or more of eight colors of different shades, or notes of an octave of different intensities. Their manifestations can be doubled through the counterpoints of adaptive and maladaptive (fulfillment and trauma) aspects and trebled through their biological, psychological, and social aspects. Absence of colors and silences representing defenses may be as significant as their presence (avoidance being as important as reliving). Including the other axes with similar multiple possibilities greatly increases the potential permutations and combinations at any triaxial intersection, adding overtones and harmonics to the themes of the symphony.

It is suggested that responses, which are at their starkest and most unambiguous near the trauma, press for linguistic designation, and words allow grasp of otherwise only felt or acted phenomena. It is suggested that experiences in the denser stippled areas in Figure 7 are relatively more clearly delineated by words, whereas in the lightly stippled areas of survival strategy ramifications words tend to be vaguer and more inclusive. It is suggested that the wholist framework may help to clarify concepts and hone nuances throughout the tri-axial framework. The wholist perspective may contribute to a view of the complexity of language and the logic in its ever more complex nuances. It may also increase awareness of specific semantic possibilities. For instance, in time different anxieties, guilts, and so on may be designated by different words.

Language of traumatic stress and language in general may have a deep evolutionary connection. The former is denoted as wholist language, and its translation to common language is shown to have therapeutic implications (Valent, in press, a). Both types of language may be wanting because of developmental lags or energy being devoted to stave off trauma through defenses.

Developmental Lags   It may be that introspective recognition of emotions and their nuances is in a process of evolution, and this is reflected in individual development. For instance, it was noted that depression is not universally recognized or labeled, and emotions may be conveyed through physiological body language, which is sometimes a symptom.

Defenses   Ambiguity of conflicting desires for healing but not to tear apart again is reflected not only in the ripples and troughs of reliving and avoidance of traumatic sequelae, but also in the language of biological, psychological, and social symbols.

Defensive gaps in awareness are associated with much of the symptomatology in traumatology (chapter 6). It may take much dedication and skill to read between the lines and to understand nonverbal and fragmented symbols and symptoms of people's traumas. It is suggested that the wholist perspective provides a means of understanding not only the great variety of stress and trauma responses, but also their disconnections and obfuscations. The wholist perspective can now extend previously described concepts of defenses (chapter 3) by noting disconnections, fragmentations, and substitutions of survival strategies and shifts within and across points of the triaxial framework.

Disconnections and fragmentations of survival strategies can be seen to account for dissociated biological, psychological, and social fragments that have lost connections with their original contexts. However, characteristic survival strategy content of such fragments may be clues to their origins and meaning. For instance, panic, avoidance, and palpitations may indicate clues of an original flight context. If only one or two specific survival strategy fragments present, often questioning reveals further such survival strategy manifestations.

Defensive survival strategy substitutions include substitution of adaptive fantasies for maladaptive and traumatic realities and substitutions of one survival strategy for another. The former may explain the mechanism of splitting, whereas the latter may explain the mechanism of repression. In repression, whole survival strategies and their original traumatic contexts, negative judgments, and unacceptable meanings are kept out of awareness. For instance, overwhelming loss that could lead to adaptation trauma of giving in and succumbing, judgment of weakness and being despicable, and meaning that to love is dangerous may be substituted by its complementary survival strategy of assertiveness, where compulsive work, achievement, and sense of control keep the traumatic alternative at bay. The compulsive nature of apparently adaptive survival strategies can be clues to repressed alternative traumatic survival strategy. Fragmentation, splitting, and repression may be seen as primary defenses, though the latter maintains more connections.

Shifts within and across triaxial points extend secondary defense concepts such as displacement, regression, and sublimation. Replacements of religions and ideologies with one another are examples of displacement shifts within triaxial points. Appeasement of individual problems by joining groups, transfer of anger across time or onto scapegoats, and regression or precocity as means of coping are parameter axis displacements. Defensive shifts along the depth axis may describe sublimation. Examples include appeasement of alienation through religion or ideology or avoidance of disintegration through artistic creativity. Again, the compulsive unhappy nature of the activities provides clues that they cover problematic alternatives.

Defenses may combine. For instance, attachment helplessness may be substituted by rescue occupations, which may be sublimated toward high-level caring professions.

It is suggested that as the wholist perspective lent itself to exploration of language and defenses, it can in a similar vein serve as a perspective to explore other issues, such as love and violence.

Clinical Applications

Only a brief indication can be given of the application of the wholist perspective to trauma and fulfillment therapy whose components (Figure 6) ramify across the triaxial framework. A fuller exposition is provided in a separate book (Valent, in press, a).

Treatment includes expertise in provision of safety, listening to the poetic fragments and metaphors of trauma and fulfillment language, orienting and diagnosing responses on multiple levels and translating them into words, contrasting traumatic responses in the past with potential fulfillment ones in the present, integrating the two into a new wholist perspective, and owning the whole process as one's narrative, within a meaningful and purposeful life.

The wholist perspective can contribute significantly at each step of the process. It may help retrieval of memory or reconstruction of traumatic events by helping to understand the sources and contexts of disconnected traumatic responses, negative judgments, meanings, and ramifications. Specific traumatic content of the past can be contrasted with specific adaptive triaxial survival strategy hopes and fulfillment prospects in the present.

It can be seen that treatment can be extremely complicated, and tailoring needs to be optimal for the conjunction of helper and helped wholist perspectives. For instance, in Case 1 triaxial conjunctions included communities of helpers and communities of bush fire victims over a period of time. In Case 2, the physical symptoms of the parents whose daughter died were in part poetic metaphors representing the stress of the substitute daughter's approach to the age at which the first daughter died. This complex language needed to be heard by people who understood angina, were interested in the tapestry of life, and were aided by a wholist approach. In Case 3, Anne's early and complex problems required intense and complex conjunctions over the range of the wholist perspective within psychotherapy.

Planning and Education

A wholist approach in planning and education such as in emergency and medical services ensures that process axis biopsychosocial responses are anticipated and catered for in all parameters and depths, and that at each triaxial point specific categories of responses are anticipated. At each such point, adaptive survival strategies are facilitated and maladaptive aspects preempted or treated.

For example, in loss situations education and planning may span facilitating adaptive grief and mourning at all social levels for all age groups in all disaster phases and at all depth axis levels. On the latter, suppose one wants to educate and plan to facilitate victim or patient dignity. To do so, adaptive survival strategies on this level are supported. Respectively, victims' own altruism, caretaking, and helping networks are acknowledged and facilitated. At the same time, victims are offered support in a nonpatronizing manner. They are encouraged to be as autonomous as possible. Losses are recognized, and grief and mourning are facilitated with respect. Victims' aggressiveness and fears are also treated with respect, recognizing their validity in the present or as belonging to particular trauma contexts. Previous and current hierarchical positions and status are honored, and the dignity to be able to give and reciprocate is facilitated, even if only with a cup of tea. Broad and detailed planning and education may be applied similarly to other triaxial points.

Lack of a wholist perspective may result in one of the biological, psychological, and social arenas being ignored, families or communities or children and the old being forgotten, and planning for later phases being deficient, or a range of humanist approaches being lost.

Research

Increased Sharpness and Focus of Research Questions   As with symptoms, particular manifestations such as specific emotions or stress compounds may be seen as fragments (not as the traumatic stress marker) whose hypothetical significance may be diagnosed retrospectively by finding their triaxial points and specific survival strategy associations. To confirm this, laboratory situations may need to reproduce the manifestations. To make sure that the particular associations are valid, other triaxial points and survival strategies need to be controlled.

Alternately, the wholist perspective can contribute to abstracting individual meaningful in vivo or prospective observations from among the great variety of responses. For instance, one may inquire what emotions or stress compounds are found in particular disaster phases among particular people (such as widows) when they are psychologically defended against their losses and when they are not, or what positive and negative meanings may occur in the reconstructive phase of particular disasters.

It may be seen, that as with language, the wholist perspective helps to hone and refine research through triaxial and survival strategy specifications.

Further Categorizations and Interests of Various Disciplines   It is suggested that the contents of many other triaxial points may be usefully categorized, according to the interests and professional discipline of the observer. For instance, categorizations of justice at different triaxial points may be of interest to jurisprudence, and categorizations of morals and values may be of interest to those interested in ethics and philosophy. The evolutionary structure of preverbal (wholist) communication may be of interest to linguists.

The framework may help research in those fields. Particular manifestations may be traced retrospectively along the wholist perspective for their significance, or particular fields of observation may be chosen to be categorized. For instance, research into violence may find that hatred and scapegoating are associated with maladaptive fight responses learned as an abused child terrified of bodily destruction. Alternatively, children who suffered such terrors may be followed up to see what survival strategies they use in which circumstances.

In summary, the wholist perspective adds color, music, and a deep meaningful sense to trauma and fulfillment phenomena. In a pragmatic way, it helps both to enrich and specify them and to help fill the gaps in their developments. The perspective reverberates with and explains the world of trauma and fulfillment in such a way that it helps to translate it into understandable significant narrative language. In a sense, it is like a formula that meaningfully connects otherwise disparate information. This formula is applicable to research in traumatology and other disciplines.

Perhaps by giving trauma a language, the wholist perspective ensures that it is not forgotten. At the same time, it replaces it with its complementary vocabulary of fulfillment.

A summary of this chapter is included in the conclusion, which follows.

Chapter 17

Conclusion: From Survival to Fulfillment

Throughout this book, it was noted that trauma encompasses a wide area. As an essential partner in the life–trauma dialectic, trauma was seen to interfere with the purpose of life—to survive and fulfill oneself according to the life cycle and to help others do the same. As such, a study of trauma is almost a study of life.

Other traumatologists have noted the need for wide perspectives. Kleber and Brom (1992, p. 257) said, "Coping with trauma entails a process of attributing meaning to events." Similarly, Herman (1992) noted that a trauma therapist has to be a jurist and a philosopher in the existential encounter with the severely traumatized person. McFarlane and van der Kolk (1996, p. 573) concluded that the experience of trauma "cannot be captured in medical and scientific models, but . . . go[es] to the core of what it is like to be human." They noted that trauma involves intense emotions such as hope, lust and revenge, and moral judgments. These emotions are important because they give personal and social knowledge and existential meaning. It is hoped that this book has provided a framework within which the important experiences of trauma and fulfillment can be meaningfully explored.

The book started with questions about the variable and contradictory nature of stress responses in traumatic situations, as well as the variable backdrops in which they occurred. Three clinical cases illustrated these problems.

Next, different traumatic situations were looked at separately, each one high-lighting special features. For instance, combat soldiers highlighted the vivid reliving of events, whereas childhood sexual abuse victims highlighted distortions in identities, relationships, morality, and values. Dying patients confirmed that it was trauma, not death, that was the counterpoint in the life–trauma dialectic.

The various components of traumatic stress were described along three axes. Components in the process from stressors to illnesses were described as part of the process axis. The parameters describing phases of disasters, social systems, and ages of those affected make up the parameter axis. The depth axis includes human function levels, from the instinctive to the spiritual. Traumas involve all three axes. A triaxial view of trauma illnesses that subsumes the major phenomenological (including PTSD) and dynamic views was presented.

Next, eight survival strategies were described in detail. Survival strategies are specific templates associated with midbrain circuits serving basic biopsychosocial patterns of survival and life-fulfilling responses. Survival strategies were followed through their ramifications of the triaxial framework, akin to following midbrain ramifications into the cerebrum.

The triaxial framework and survival strategies were combined in the wholist perspective. The advantages of the framework are multiple. It includes linear as well as nonlinear scientific paradigms, the latter being particularly applicable to traumatology. The perspective overcomes mind–body dualism within a biopsychosocial view, overcomes reductionist–whole dichotomies within a wholist view, and bridges the scientific–humanist gap.

Application of the wholist perspective in traumatology includes understanding that the wide variety of fluctuating and often contradictory traumatic stress and fulfillment responses are different survival strategy manifestations at different triaxial points. Their sense can be gleaned by tracing them back along the axes to their contexts. The framework allows understanding of what was relived and avoided and why in PTSD and in the wide variety of comorbid illnesses following trauma.

Although maladaptive responses form the foundations of traumatic stress responses, adaptive ones form the foundations for fulfillment responses. Orientation and meaning can be made of the latter just as of the former, and it is possible to note what corresponding fulfillment responses are damaged in trauma.

Contents of triaxial points can be categorized according to survival strategies. Perhaps for the first time, meaningful categorizations were initiated for acute stress responses and their emotional, social, and physiological components and for moral components of good and bad, worth and justice, and other depth axis components such as meanings, ideology, and the sacred.

Ramifications of survival strategies in the depth axis contribute to solution of the conundrum (paralleling responses in traumatology) of the great variability and often contradictory nature of morals, values, principles, and ideologies. Their survival strategy sources also explain the mystery of their naturalness (as in natural law and natural justice), in spite of their variability and seemingly paradoxical contradictions. The relativity of higher function-level contents stemming from variable circumstances and different survival needs does not detract from their spiritual value or fulfillment of the soul. Their value may increase through added understanding and wisdom.

Such wisdom may have pragmatic clinical applications in trauma treatment, planning and education, and research.

Last, the dialectic of life and trauma was seen to use a complex language. Its defensive obfuscations and symbolism reflect the ambiguity of the desire for communication for the sake of healing and hiding communication for the sake of mitigating and avoiding repetition of traumas. Symptoms and illnesses arise in compromise equilibria arising from such ambiguities. However, it is suggested that maintenance of such illnesses when circumstances have changed to normal is the basic irrationality in the maintenance of trauma sequelae. It is nature's appendix in traumatology, which can cause unnecessary trouble. The essence of trauma treatment is to understand the language and meaning of trauma and in safety reverse this irrationality. This may be a complex process that uses variable scientific knowledge, often supplemented intuitively by helpers using their wholist selves. However, conscious use of the wholist framework may enhance such treatment. This is explored in a separate volume (Valent, in press, a).

Historically, perhaps for the first time there is sufficient critical mass of sustained well-being for the high frequency of trauma to be able to be acknowledged and not be suppressed. There may be sufficient hope to be able to look at the widespread trauma of body, mind, spirit, and soul. The life–trauma dialectic may be recognized more widely and fruitfully.

The wholist framework requires much discussion and research. In a way, a first, wide brush painted a picture that needs much questioning, refinement, and testing. However, it is hoped that it may add to the critical mass of realistic hope and tilt the balance a little from survival to fulfillment.

References

Abramson, L. Y., Garber, J., & Seligman, M. (1980). In J. Garber & M. Seligman (Eds.), *Human helplessness*. New York: Academic Press.

Ader, R. (1980). Psychosomatic and psychoimmunologic research. *Psychosomatic medicine, 42*, 307–321.

Alexander, F. (1950). *Psychosomatic medicine*. New York: Norton.

Allen, J. G. (1995). *Coping with trauma*. Washington, DC: American Psychiatric Press.

American Psychiatric Association. (1980). *Diagnostic and statistical manual of mental disorders*. Washington, DC: Author.

American Psychiatric Association. (1987). *Diagnostic and statistical manual of mental disorders* (3rd ed., rev.). Washington, DC: Author.

American Psychiatric Association. (1994). *Diagnostic and statistical manual of mental disorders* (4th ed.). Washington, DC: Author.

Appel, J. W., & Beebe, G. W. (1946). Preventive psychiatry. *Journal of the American Medical Association, 131*, 1469–1475.

Appels, A., & Mulder, P. (1989). Fatigue and heart disease. The association between "vital exhaustion" and past, present and future coronary heart disease. *Journal of Psychosomatic Research, 33*, 727–738.

Ardrey, R. (1967). *The territorial imperative. A personal inquiry into the animal origins of property and nations*. London: Collins.

Ardrey, R. (1976). *The hunting hypothesis*. London: Collins.

Arendt, H. (1963). *Eichmann in Jerusalem*. New York: Penguin.

Aristotle. (1988). Nicomachean ethics (Trans., W. D. Ross). In *Brittanica Great Books* (Volume 9, pp. 339–444). Chicago: William Benton.

Asch, S. E. (1952). *Social psychology*. New York: Prentice Hall.

Athens, L. H. (1989). *The creation of dangerous violent criminals*. London: Routledge.

Baker, H. S., & Baker, M. N. (1987). Heinz Kohut's self psychology: An overview. *American Journal of Psychiatry, 144*, 1–9

Baldessarini, R. J. (1975). An overview of the basis for amine hypotheses in affective illness. In J. Mendels (Ed.), *The psychobiology of depression* (pp. 69–83). New York: Spectrum.

Balint, E. (1963). On being empty of oneself. *International Journal of Psycho-Analysis, 44*, 470–480.

Barefoot, J. C., Dodge, K. A., Peterson, B. L., Dahlstrom, W. G., & Williams, X. B. (1989). The Cook-Medley hostility scale: Item content and ability to predict survival. *Psychosomatic Medicine, 51*, 46–57.

Bar-On, D. (1990). The use of a limited personal morality to rationalize horrendous evil: Interviews with an Auschwitz doctor and his son. *Journal of Traumatic Stress, 3*, 415–428.

Bartemeier, L. H., Kubie, L. S., Menninger, K. A., Romano, J., & Whitehorn, J. C. (1946). Combat exhaustion. *Journal of Nervous and Mental Disease, 104*, 358–389.

Bartrop, R. W., Lazarus, L., Luckhurst, E., Kiloh, I. G., & Penny, R. (1977). Depressed lymphocyte function after bereavement. *Lancet, 1*, 834–836.

Batson, C. D., Darley, J. M., & Coke, J. S. (1978). Altruism and human kindness; internal and external determinants of helping behavior. In L. A. Pervin & M. Lewis (Eds.), *Perspectives in interactional psychology* (pp. 11–140). New York: Plenum Press.

Bauer, M., Priebe, S., Häring, B., & Adamczak, K. (1993). Long-term sequelae of political imprisonment in East Germany. *Journal of Nervous and Mental Disease, 181*, 257–262.

Bayles, M. D., & Henley, K. (Eds.). (1983). *Right conduct: Theories and applications.* New York: Random House.

Beaton, R. D., & Murphy, S. A. (1995). Working with people in crisis: Research implications. In C. R Figley (Ed.), *Compassion fatigue: Secondary traumatic stress disorder in helpers* (pp. 51–81). New York: Brunner/Mazel.

Beck A. T., Rush A. J., Shaw, B. F., and Emery, G. (1979). *Cognitive therapy of depression.* New York: Guilford Press.

Becker, E. (1973). *The denial of death.* New York: Free Press.

Beebe, G. W. (1975). Follow-up studies of World War II and Korean War prisoners. *Journal of Epidemiology, 101*, 400–422.

Benedict, R. (1963). *Patterns of culture.* London: Routledge & Kegan Paul.

Bennet, G. (1970). Bristol floods 1968. Controlled survey of effects on health of local community disaster. *British Medical Journal, 3*, 454–458.

Bennett, A. E. (1969). Psychiatric and neurologic problems in head injury with medicolegal implications. *Diseases of the Nervous System, 30*, 314–317.

Benyakar, M., Kutz, I., Dasberg, H., & Stern, M. J. (1989). The collapse of a structure: A structural approach to trauma. *Journal of Traumatic Stress, 2*, 431–449.

Berah, E., Jones, H. J., & Valent, P. (1984). The experience of a mental health team involved in the early phase of a disaster. *Australian and New Zealand Journal of Psychiatry, 18*, 354–358.

Bergland, R. (1985). *Fabric of the mind.* London: Penguin.

Bergman, M. S., & Jucovy, M. E. (Eds.). (1982). *Generations of the Holocaust.* New York: Columbia University Press.

Bernard, C. (1930). *Lecons sur les phenomenes de la vie communs aux animaux et aux vegetaux* [Findings on manifestations of life common to animals and vegetables]. In J. F. Fulton (Trans.), *Selected readings in the history of physiology.* Springfield, IL: Charles C Thomas. (Original published 1878)

Bettelheim, B. (1943). Individual and mass behaviour in extreme situations. *The Journal of Abnormal and Social Psychology, 38*, 417–452.

Bettelheim, B. (1960). *The informed heart.* City, IL: Free Press of Glencoe.

Bey, D. R., & Zecchinelli, V. A. (1974). G.I.s against themselves—Factors resulting in explosive violence in Vietnam. *Psychiatry, 37*, 221–227.

Bion, W. R. (1961). *Experiences in groups.* London: Tavistock.

Bion, W. R. (1962). The psycho-analytic study of thinking. *International Journal of Psychoanalysis, 43*, 306–310.

Blanchard, D. C., & Blanchard, R. J. (1988). Ethoexperimental approaches to the biology of emotion. *Annual Review of Psychology, 39*, 43–68.

Blank, A. S. (1993). Suggested recommendations for DSM-IV on course and subtypes. In J. R. T. Davidson & E. B. Foa (Eds.), *Posttraumatic stress disorder: DSM-IV and beyond* (pp. 237–240). Washington, DC: American Psychiatric Press.

Bloch, D. A., Silber, E., & Perry, S. E. (1956). Some factors in the emotional reaction of children to disaster. *American Journal of Psychiatry, 113*.

Bloch, H. S. (1970). The psychological adjustment of normal people during a year's tour in Vietnam. *Psychiatric Quarterly, 44*, 613–626.

Boman, B. (1982a). Psychosocial stress and ischaemic heart disease: A response to Tennant. *Australian and New Zealand Journal of Psychiatry, 16,* 265–278.

Boman, B. (1982b). The Vietnam veteran ten years on. *Australian and New Zealand Journal of Psychiatry, 16,* 107–127.

Booth, A., Shelley, G., & Mazur, A. (1990). Testosterone, and winning and losing in human competition. *Journal of Cell Biology, 110,* 43–52.

Bourne, P. G. (1969). Urinary 17-OHCS levels in two combat situations. In P. G. Bourne (Ed.), *The psychology and physiology of stress* (pp. 95–116). New York: Academic Press.

Bourne, P. G. (1970). Psychological aspects of combat. In H. S. Abram & C. C. Thomas (Eds.), *Psychological aspects of stress* (pp. 70–85). Springfield, IL: Charles Thomas.

Bourne, P. G., Rose, R. M., & Mason, J. W. (1967). Urinary 17-OHCS levels. *Archives of General Psychiatry, 17,* 104–10.

Bourne, P. G., Rose, R. M., & Mason, J. W. (1968). 17-OHCS levels on combat special forces "A" team under threat of attack. *Archives of General Psychiatry, 19,* 135–140.

Bowlby, J. (1971). *Attachment and loss: Vol. 1. Attachment.* Harmondsworth, England: Pelican.

Bowlby, J. (1975). *Attachment and loss: Vol. 2. Separation.* Harmondsworth, England: Pelican.

Bowlby, J. (1981). *Attachment and loss: Vol. 3. Loss: Sadness and depression.* New York: Penguin.

Brainerd, C. J. (1978). *Piaget's theory of intelligence.* Englewood Cliffs, NJ: Prentice Hall.

Braun, B. G. (1993). Multiple personality disorder and posttraumatic stress disorder. In J. Wilson & B. Raphael (Eds.), *International handbook of traumatic stress syndrome* (pp. 35–48). New York: Plenum Press.

Bremner, J. D., Krystal, J. H., Southwick, S. M., & Charney, D. S. (1995). Functional neuroanatomical correlates of the effects of stress on memory. *Journal of Traumatic Stress, 8*(4), 527–554.

Brende, J. O. (1983). A psychodynamic view of character pathology in Vietnam combat veterans. *Bulletin of the Menninger Clinic, 47*(3), 193–216.

Brett, E. A. (1996). The classification of posttraumatic stress disorder. In B. A. Van der Kolk, A. C. McFarlane, & L. Weisath (Eds.), *Traumatic stress: The effects of overwhelming experience on mind, body, and society* (pp. 117–128). New York: Guilford.

Breuer, J., & Freud, S. (1975). Studies in hysteria. In J. Strachey (Ed.), *The standard edition of the complete psychological works of Sigmund Freud* (Vol. 2, pp. ix–251). London: Hogarth Press. (Original published 1895)

Brown, N. O. (1968). *Life against death.* London: Sphere Books.

Browning, C. R. (1992). *Ordinary men: Reserve Police Battalion 101 and the final solution in Poland.* New York: Harper Perennial.

Burges Watson, I. P., Muller, H. K., Jones, I. H., & Bradley, A. J. (1993). Cell-mediated immunity in combat veterans with post-traumatic stress disorder. *Medical Journal of Australia, 159,* 513–516.

Burgess, A. W., & Holstrom, L. (1974). Rape trauma syndrome. *American Journal of Psychiatry, 131,* 981–986.

Burnett, P., Middleton, W., Raphael, B., Dunne, M., Moylan, A., & Martinek, N. (1994). Concepts of normal bereavement. *Journal of Traumatic Stress, 7,* 123–128.

Burton, D., Foy, D., Bwanausi, C., Johnson, J., & Moore, L. (1994). The relationship between traumatic exposure, family dysfunction, and post-traumatic stress symptoms in male juvenile offenders. *Journal of Traumatic Stress, 7,* 83–94.

Bychowski, G. (1968). Permanent character changes as an aftereffect of persecution. In H. Krystal (Ed.), *Massive psychic trauma* (pp. 75–86). New York: International Universities Press.

Calabrese, J. R., Kling, M. A., & Gold, P. W. (1987). Alterations in immunocompetence during stress, bereavement, and depression: Focus on neuroendocrine regulation. *American Journal of Psychiatry, 144,* 1123–1134.

Campbell, D. (1994). *Voices from the silence.* Castle Hill, New South Wales, Australia: Shofarot.

Camus, A. (1961). *The outsider.* Harmondsworth, England: Penguin.

Canetti, E. (1973). *Crowds and power.* Harmondsworth, England: Penguin.

Cannon, W. B. (1939). *The wisdom of the body.* New York: Norton.

Cannon, W. B. (1963). *Bodily change in pain, hunger, fear, and rage.* London: Appleton.

Caplan, G. (1964). *Principles of preventive psychiatry.* New York: Basic Books.

Cass, E. L., & Zimmer, F. G. (1975). The Hawthorne studies: A synopsis. In E. L. Cass & F. G. Zimmer (Eds.), *Man and work in society* (pp. 278–306). New York: Van Nostrand Reinhold.

Chan, A. W. K. (1987). Factors affecting the drinking driver. *Drug and Alcohol Dependence, 19,* 99–119.

Chodoff, P. (1970). The German concentration camp. *Archives of General Psychiatry, 22,* 78–87.

Christie, G. L. (1969). Falling in love and infatuation. *Australian and New Zealand Journal of Psychiatry, 3,* 17–21

Cobb, S., & Lindemann, E. (1943). Neuropsychiatric observations during the Cocoanut Grove fire. *Annals of Surgery, 117,* 814–824.

Coe, C. L., Lubach, G., & Ershler, W. B. (1989). Immunological consequences of maternal separation in infant primates. *New Directions for Child Development, 45,* 65–91.

Coe, C. L., Wiener, S. G., Rosenberg, L. T., Levine, S. (1985). Endocrine and immune responses to separation and maternal loss in nonhuman primates. In M. Reite & T. Field (Eds.), *The psychobiology of attachment and separation* (pp. 163–200). New York: Academic Press.

Cohen, F. (1981). Stress and bodily illness. *Psychiatric Clinics of North America, 4,* 269–286.

Collins, J. J., & Bailey, S. L. (1990). Traumatic stress disorder and violent behavior. *Journal of Traumatic Stress, 3,* 203–220.

Craighill, M. D. (1954). Psychiatric aspects of women serving in the army. In D. C. Nolan, L. Engle, & B. Engle (Eds.), *Wartime psychiatry: A compendium of the international literature.* New York: Oxford University Press. (Original published 1948)

Crutchfield, R. S. (1955). Conformity and character. *American Psychologist, 10,* 191.

Cummings, E. M., Hollenbeck, B., & Ianotti, R. (1986). Early organization of altruism and aggression: Developmental patterns and individual differences. In C. Zahn-Waxler, E. M. Cummings, & R. Ianotti (Eds.), *Altruism and aggression (biological and social origins)* (pp. 165–188). Cambridge, England: Cambridge University Press.

Czikszentmihalyi, M., & Rathunde, K. (1993). The psychology of wisdom: An evolutionary interpretation. In R. J. Sternberg (Ed.), *Wisdom: Its nature, origins, and development* (pp. 25–51). New York: Cambridge University Press.

Dabbs, J. M. Jr., Frady, R. L., Carr, T. S., & Besch, N. F. (1987). Saliva testosterone and criminal violence in young adult prison inmates. *Psychosomatic Medicine, 49,* 174–182.

Da Costa, J. M. (1871). On irritable heart: A clinical case study of a form of functional cardiac disorder and its consequences. *American Journal of Medical Science, 16,* 17–52.

Darwin, C. (1965). *The expressions of the emotions in man and animals.* Chicago: University of Chicago Press. (Original published 1872)

Darwin, C. (1974). *The origin of species.* Pelican/Penguin. (Original published 1859)

Dasberg, H. (1976). Belonging and loneliness in relation to mental breakdown in battle. *Israeli Annals of Psychiatry, 14,* 307–321.

Davidson, L. M., Fleming, I., & Baum, A. (1986). Post-traumatic stress as a function of chronic stress and toxic exposure. In C. R. Figley (Ed.), *Trauma and its wake. Vol. II: Traumatic stress theory, research, and intervention* (pp. 57–77). New York: Brunner/Mazel.

Davies, P. (1984). *Superforce: The search for a grand unified theory of nature.* Boston: Unwin Paperbacks.

De Board, R. (1978). *The psychoanalysis of organizations.* London: Tavistock.

DeFazio, V. J. (1978). Dynamic perspectives on the nature and effects of combat stress. In C. R. Figley (Ed.), *Stress disorders among Vietnam veterans* (pp. 23–42). New York: Brunner/Mazel.

Dengerink, H. A. (1976). Personality variables as mediators of attack-instigated aggression. In R. G. Geen & E. C. O'Neal (Eds.), *Perspectives on aggression* (pp. 61–98). New York: Academic Press.

Deutsch, H. (1937). Absence of grief. *Psychoanalytic Quarterly, 6*, 12–22.

Dicks, H. V. (1972). *Licensed mass murder: A sociopsychological study of some SS killers.* London: Tavistock.

Dienstbier, R. A. (1989). Arousal and physiological toughness: Implications for mental and physical health. *Psychological Review, 96*, 84–100.

Dimsdale, J. E. (1974). The coping behaviour of Nazi concentration camp survivors. *American Journal of Psychiatry, 131*, 792–797.

Dixon, A. K., & Kaesermann, H. P. (1987). Ethopharmacology of flight behaviour. In B. Olivier, J. Mos, & P. F. Brain, *Ethopharmacology of agonistic behaviour in animals and humans.* (pp. 46–79). Dordrecht, The Netherlands: Nijhoff.

Dollard, J., & Miller, N. E. (1950). *Personality and psychotherapy: An analysis in terms of learning, thinking and culture.* New York: McGraw-Hill.

Donovan, D. M. (1991). Traumatology: A field whose time has come. *Journal of Traumatic Stress, 4*, 433–437.

Donovan, D. M. (1993). Traumatology: What's in a name? *Journal of Traumatic Stress, 6*, 409–412.

Donovan, D. M., Marlatt, G. A., & Salzberg, P. (1983). Drinking behaviour, personality factors and high-risk driving: A review and theoretical formulation. *Journal of Studies on Alcohol, 44*, 395–428.

Dubos, R. (1968). *Man, medicine and environment.* London: Pall Mall Press.

Dunbar, R. (1985). The sociobiology of war. *Medicine and War, 1*, 169–176.

Dunn, W. H. (1942). Gastroinduodenal disorders: An important wartime medical problem. *War Medicine. 2*, 967–983.

Dutton, M. A., Burghardt, K. J., Perrin, S. G., Chrestman, K. R., & Halle, P. M. (1994). Battered women's cognitive schemata. *Journal of Traumatic Stress, 7*, 237–256.

Dwork, D. (1991). *Children with a star: Jewish youth in Nazi Europe.* New Haven, CT: Yale University Press.

Dynes, R. R., & Quarantelli, E. L. (1976). The family and community context of individual reactions to disaster. In H. Parad, H. L. P. Resnik, & L. G. Parad (Eds.), *Emergency and disaster management* (pp. 231–244). Bowie, MD: Charles Press.

Dyregrov, A., & Raundalen, M. (1992, June). *The impact of the Gulf War on children in Iraq.* Paper presented at the World Conference of the International Society for Traumatic Stress Studies, Amsterdam.

Editorial comment. (1992). Acute psychological stressors and short-term immune changes: What, why, for whom, and to what extent? *Psychosomatic Medicine, 54*, 680–685.

Eibl-Eibesfeldt, I. (1980). Strategies of social interaction. In R. Plutchik & H. Kellerman (Eds.), *Emotion: Theory, research and experience* (Vol. 3, pp. 57–80). New York: Academic Press.

Eisdorfer, C. (1985). The conceptualization of stress and a model for further study. In M. R. Zales (Ed.), *Stress in health and disease* (pp. 5–23). New York: Brunner/Mazel.

Eitinger, L. (1973). A follow-up study of the Norwegian concentration camp survivors' mortality and morbidity. *Israel Annals of Psychiatry and Related Disciplines, 2*, 199–209.

Ejiofo-Mbanefo, S. (1971). The effect of crisis on the mental health of a community (Onitsha). *Journal of the Royal College of General Practitioners, 21*, 102.

Elliott, D. M., & Briere, J. (1995). Posttraumatic stress associated with delayed recall of sexual abuse: A general population study. *Journal of Traumatic Stress, 8*, 629–648.

Ellis, P. S. (1984). The origins of the war neuroses. *Journal of the Royal Navy Medical Service, 70*, 168–177.

Emery, V. O., Emery, P. E., Shama, D. K., Quiana, N. A., & Jassani, A. K. (1991). Predisposing variables in PTSD patients. *Journal of Traumatic Stress, 4*, 325–343.

Engel, G. L.(1961). Is grief a disease? *Psychosomatic Medicine, 23*, 18–22.

Engel, G. L. (1977). The need for a new medical model: A challenge for biomedicine. *Science, 196*, 129–135.

Engel, G. L., & Reichsman, F. (1956). Spontaneous and experimentally induced depressions in an infant with a gastric fistula. *American Psychoanalytic Association Journal, 4,* 428–452.

Engel, G. L., & Schmale, A. H. (1972). Conservation-withdrawal: A primary regulatory process for organismic homeostasis. In *Ciba Foundation Symposium: Physiology of emotion and psychosomatic illness* (pp. 57–85). New York: Elsevier.

Epstein, H. (1979). *Children of the Holocaust.* New York: Penguin.

Epstein, S. H. (1944). War neurosis. *New England Journal of Medicine, 231,* 447–449.

Erichsen, J. E. (1866). *On railway and other injuries of the nervous system.* London: Walton & Moberly.

Erikson, E. H. (1965). *Childhood and society.* Harmondsworth, England: Penguin.

Esser, A. H., & Deutsch, R. D. (1977). Private and interaction territories on psychiatric wards: Studies on nonverbal communication of spatial needs. In M. T. McGuire & L. A. Fairbanks (Eds.) *Ethological psychiatry: Psychopathology in the context of evolutionary biology* (pp. 127–152). New York: Grune & Stratton.

Eth, S., & Pynoos, R. S. (1985). Interaction of trauma and grief in childhood. In S. Eth & R. S. Pynoos (Eds.), *PTSD in children.* Washington, DC: American Psychiatric Press.

Evans-Pritchard, E. E. (1967). The morphology and function of magic: A comparative study of Trobriand and Zande rituals and spells. In J. Middleton (Ed.), *Magic, witchcraft and curing* (pp. 1–22). New York: Natural History Press.

Everly, G. S. (1995). Psychotraumatology. In G. S. Everly & J. M. Lating (Eds.), *Psychotraumatology: Keypapers and concepts in post-traumatic stress* (pp. 3–8). New York: Plenum Press

Field, T., & Reite, M. (1985). The psychobiology of attachment and separation: A summary. In M. Reite & T. Field (Eds), *The psychobiology of attachment and separation* (pp. 455–480). New York: Academic Press.

Figley, C. R. (1978). Psychosocial adjustment among Vietnam veterans: An overview of the research. In C. R. Figley (Ed.), *Stress disorders among Vietnam veterans* (pp. 57–70). New York: Brunner/Mazel.

Figley, C. R. (1985). Introduction. In C. R. Figley (Ed.), *Trauma and its wake: The study and treatment of post-traumatic stress disorder* (pp. xvii–xxvi). New York: Brunner/Mazel.

Figley, C. R. (1988). Introductory statement. *Journal of Traumatic Stress, 1,* 1–2.

Figley, C. R. (1995a). Compassion fatigue as secondary traumatic stress disorder: An overview. In C. R . Figley (Ed.), *Compassion fatigue: Secondary traumatic stress disorder in helpers* (pp. 1–20). New York: Brunner/Mazel.

Figley, C .R. (Ed.). (1995b). *Compassion fatigue: Coping with secondary traumatic stress disorder in those who treat the traumatized.* New York: Brunner/Mazel.

Finkelhor, D. (1986). *A sourcebook on child sexual abuse.* London: Sage.

Finnis, J. (1980). *Natural law and natural rights.* Oxford, England: Clarendon Press.

Flannery, R. B. (1987). From victim to survivor: A stress management approach in the treatment of learned helplessness. In B. A. van der Kolk (Ed.), *Psychological trauma* (pp. 217–232). Washington, DC: American Psychiatric Press.

Fleming, A. S., & Anderson, V. (1987). Affect and nuturance: Mechanisms mediating maternal behavior in two female mammals. *Progressive Neuro-Psychopharmacology and Biological Psychiatry, 11,* 121–127.

Fleshner, M., Laudenslager, M. L., Simons, L., & Maier, S. F. (1989). Reduced serum antibodies associated with social defeat in rats. *Physiology and Behavior, 45,* 1183–1187.

Foa, E. B., Molnar, C., & Cashman, L. (1995). Change in rape narratives during exposure therapy for posttraumatic stress disorder. *Journal of Traumatic Stress, 8,* 675–690.

Folks, D. G., & Kinney, F. C. (1992). The role of psychological factors in gastrointestinal conditions. *Psychosomatics,* 33(3), 257–270.

Folks, D. G., & Kinney, F. C. (1995). Gastrointestinal conditions. In A. Stoudemire (Ed.), *Psychological factors affecting medical conditions* (pp. 99–122). Washington, DC: American Psychiatric Press.

Fornari, F. (1975). *The psychoanalysis of war.* London: Doubleday.

Fox, D. (1974). Narcissistic rage and the problem of combat aggression. *Archives of General Psychiatry, 31,* 807–811.

Frankenhaeuser, M. (1980). Psychoneuroendocrine approaches to the study of stressful person-environment transactions. In H. Selye (Ed.), *Selye's guide to stress research* (Vol. 2, pp. 46–70). New York: Van Nostrand Reinhold.

Frankl, V. E. (1959). *From death camp to existentialism.* Boston: International Universities Press/ Beacon Press.

Frederick, C. (1984). Children traumatised by catastrophic situations. In S. Eth & R. S. Pynoos (Eds.), *Post-traumatic stress disorder in children* (pp. 71–100). Washington, DC: American Psychiatric Press.

Freud, A. (1936). *The writings of Anna Freud, Vol. 2: The ego and the mechanisms of defense.* New York: International Universities Press.

Freud, S. (1975a). Extracts from the Fliess papers: Letter 69 to Fliess. In J. Strachey (Ed. and Trans.), *The standard edition of the complete psychological works of Sigmund Freud* (Vol. 1). London: Hogarth Press. (Original published in 1897)

Freud, S. (1975b). The aetiology of hysteria. In J. Strachey (Ed. and Trans.), *The standard edition of the complete psychological works of Sigmund Freud* (Vol. 3). London: Hogarth Press. (Original published in 1896)

Freud, S. (1975c). Beyond the pleasure principle. In J. Strachey (Ed. and Trans.), *The standard edition of the complete psychological works of Sigmund Freud* (Vol. 18). London: Hogarth Press. (Original published in 1920)

Freud, S. (1975d). The case of Schreber. In J. Strachey (Ed. and Trans.), *The standard edition of the complete psychological works of Sigmund Freud* (Vol. 12). London: Hogarth Press. (Original published in 1911)

Freud, S. (1975e). The future of an illusion. In J. Strachey (Ed. and Trans.), *The standard edition of the complete psychological works of Sigmund Freud* (Vol. 21). London: Hogarth Press. (Original published in 1927)

Freud, S. (1975f). Group psychology. In J. Strachey (Ed. and Trans.), *The standard edition of the complete psychological works of Sigmund Freud* (Vol. 18). London: Hogarth Press. (Original published in 1921)

Freud, S. (1975g). Hysteria. In J. Strachey (Ed. and Trans.), *The standard edition of the complete psychological works of Sigmund Freud* (Vol. 1). London: Hogarth Press. (Original published in 1888).

Freud, S. (1975h). Inhibitions, symptoms, and anxiety. In J. Strachey (Ed. and Trans.), *The standard edition of the complete psychological works of Sigmund Freud* (Vol. 20). London: Hogarth Press. (Original published in 1926)

Freud, S. (1975i) Introduction to psycho-analysis and the war neuroses. In J. Strachey (Ed. and Trans.), *The standard edition of the complete psychological works of Sigmund Freud* (Vol. 17, pp. 205–210). London: Hogarth Press. (Original published in 1919)

Freud, S. (1975j). Little Hans. In J. Strachey (Ed. and Trans.), *The standard edition of the complete psychological works of Sigmund Freud* (Vol. 10). London: Hogarth Press. (Original published in 1915)

Freud, S. (1975k). Mourning and melancholia. In J. Strachey (Ed. and Trans.), *The standard edition of the complete psychological works of Sigmund Freud* (Vol. 14). London: Hogarth Press. (Original published in 1917)

Freud, S. (1975l). The neuro-psychoses of defence. In J. Strachey (Ed. and Trans.), *The standard edition of the complete psychological works of Sigmund Freud* (Vol. 3). London: Hogarth Press. (Original published in 1894).

Freud, S. (1975m). An outline of psychoanalysis. In J. Strachey (Ed. and Trans.), *The standard edition of the complete psychological works of Sigmund Freud* (Vol. 23). London: Hogarth Press. (Original published in 1940)

Freud, S. (1975n). Report of my studies in Paris and Berlin. In J. Strachey (Ed. and Trans.), *The standard edition of the complete psychological works of Sigmund Freud* (Vol. 1, 3–15). London: Hogarth Press. (Original published in 1886)

Freud, S. (1975o). Sexuality in the neuroses. In J. Strachey (Ed. and Trans.), *The standard edition of the complete psychological works of Sigmund Freud* (Vol. 7). London: Hogarth Press. (Original published in 1906)

Freud, S. (1975p). Studies on hysteria. In J. Strachey (Ed. and Trans.), *The standard edition of the complete psychological works of Sigmund Freud* (Vol. 2). London: Hogarth Press. (Original published in 1893).

Freud, S. (1975q). Three essays on the theory of sexuality. In J. Strachey (Ed. and Trans.), *The standard edition of the complete psychological works of Sigmund Freud* (Vol. 7). London: Hogarth Press. (Original published in 1905)

Friedman, M. J. (1991). Biological approaches to the diagnosis and treatment of post-traumatic stress disorder. *Journal of Traumatic Stress, 4*(1), 67–91.

Friedman, M. J., & Rosenman, R. H. (1959). Association of specific overt behavior pattern with blood and cardiovascular findings. *Journal of American Medical Association, 169*(12), 1286–1294.

Friedrich, O. (1981). The kingdom of Auschwitz. *Atlantic Monthly,* Sept., 30–60.

Fromm, E. (1973). *The anatomy of human destructiveness.* New York: Penguin.

Fullerton, C. S., & Ursano, R. J. (1997). The other side of chaos: Understanding the patterns of posttraumatic responses. In C. S. Fullerton & R. J. Ursano (Eds*.), Posttraumatic stress disorder: Acute and long-term responses to trauma and disaster* (pp. 3–18). Washington, DC: American Psychiatric Press.

Futterman, S., & Pumpian-Mindlin, E. (1951). Traumatic war neuroses five years later. *American Journal of Psychiatry, 108,* 401–408.

Gaarder, J. (1994). *Sophie's world: An adventure in philosophy.* London: Phoenix House.

Garber, J., & Seligman, M. (Eds.). (1980). *Human helplessness.* New York: Academic Press.

Geen, R. G. (1976). The study of aggression. In R. G. Geen & E. C. O'Neal (Eds.), *Perspectives on aggression* (pp. 1–10). New York: Academic Press.

Gellhorn, E. (1970). The emotions and the ergotropic and trophotropic systems. *Psychologische Forschung, 34,* 48–94.

Gersons, B. P. R. (1989). Patterns of PTSD among police officers following shooting incidents: A two-dimensional model and treatment implications. *Journal of Traumatic Stress, 2,* 247–258.

Gibbon, E. (1978). *History of the Roman Empire.* London: Chatto & Windus.

Gibbs, M. S. (1989). Factors in the victim that mediate between disaster and psychopathology: A review. *Journal of Traumatic Stress, 2*(4), 489–514.

Gibran, K. (1972). *The prophet.* London: Heinemann.

Gilman, T. T., & Marcuse, F. L. (1942). Animal hypnosis. *Psychological Bulletin, 46,* 151–165.

Glass, A. J. (1959). Psychological aspects of disaster. *Journal of American Medical Association, 171,* 222–225.

Glass, A. J. (1966). Army psychiatry before World War II. In R. S. Anderson, A. J. Glass, & R. J. Bernucci (Eds), *Neuropsychiatry in World War II* (Vol. I, pp. 3–23). Washington, DC: Office of the Surgeon General, Department of the Army.

Gleick, J. (1987). *Chaos: Making a new science.* New York: Penguin.

Glover, H. (1992). Emotional numbing: A possible endorphin-mediated phenomenon associated with post-traumatic stress disorders and other allied psychopathologic states. *Journal of Traumatic Stress, 5,* 643–675.

Goldhagen, D. J. (1996). *Hitler's willing executioners: Ordinary Germans and the Holocaust.* London: Abacus.

Goldstein, M. G., & Niaura, R. (1992). Psychological factors affecting physical condition. *Psychosomatics, 33,* 134–145.

Goldstein, M. G., & Niaura, R. (1995). Cardiovascular disease, Part I and II. In A. Stoudemire

(Ed.), *Psychological factors affecting medical conditions* (pp. 19–56). Washington, DC: American Psychiatric Press.

Good News Bible: Today's English Version. New York: American Bible Society.

Goodall, J. (1988). *In the shadow of man.* London: Weidenfeld & Nicolson.

Gordon, R., & Wraith, R. (1993). Responses of children and adolescents to disaster. In J. Wilson & B. Raphael (Eds.), *International handbook of traumatic stress syndromes* (pp. 561–576). New York: Plenum Press.

Goulston, K. J., Dent, O. F., Chapais, P. H., Chapman, G., Smith, C. I., Tait, A. D., & Tennant, C. C. (1985). Gastrointestinal morbidity among World War II prisoners of war: 40 years on. *Medical Journal of Australia, 143,* 6–10.

Green, A. H. (1985). Children traumatized by physical abuse. In. S. Eth & R. S. Pynoos (Eds), *Post-traumatic stress disorder in children* (pp. 133–154). Washington, DC: American Psychiatric Press.

Greenson, R. (1953). On boredom. *Journal of the American Psychoanalytic Association, 1,* 7–21.

Grinker, R. R., & Spiegel, J. P. (1945). *Men under stress.* New York: Irvington.

Grossarth-Maticek, R., Kanazir, D. T., Schmidt, P., & Vetter, H. (1982). Psychosomatic factors in the process of cancerogenesis. *Psychotherapy and Psychosomatics, 38,* 284–302.

Guntrip, H. (1973). *Psychoanalytic theory, therapy, and the self.* New York: Basic Books.

Haley, S. A. (1974). When the patient reports atrocities: Specific treatment considerations of the Vietnam Veteran. *Archives of General Psychiatry, 30,* 191–196.

Hall, J. (1960). *General principles of criminal law.* New York: Bobbs Merril.

Halliday, T. R. (1981). Sexual behavior and group cohesion. In H. Kellerman (Ed.), *Group cohesion: Theoretical and clinical perspectives* (pp. 170–189). New York: Grune & Stratton.

Hanson, F. R. (1949). The factor of fatigue in the neuroses of combat. In F. R. Hanson (Ed.), *Combat psychiatry.* Washington, DC: U.S. Government Printing Office.

Harkness, L. L. (1993). Transgenerational transmission of war-related trauma. In J. Wilson & B. Raphael (Eds.), *International handbook of traumatic stress syndromes* (pp. 635–644). New York: Plenum Press.

Hartman, C. R., & Burgess, A. W. (1988). Rape trauma and treatment of the victim. In F. M. Ochberg (Ed.), *Post-traumatic therapy and victims of violence* (pp. 152–174). New York: Brunner/Mazel.

Hatfield, E., & Rapson, R. (1993). Love and attachment processes. In M. Lewis & J. M. Haviland (Eds.), *Handbook of emotions* (pp. 595–604). New York: Guilford.

Hawking, S. (1988). *A brief history of time.* London: Bantam Press.

Heath, R. G. (1992). Correlation of brain activity with emotion: A basis for developing treatment of violent-aggressive behavior. *Journal of the American Academy of Psychoanalysis, 20*(3), 335–346.

Henderson, S., & Bostock, T. (1977). Coping behaviour after shipwreck. *British Journal of Psychiatry, 131,* 15–20.

Henry, J. P. (1986). Neuroendocrine patterns of emotional response. *Emotion: Theory, Research, and Experience, 3,* 37–60.

Herman, J. L. (1981). *Father-daughter incest.* Cambridge, MA: Harvard University Press.

Herman, J. L. (1992). *Trauma and recovery.* New York: Basic Books.

Hill, R., & Hansen, D. A. (1962). Families in disaster. In G. W. Baker & D. W. Chapman (Eds.), *Man and society in disaster* (pp. 185–221). New York: Basic Books.

Hirschfeld, A. H., & Behan, R. C. (1969). Disability. *International Psychiatry Clinics, 6*(4), 239–248.

Hobbes, T. (1651). Leviathan. In *Brittanica Great Books* (Vol. 23, pp. 41–283). Chicago: Benton.

Hoch, F., Werle, E., & Weicker, H. (1988). Sympathoadrenergic regulation in elite fencers in training and competition. *International Journal of Sports Medicine, 9*(Suppl. 2), 141–145.

Hocking, F. (1965). Human reactions to extreme environmental stress. *Medical Journal of Australia, 2,* 477–483.

Hocking, F. H. (1970). Psychiatric aspects of extreme environmental stress. *Diseases of the Nervous System, 31,* 542–545.

Holloway, H. C., & Fullerton, C. S. (1994). The psychology of terror and its aftermath. In R. J. Ursano, B. G. McCaughey, & C. S. Fullerton (Eds.), *Individual and community responses to trauma and disaster: The structure of human chaos* (pp. 31–45). Cambridge, England: Cambridge University Press.

Holmes, T. H., & Rahe, R. H. (1967). The social readjustment rating scale. *Journal of Psychosomatic Research, 11,* 213–218.

Horne, D. (1993). Traumatic stress reactions to motor vehicle accidents. In J. Wilson & B. Raphael (Eds.), *International handbook of traumatic stress syndromes* (pp. 499–506). New York: Plenum Press.

Horowitz, M. (1992). *Stress response syndromes.* New York: Aronson. (Original published 1976)

Hunter, E. J. (1993). The Vietnam prisoner of war experience. In J. P. Wilson & B. Raphael (Eds.), *International handbook of traumatic stress syndromes* (pp. 297–304). New York: Plenum Press.

Ingersoll, D. E., & Matthews, R. K. (1986). *The philosophic roots of modern ideology: Liberalism, communism, fascism.* Englewood Cliffs, NJ: Prentice-Hall.

Irwin, M., Daniels, M., & Weiner, H. (1987). Immune and neuroendocrine changes during bereavement. *Psychiatric Clinics of North America, 10,* 449–465

Isaac, G. L. (1977). Traces of Pleistocene hunters: An African example. In R. B. Lee & I. DeVore (Eds.), *Man the hunter* (pp. 253–274). Chicago: Aldine.

Isherwood, J., Adam, K. S., & Hornblow, A. R. (1982). Life event stress, psychosocial factors, suicide attempt and auto-accident proclivity. *Journal of Psychosomatic Research, 26,* 371–383.

Jacobson, S. R. (1973). Individual and group responses to confinement in a skyjacked plane. *American Journal of Orthopsychiatry, 43*(3), 459–469.

Janis, I. L. (1951). *Air war and emotional stress, psychological studies of bombing and civilian defence.* New York: McGraw-Hill.

Janis, I. L. (1962). Psychological effects of warnings. In G. W. Baker & D. W. Chapman (Eds.), *Man and society in disaster* (pp. 55–92). New York: Basic Books.

Janis, I. L. (1972). *Victims of groupthink.* Boston: Houghton Mifflin.

Janis, I. L., & Mann, L. (1977). Emergency decision making: A theoretical analysis of responses to disaster warnings. *Journal of Human Stress, 3,* 34–45.

Janoff-Bulman, R. (1988). Victims of violence. In G. S. Everly & J. M. Lating (Eds.), *Psychotraumatology: Key papers and concepts in post-traumatic stress.* New York: Plenum Press.

Jemmott, J. B. (1987). Social motives and susceptibility to disease: Stalking individual differences in health risks. *Journal of Personality, 55,* 267–298.

Joseph, S., Yule, W., & Williams, R. (1993). Post-traumatic stress: Attributional aspects. *Journal of Traumatic Stress, 6*(4), 501–514.

Kant, I. (1786). Fundamental principles of the metaphysics of morals. *In Britannica Great Books* (Vol. 42, pp. 251–287). Chicago: Benton.

Kardiner, A. (1941). *The traumatic neuroses of war.* New York: Paul B. Hoeber.

Kasfir, N. (1979). Explaining ethnic political participation. *World Politics, 31,* 365–388.

Kaufman, I. C., & Rosenblum, L. A. (1967). The reaction to separation in infant monkeys: Anaclitic depression and conservation-withdrawal. *Psychosomatic Medicine, 29*(6), 648–675.

Keegan, J. (1985). *The face of battle.* Harmondsworth, England: Penguin.

Keegan, J., & Holmes, R. (1985). *Soldiers: A history of men in battle.* London: Hamish Hamilton.

Kellerman, H. (1980). A structural model of emotion and personality: Psychoanalytic and sociobiological implications. In R. Plutchik & H. Kellerman (Eds.), *Emotion: Theory, research, and experience. Vol. I: Theories of emotion* (pp. 349–384). New York: Academic Press.

Kelley, D. M. (1947). *Twenty two cells in Nuremberg: A psychiatrist examines the Nazi criminals.* New York: Greenberg.

Kernberg, O. (1975). *Borderline conditions and pathological narcissism.* New York: Science House.

Kestenberg, J. (1988). Memories from early childhood. *Psychoanalytic Review, 75,* 561–571.

Kestenberg, J. (1989). Transposition revisited: Clinical, therapeutic and developmental considerations. In P. Marcus & A. Rosenberg (Eds.), *Healing their wounds: Psychotherapy with Holocaust survivors and their families* (pp. 67–82). New York: Praeger.

Kestenberg, J. (1992). Children of survivors and child survivors. *Echoes of the Holocaust, 1,* 26–50.

Kestenberg, J., & Brenner, I. (1986). Children who survived the Holocaust: The role of rules and routines in the development of the superego. *International Journal of Psychoanalysis, 67,* 309–316.

Khan, M. M. R. (1964). Ego distortion, cumulative trauma, and the role of reconstruction in the analytic situation. *International Journal of Psychoanalysis, 45,* 272–279.

Kiecolt-Glaser, J. K., Cacioppo, J. T., Malarkey, W. B., & Glaser, R. (1992). Acute psychological stressors and short-term immune changes: What, why, for whom, and to what extent? *Psychosomatic Medicine, 54,* 680–685.

Kilpatrick, D. G., Veronen, L. J. & Best, C. L. (1985). Factors predicting psychological distress among rape victims. In C. R. Figley (Ed.), *Trauma and its wake: The study and treatment of post-traumatic stress disorder* (pp. 113–141). New York: Brunner/Mazel.

Kimball, C. D. (1987). Do opioid hormones mediate appetites and love bonds. *American Journal of Obstetrics and Gynecology, 156(6),* 1463–1466.

Kleber, R. J., & Brom, D. (1992). *Coping with trauma: Theory, prevention and treatment.* Amsterdam: Swets & Zeitlinger.

Klein, H (1968). Problems in the psychotherapeutic treatment of Israeli survivors of the Holocaust. In H. Krystal (Ed.), *Massive psychic trauma* (pp. 233–248). New York: International Universities Press.

Klein, M. (1975a). Some theoretical conclusions regarding the emotional life of the infant. In M. Klein, *Envy and gratitude, and other works 1946-1963* (pp. 61–93). London: Hogarth Press. (Original published in 1952)

Klein, M. (1975b). Envy and gratitude. In M. Klein, *Envy and gratitude, and other works 1946-1963* (pp. 176–235). London: Hogarth Press. (Original published in 1957)

Kleiner, J. (1970). On nostalgia. *Bulletin of Philadelphia Association of Psychoanalysis, 20,* 11–30.

Kleinman, S. B. (1989). A terrorist hijacking: Victims' experiences initially and nine years later. *Journal of Traumatic Stress, 2,* 49–58.

Klerman, G. L. (1984). The advantages of DSM-III (a debate on DSM-III). *American Journal of Psychiatry, 141,* 539–542.

Kliman, A. S. (1976). The Corning flood project: Psychological first aid following a natural disaster. In H. Parad, H. L. P. Resnik, & L. G. Parad (Eds.), *Emergency and disaster management* (pp. 325–335). Bowie, MD: Charles Press.

Kling, A. S. (1986). The anatomy of aggression and affiliation. In R. Plutchik & H. Kellerman (Eds.), *Emotion: Theory, research and experience* (Vol. 3) (pp. 237–264). New York: Academic Press.

Klonoff, H. M., McDougall, G., Clark, C., Kramer, P., & Horgan, J. (1976). The neuropsychological, psychiatric and physical effects of prolonged and severe stress: 30 years later. *Journal of Nervous and Mental Disease, 163,* 246–252.

Knapp, P. H., Levy, E. M., Giorgi, R. G., Black, P. H., Fox, B. H., & Heeren, T. C. (1992). Short-term immunological effects of induced emotion. *Psychosomatic Medicine, 54,* 133–148.

Knol, B. W., & Egbering-Alink, S. T. (1989). Androgens, progestatens and agonistic behaviour: A review. *The Veterinary Quarterly, 11(2),* 94–101.

Koepping, K.-P. (1989). Nature and nurture: The continuing relevance of Darwin. *Medical Journal of Australia, 151,* 672–677.

Koestler, A. (1974). *The urge to self-destruction: The heel of Achilles essays.* London: Hutchinson.

Koestler, A. (1983). *Janus: A summing up.* London: Picador.

Kohlberg, L. (1981). *The meaning and measurement of moral development* (Heinz Warner Lecture Series). Worcester, MA: Clark University Press.

Kohlberg, L. (1985). A current statement on some theoretical issues. In J. Modgil & C. Modgil (Eds), *Consensus and controversy* (pp. 487–489). London: Falmer Press.

Kohut, H. (1971). The analysis of the self. In *Psychoanalytic study of the child* (monograph). New York: International Universities Press.

Kolb, L. C. (1993). The psychobiology of PTSD: Perspectives and reflections on the past, present and future. *Journal of Traumatic Stress, 6,* 293–304.

Kraemer, G. W. (1985). Effects of differences in early social experience on primate neurobiological-behavioral development. In M. Reite & T. Field (Eds.), *The psychobiology of attachment and separation* (pp. 135–162). New York: Academic Press.

Kral, V. A. (1951). Psychiatric observations under severe chronic stress. *American Journal of Psychiatry, 108,* 185–192.

Krell, R. (1985). Therapeutic value of documenting child survivors. *Journal of the American Academy of Child Psychiatry, 24,* 397–400.

Krell, R., & Sherman, M. I. (Eds.). (1997). Medical and psychological effects of concentration camps on Holocaust survivors. New Brunswick, CT: Transaction Press.

Kroeber, A. L. (1948). *Anthropology.* London: Harcourt, Brace & World.

Krueger, D. (Ed.). (1984). *Emotional rehabilitation of physical trauma and disability.* New York: Spectrum.

Krull, M. (1987). *Freud and his father.* London: Hutchinson.

Krystal, H. (1971). Trauma: Considerations of its intensity and chronicity. In H. Krystal & W. G. Niederland (Eds.), *Psychic traumatization: Aftereffects in individuals and communities* (International Psychiatry Clinics 8:1, pp. 11–28). Boston: Little, Brown.

Krystal, H., & Niederland, W. G. (1968). Clinical observations on the survivor syndrome. In H. Krystal (Ed.), *Massive psychic trauma* (pp. 327–348). New York: International Universities Press.

Kubany, E. S., Gino, A., Denny, N. R., & Torigoe, R. Y. (1994). Relationship of cynical hostility and PTSD among Vietnam combat veterans. *Journal of Traumatic Stress, 7,* 21–32.

Kübler-Ross, E. (1969). *On death and dying.* New York: Macmillan.

Kuhn, T. S. (1962). *The structure of scientific revolutions.* Chicago: University of Chicago Press.

LaBarre, W. (1979). Species-specific biology, magic and religion. In R. H. Hook (Ed.), *Fantasy and symbol: Studies in anthropological interpretation* (pp. 55–63). London: Academic Press.

Lacan, J. (1966). *Ecrits.* Paris: Editions du Seuil.

Lane, R. D., & Schwartz, G. E. (1987). Levels of emotional awareness: A cognitive-developmental theory and its application to psychopathology. *American Journal of Psychiatry, 144*(2), 133–143.

Laub, D., & Auerhahn, N. C. (1993). Knowing and not knowing massive psychic trauma: Forms of traumatic memory. *International Journal of Psychoanalysis, 74,* 287–302.

Laughlin, W. S. (1977). An integrating biobehavior system and its evolutionary importance. In R. B. Lee & I. DeVore (Eds.), *Man the hunter* (pp. 304–320). Chicago: Aldine.

Lavee, Y., & Ben-David, A. (1993). Families under war: Stresses and strains of Israeli families during the Gulf War. *Journal of Traumatic Stress, 6,* 239–254.

Lazarus, R. S. (1966). *Psychological stress and the coping process.* New York: McGraw-Hill.

Lazarus, R. S., & Cohen, J. B. (1977). Environmental stress. In I. Altman & J. F. Wohlwill (Eds.), *Human behavior and the environment: Current theory and research* (Vol. 2). (pp. 90–128). New York: Plenum.

Lazarus, R. S., & Folkman, S. (1984). *Stress, appraisal, and coping.* New York: Springer.

Leavitt, F. (1997). False attribution of suggestibility to explain recovered memory of childhood sexual abuse following extended amnesia. *Child Abuse and Neglect, 21,* 265–272.

Lebowitz, L., & Roth, S. (1994). "I felt like a slut": The cultural context and women's response to being raped. *Journal of Traumatic Stress, 7*, 363–390.

Lee, R. B. (1977). What hunters do for a living, or, how to make out on scarce resources. In R. B. Lee & I. DeVore (Eds.), *Man the hunter* (pp. 30–48). Chicago: Aldine.

Lee, R. B., & DeVore, I. (Eds.). (1977). *Man the hunter.* Chicago: Aldine.

Lemerise, E. A., & Dodge, K. A. (1993). The development of anger and hostile interactions. In M. Lewis & J. M. Haviland (Eds.), *Handbook of emotions* (pp. 537–546). New York: Guilford.

Leopold, R. L., & Dillon, H. (1963). Psycho-anatomy of a disaster: A long term study of post-traumatic neuroses in survivors of a marine explosion. *American Journal of Psychiatry, 119*, 913–921.

Leshner, A. I. (1983). Pituitary-adrenocortical effects on inter-male agonistic behavior. In B. B. Svare (Ed.), *Hormones and aggressive behavior* (pp. 27–38). New York: Plenum Press.

Levi, P. (1979). If this is a man. London: Abacus.

Levinson, J. L., & Bemis, C. (1995). Cancer onset and progression. In A. Stoudemire (Ed.), *Psychological factors affecting medical conditions* (pp. 81–98). Washington, DC: American Psychiatric Press.

Lewis, A. (1942). Incidence of neurosis—England under war conditions. *Lancet, 2*, 175–183.

Lewis, M. (1995). Memory and psychoanalysis: A new look at infantile amnesia and transference. *Journal of the American Academy of Child and Adolescent Psychiatry, 34*, 405–417.

Lewis, M., & Haviland, J. M. (Eds.). (1993). *Handbook of emotions.* New York: Guilford.

Lidz, T. (1946). Psychiatric casualties from Guadalcanal. *Psychiatry, 9*, 193–213.

Liebowitz, M. R. (1983). *The chemistry of love.* Boston: Little, Brown.

Lienhardt, G. (1966). *Social anthropology.* Oxford, England: Oxford University Press.

Lifton, R. J. (1967). *Death in life.* New York: Touchstone/Simon & Schuster.

Lifton, R. J. (1973). *Home from the war.* New York: Touchstone/Simon & Schuster.

Lifton, R. J. (1980). *The broken connection.* New York: Touchstone.

Lifton, R. J. (1986). *The Nazi doctors.* London: Papermac.

Lilar, S. (1965). *Aspects of love in western society.* London: Thames & Hudson.

Lindemann, E. (1944). Symptomatology and management of acute grief. *American Journal of Psychiatry, 101*, 141–148.

Lindy, J. D. (Ed.). (1988). *Vietnam: A casebook.* New York: Brunner/Mazel.

Lishman, W. A. (1973). The psychiatric sequelae of head injury: a review. *Psychological Medicine, 3*, 304–318.

Loftus, E. F. (1993). The reality of repressed memories. *American Psychologist, 48*, 518–537.

Lonetto, R. (1980). *Children's conceptions of death.* New York: Springer.

The Longest Hatred (1993). Documentary Film.

Lonie, I. (1991). Chaos theory: A new paradigm for psychotherapy. *Australian and New Zealand Journal of Psychiatry, 25*, 548–560.

Lorenz, E. N. (1979, December). *Predictability: Does the flap of a butterfly in Brazil set off a tornado in Texas?* Paper presented at annual meeting of American Association for Advancement of Science.

Lorenz, K. (1968). *On aggression.* City, England: University Paperback.

Lum, L. C. (1975). Hyperventilation: The tip and the iceberg. *Journal of Psychosomatic Research, 19*, 375–383.

Lundin, T. (1995). Transportation disasters—A review. *Journal of Traumatic Stress, 8*, 381–390.

Machiavelli, N. (1988). *The prince* (W. K. Marriott, Trans.). Chicago: William Benton. (Original published in 1513)

MacLean, P. D. (1973). *A triune concept of the brain and behaviour.* Toronto: Toronto University Press.

MacLean, P. D. (1985). Brain evolution relating to family, play, and the separation call. *Archives of General Psychiatry, 42*, 405–417.

Macy, J. (1981). Despair work. In D. Hoffman & A. Johnson (Eds.), *Evolutionary blues* (Vol. 1, No. 1, pp. 36–47). Agenta, CA: Summer-Hall.

Mahler, M. S., Pine, F., & Bergman, A. (1975). *The psychological birth of the human infant.* London: Hutchinson.

Maier, S. F., & Seligman, M. E. P. (1976). Learned helplessness: Theory and evidence. *Journal of Experimental Psychology, 105,* 3–46.

Malt, U. F. (1994). Traumatic effects of accidents. In R. J. Ursano, B. G. McCaughey, & C. S. Fullerton (Eds.), *Individual and community responses to trauma and disaster: The structure of human chaos* (pp. 103–135). Cambridge, England: Cambridge University Press.

Manolias, M. B., & Hyatt-Williams, A. (1993). Effects of postshooting experiences on police-authorised firearms officers in the United Kingdom. In J. Wilson & B. Raphael (Eds.), *International handbook of traumatic stress syndromes* (pp. 385–394). New York: Plenum.

Maoz, Z. (1981). The decision to raid Entebbe. *Journal of Conflict Resolution, 25,* 677–707.

Marmar, C. R., Weiss, D. S., Schlenger, W. E., Fairbank, J. A., Kulka, R. A. & Hough, R. L. (1994). Peritraumatic dissociation and posttraumatic stress in male Vietnam theater veterans. *American Journal of Psychiatry, 151,* 902–907.

Marris, P. (1991). The social construction of uncertainty. In C. M. Parkes, J. Stevenson-Hinde, & P. Marris (Eds.), *Attachment across the life cycle* (pp. 77–90). London: Routledge.

Maslow, A. H. (1970). *Motivation and personality.* New York: Harper & Row.

Mason, J. W. (1968). The scope of psychoendocrine research. *Psychosomatic Medicine, 30,* 565–574.

Masson, J. M. (1984). *The assault on truth: Freud's suppression of the seduction theory.* New York: Penguin.

Mattsson, E. I. (1975). Psychological aspects of severe physical injury and its treatment. *Journal of Trauma, 15,* 217–234.

Maxwell, M. (1984). *Human evolution: A philosophical anthropology.* London: Croom Helm.

Mazur, A. (1983). Hormones, aggression, and dominance in humans. In B. B. Svare (Ed.), *Hormones and aggressive behavior* (pp. 563–576). New York: Plenum Press.

McClelland, D. C. (1975). *Power: The inner experience.* New York: Irvington.

McFarlane, A. C. (1988). The longitudinal course of posttraumatic morbidity: The range of outcomes and their predictors. *Journal of Nervous and Mental Disease, 176,* 30–39.

McFarlane, A. C., & de Girolamo, G. (1996). The nature of traumatic stressors and the epidemiology of posttraumatic reactions. In A. C. McFarlane & L. Weisath (Eds.), *Traumatic stress: The effects of overwhelming experience on mind, body, and society* (pp. 129–154). New York: Guilford.

McFarlane, A. C., & Papay, P. (1992). Multiple diagnoses in posttraumatic stress disorder in the victims of a natural disaster. *The Journal of Nervous and Mental Disease, 180,* 498–504.

McFarlane, A. C., & van der Kolk, B. A. (1996). Conclusions and future directions. In B. A. Van der Kolk, McFarlane, A. C., & Weisath, L. (Eds.), *Traumatic stress: The effects of overwhelming experience on mind, body, and society* (pp. 559–575). New York: Guilford.

McFarlane, A. C., & Yehuda, R. (1995). Conflict between current knowledge about posttraumatic stress disorder and its original conceptual basis. *American Journal of Psychiatry, 152,* 1705–1713.

McGregor, D. (1960). *The human side of enterprise.* New York: McGraw-Hill.

McNamara, E. (1995). Neurological conditions. In A. Stoudemire (Ed.), *Psychological factors affecting medical conditions* (pp. 57–79). Washington, DC: American Psychiatric Press.

Mendelson, G. (1988). *Psychiatric aspects of personal injury claims.* Springfield, IL: Charles C Thomas.

Menninger, W. C. (1947). Psychiatric experience in the war, 1941-1946. *American Journal of Psychiatry, 103,* 577–586.

Meyerhoff, J. L., Oleshansky, M. A., & Mougey, E. H. (1988). Psychologic stress increases plasma levels of prolactin, cortisol, and POMC-derived peptides in man. *Psychosomatic Medicine, 50,* 295–303.

Mileti, D., Drabek, T. E., & Haas, J. E. (1975). *Human systems in extreme environments: A sociological perspective.* Denver: University of Colorado, Institute of Behavioral Science.

Milgram, N. A. (Ed.). (1986). *Stress and coping in time of war: Generalizations from the Israeli experience.* New York: Brunner/Mazel.

Milgram, S. (1963). Behavioral study of obedience. *Journal of Abnormal Social Psychology, 67,* 371–378.

Mill, J. S. (1863). Utilitarianism. In *Brittanica Great Books* (pp. 445–476). Chicago: Benton.

Miller, E. J. (Ed.). (1976). *Task and organization.* Chichester, England: Wiley.

Miller, H. (1961). Accident neurosis. *British Medical Journal, 1,* 919–925.

Miller, M. L. (1944). Aftermath of operational fatigue in combat aircrews. *American Journal of Psychiatry, 101,* 325–330.

Mintzberg, H. (1973). *The nature of managerial work.* New York: Harper & Row.

Mitchell, J. T., & Dyregrov, A. (1993). Traumatic stress in disaster workers and emergency personnel: Prevention and intervention. In J. Wilson & B. Raphael (Eds.), *International handbook of traumatic stress syndromes* (pp. 905–914). New York: Plenum.

Moran, M. G. (1995). Pulmonary and rheumatologic diseases. In A. Stoudemire (Ed.), *Psychological factors affecting medical conditions* (pp. 141–158). Washington, DC: American Psychiatric Press.

Morstyn, R. (1992). The quantum of meaning: An approach to the paradox of self-observation. *Australian and New Zealand Journal of Psychiatry, 26,* 287–294.

Murphy, J. M. (1975). Psychological responses to war stress. *Acta Psychiatrica Scandinavica, 263*(Suppl.), 16–21.

Myers, C. S. (1990). *Shell shock in France 1914–1918.* Cambridge, England: Cambridge University Press.

Nader, K. (1993). Talk to Australasian Society for Traumatic Stress Studies.

Needles, W. (1946). The regression of psychiatry in the army. *Psychiatry, 9,* 167–185.

The New York Review (1994, Nov. 17, Dec. 1). The revenge of the repressed, pp. 54–60, 49–58.

Newman, E., Kaloupek, D. G., & Keane, T. M. (1996). Assessment of posttraumatic stress disorder in clinical and research settings. In B. A. Van der Kolk, A. C. McFarlane, & L. Weisath (Eds.), *Traumatic stress: The effects of overwhelming experience on mind, body, and society* (pp. 242–275). New York: Guilford Press.

Niaura, R., & Goldstein, M. G. (1992). Psychological factors affecting physical condition: Cardiovascular disease literature review. *Psychosomatics, 33,* 146–153.

Nolan, D. C., Engle, L., & Engle, B. (Eds.). (1954). *Wartime psychiatry: A compendium of the international literature.* New York: Oxford University Press.

Ochberg, F. M. (Ed.). (1988). *Post-traumatic therapy and victims of violence.* New York: Brunner/Mazel.

Ochberg, F. M. (1989). Cruelty, culture, and coping: Comment on the Westermeyer paper. *Journal of Traumatic Stress, 2,* 537–541.

Öhman, A. (1993). Fear and anxiety as emotional phenomena: Clinical phenomenology, evolutionary perspectives, and information-processing mechanisms. In M. Lewis & J. M. Haviland (Eds.), *Handbook of emotions* (pp. 511–536). New York: Guilford Press.

Olweus, D., Mattsson, A., Schalling, D., & Low, H. (1988). Circulating testosterone levels and aggression in adolescent males: A causal analysis. *Psychosomatic Medicine, 50,* 241–272.

Orne, M. T., & Evans, F. J. (1965). Social control in the psychological experiment: Antisocial behavior and hypnosis. *Journal of Personality and Social Psychology, 1,* 189–200.

Panksepp, J. (1986a). The anatomy of emotions. In R. Plutchik & H. Kellerman (Eds.), *Emotion: Theory, research and experience* (Vol. 3, pp. 100–106). New York: Academic Press.

Panksepp, J. (1986b). The neurochemistry of behavior. *Annual Review of Psychology, 37,* 77–107.

Panksepp, J. (1989a). The neurobiology of emotions: Of animal brains and human feelings. In H. Wagner & A. Manstead (Eds.), *Handbook of social psychophysiology* (pp. 5–26). New York: Wiley.

Panksepp, J. (1989b). The psychobiology of emotions: The animal side of human feelings. *Experimental Brain Research Series, 18,* 31–55.

Panksepp, J. (1993). Neurochemical control of moods and emotions: Amino acids to neuropeptides. In M. Lewis & J. M. Haviland (Eds.), *Handbook of emotions* (pp. 87–107). New York: Guilford Press.

Panksepp, J., Meeker, R., & Bean, J. (1980). The neurochemical control of crying. *Pharmacology Biochemistry and Behavior, 12,* 437–443.

Panksepp, J., Siviy, S. M., & Normansell, L. A. (1985). Brain opioids and social emotions. In M. Reite & T. Field (Eds), *The psychobiology of attachment and separation.* New York: Academic Press.

Parker, N. (1977). Accident litigants with neurotic symptoms. *Medical Journal of Australia, 2,* 318–322.

Parkes, C. M. (1972). *Bereavement: Studies of grief in adult life.* London: Tavistock.

Parkes, C. M., & Weiss, R. S. (1983). *Recovery from bereavement.* New York: Basic Books.

Parson, E. R. (1993). Posttraumatic narcissism: Healing traumatic alterations in the self through curvilinear group psychotherapy. In J. Wilson & B. Raphael (Eds.), *International handbook of traumatic stress syndromes* (pp. 821–840). New York: Plenum.

Pearlman, K. W., & Saakvitne, L. A. (1995). *Trauma and the therapist.* New York: Norton.

Perini, C., Müller, F. B., Rauchfleisch, U., Battegay, R., & Bühler, F. R. (1986). Hyperadrenergic borderline hypertension is characterized by suppressed aggression. *Journal of Cardiovascular Pharmacology, 8,* S53–S55.

Plato. (1988). Timaeus (R. M. Hutchins, Ed.). In *Brittanica Great Books.* Chicago: Benton.

Plutchik, R. (1980). A general psychoevolutionary theory of emotion. In R. Plutchik & H. Kellerman (Eds.), *Emotion: Theory, research, and experience. Vol. 1: Theories of emotion* (pp. 3–33) New York: Academic Press.

Plutchik, R. (1993). Emotions and their vicissitudes: Emotions and psychopathology. In M. Lewis & J. M. Haviland (Eds.), *Handbook of emotions* (pp. 53–66). New York: Guilford Press.

Posner, G. L. (1991). *Hitler's children.* New York: Random House.

Pynoos, R. S. (1993). Traumatic stress and developmental psychopathology in children and adolescents. In J. M. Oldham, M. B. Riba, & A. Tasman (Eds.), *American Psychiatric Press review of psychiatry* (Vol. 12, pp. 206–238). Washington, DC: American Psychiatric Press.

Pynoos, R. S, & Eth, S. (1985). Developmental perspective on psychic trauma in childhood. In C. R. Figley (Ed.), *Trauma and its wake* (pp. 36–52). New York: Brunner/Mazel.

Pynoos, R. S., & Nader, K. (1990). Children's exposure to violence and traumatic death. *Psychiatric Annals, 20,* 334–344.

Pynoos, R. S., & Nader, K. (1993). Issues in the treatment of posttraumatic stress in children and adolescents. In J. Wilson & B. Raphael (Eds.), *International handbook of traumatic stress syndromes.* New York: Plenum.

Pynoos, R. S., Steinberg, A. M., & Goenjian, A. (1996). Traumatic stress in childhood and adolescence: Recent developments and current controversies. In B. A. Van der Kolk, A. C. McFarlane, & L. Weisath (Eds.), *Traumatic stress: The effects of overwhelming experience on mind, body, and society* (pp. 331–358). New York: Guilford Press.

Quanty, M. B. (1976). Aggression catharsis: Experimental investigations and implications. In R. G. Geen & E. C. O'Neal (Eds.), *Perspectives on aggression* (pp. 99–132). New York: Academic Press.

Quarantelli, E. L. (1954). The nature and conditions of panic. *American Journal of Sociology, 60,* 267–275.

Quarantelli, E. L. (1985). An assessment of conflicting views on mental health: The consequences of traumatic events. In C. R. Figley (Ed.), *Trauma and its wake* (pp. 173–215). New York: Brunner/Mazel.

Quarantelli, E. L., & Dynes, R. R. (1972). When disaster strikes. *Psychology Today, 5,* 67–70.

Quarantelli, E. L., & Dynes, R. R. (1977). Response to social crisis and disaster. *Annual Review of Sociology, 3,* 23–49.

Raphael, B. (1984). *The anatomy of bereavement.* London: Hutchinson.

Raphael, B. (1986). *When disaster strikes.* London: Hutchinson.

Realmuto, G. M., Masten, A., Carole, L. F., Hubbard, J., Groteluschen, A., & Chhun, B. (1992). Adolescent survivors of massive childhood trauma in Cambodia: Life events and current symptoms. *Journal of Traumatic Stress, 5*, 589–600.

Reder, P. (1989). Freud's family. *British Journal of Psychiatry, 154*, 93–98.

Rees, W. D., & Lutkins, S. (1967). Mortality of bereavement. *British Medical Journal, 4*, 13–16.

Reite, M., & Capitano, J. P. (1985). On the nature of social separation and social attachment. In M. Reite & T. Field (Eds.), *The psychobiology of attachment and separation* (pp. 223–257). New York: Academic Press.

Renner, J. A., Jr. (1973). The changing patterns of psychiatric problems in Vietnam. *Comprehensive Psychiatry, 14*(2), 169–181.

Reviere, S. L. (1996). *Memory of childhood trauma: A clinician's guide to the literature.* New York: Guilford Press.

Robbins, S. P. (1991). *Organizational behavior: Concepts, controversies, and applications.* Englewood Cliffs, NJ: Prentice-Hall.

Robertson, J., & Robertson, J. (1967) (Prod., Dir.). *No. 1 Kate.* [Young children in brief separation series]. (Available from Tavistock Institute of Human Relations, Child Development Research Unit, London, England, or the New York University Film Library, New York, NY).

Robertson, J., & Robertson, J. (1968) (Prod., Dir.). *No. 2 Jane.* [Young children in brief separation series]. (Available from Tavistock Institute of Human Relations, Child Development Research Unit, London, England, or the New York University Film Library, New York, NY).

Robertson, J., & Robertson, J. (1967) (Prod., Dir.). *No. 3 John.* [Young children in brief separation series]. (Available from Tavistock Institute of Human Relations, Child Development Research Unit, London, England, or the New York University Film Library, New York, NY).

Robertson, J., & Robertson, J. (1967) (Prod., Dir.). *No. 4 Thomas.* [Young children in brief separation series]. (Available from Tavistock Institute of Human Relations, Child Development Research Unit, London, England, or the New York University Film Library, New York, NY).

Robertson, J., & Robertson, J. (1967) (Prod., Dir.). *No. 5 Lucy.* [Young children in brief separation series]. (Available from Tavistock Institute of Human Relations, Child Development Research Unit, London, England, or the New York University Film Library, New York, NY).

Robertson, J., & Robertson, J. (1971). Young children in brief separation: A fresh look. *Psychoanalytic Study of the Child, 8*, 288–309.

Robinson, D. M. (1993). Wisdom through the ages. In R. J. Sternberg (Ed.), *Wisdom: Its nature, origins and development* (pp. 13–24). New York: Cambridge University Press.

Robinson, R. C., & Mitchell, J. T. (1993). Evaluation of psychological debriefings. *Journal of Traumatic Stress, 6*, 367–383.

Rogers, M. L. (1995). Factors influencing recall of childhood sexual abuse. *Journal of Traumatic Stress, 8*, 691–716.

Rogers, M. P., Dubey, D., & Reich, P. (1979). The influence of the psyche and the brain on immunity and disease susceptibility: A critical review. *Psychosomatic Medicine, 41*, 147–164.

Roheim, G. (1968). *Psychoanalysis and anthropology.* New York: International Universities Press.

Rose, R. M. (1969). Androgen excretion in stress. In P. G. Bourne (Ed.), *The psychology and physiology of stress, with reference to special studies of the Viet Nam War* (pp. 117–147). New York: Academic Press.

Rosenblatt, J. S. (1989). The physiological and evolutionary background of maternal responsiveness. *New Directions for Child Development, 43*, 15–30.

Ross, W. D. (1988) (Trans.). Aristotle. Nicomachean ethics. In *Brittanica Great Books* (Volume 9, p. 1109). Chicago: Benton.

Roth, S., & Cohen, L. J. (1986). Approach, avoidance, and coping with stress. *American Psychologist, 41,* 813–819.

Rothbaum, B. O., & Foa, E. B. (1993). Subtypes of posttraumatic stress disorder and duration of symptoms. In J. R. T. Davidson & E. B. Foa (Eds.), *Posttraumatic stress disorder: DSM-IV and beyond* (pp. 23–35). Washington, DC: American Psychiatric Press.

Rozin, P., Haidt, J., & McCauley, C. R. (1993). Disgust. In M. Lewis & J. M. Haviland (Eds.), *Handbook of emotions* (pp. 575–594). New York: Guilford.

Rubenstein, R. L. (1992). *After Auschwitz.* London: Johns Hopkins University Press.

Rush, F. (1977). Freud and the sexual abuse of children. *Chrysalis, 1,* 31–45.

Russell, D. E. H. (1986). *The secret trauma: Incest in the lives of girls and women.* New York: Basic Books.

Ryn, Z. (1990). Between life and death: Experiences of concentration camp Musselmen during the Holocaust. *Genetic, Social and General Psychology Monographs, 116,* 7–19.

Sachar, E. J. (1975a). A neuroendocrine strategy in the psychobiological study of depressive illness. In J. Mendels (Ed.), *The psychobiology of depression* (pp. 123–132). New York: Spectrum.

Sachar, E. J. (1975b). *Topics in psychoendocrinology.* New York: Grune & Stratton.

Sadoff, R. L. (1977). On the nature of crying and weeping. In C. W. Socarides (Ed.), *The world of emotions: Clinical studies of affects and their expression* (pp. 377–389). New York: International Universities Press. (Original published in 1966)

Salmon, T. (1919). The war neuroses and their lesson. *New York State Journal of Medicine, 59,* 933–934.

Saul, L. J. (1966). Sudden death at impasse. *Psychoanalysis, 1,* 87–89.

Schlenger, W. E., Kulka, R. A., Fairbank, J. A., Hough, R. L., Jordan, B. K., Marmar, C. R., & Weiss, D. S. (1992). The prevalence of post-traumatic stress disorder in the Vietnam generation: A multimethod, multisource assessment of psychiatric disorder. *Journal of Traumatic Stress, 5,* 333–363.

Schmale, A. H. (1972). Giving up as a final common pathway to changes in health. *Advances in Psychosomatic Medicine, 8,* 20–40.

Schmale, A. H., & Iker, H. P. (1966). The affect of hopelessness and the development of cancer: Identification of uterine cervical cancer in women with atypical cytology. *Psychosomatic Medicine, 28,* 714.

Schmideberg, M. (1942). Some observations on individual reactions to air raids. *International Journal of Psychoanalysis, 23,* 146–176.

Schur, M. (1972). *Freud: Living and dying.* New York: International Universities Press.

Schwartz, S. H. (1994). Are there universal aspects in the structure and contents of human values? *Journal of Social Issues, 50,* 19–45.

Scott, J. P. (1977). Agonistic behavior: Adaptive and maladaptive organization. In M. T. McGuire & L. A. Fairbanks (Eds.), *Ethological psychiatry. Psychopathology in the context of evolutionary biology* (pp. 193–209). New York: Grune & Stratton.

Scott, J. P. (1980). The function of emotions in behavioral systems: A systems theory analysis. In R. Plutchik & H. Kellerman (Eds.), *Emotion: Theory, research, and experience. Vol. 1: Theories of emotion* (pp. 35–56). New York: Academic Press.

Scott, J. P. (1981). Biological and psychological bases of social attachment. In H. Kellerman (Ed.), *Group cohesion: Theoretical and clinical perspectives* (pp. 206–224). New York: Grune & Stratton.

Scott, J. P. (1989). *The evolution of social systems.* New York: Gordon & Breach Science.

Segal, M. (1975). *Introduction to the work of Melanie Klein.* London: Hogarth.

Seligman, M. (1974). Depression and learned helplessness. In R. J. Friedman & M. M. Katz (Eds.), *The psychology of depression: Contemporary theory and research* (pp. 83–126). New York: Wiley.

Selye, H. (1936). A syndrome produced by various nocuous agents. *Nature (Lond.), 148,* 84–85.

Selye, H. (1946). The general adaptation syndrome and the diseases of adaptation. *Journal of Clinical Endocrinology, 6,* 117–196.

Selye, H. (1973). The evolution of the stress concept. *American Scientist, 61(6),* 692–699.

Shaikh, M. B., Brutus, M., Siegel, H. E., & Siegel, A. (1985). Topographically organized midbrain modulation of predatory and defensive aggression in the cat. *Brain Research, 336,* 308–312.

Shalev, A. Y. (1996). Stress versus traumatic stress: From acute homeostatic reactions to chronic psychopathology. In B. A. Van der Kolk, A. C. McFarlane, & L. Weisath (Eds.), *Traumatic stress: The effects of overwhelming experience on mind, body, and society.* New York: Guilford Press.

Shalev, A. Y., Orr, S. P., & Pitman, R. K. (1993). Psychophysiologic assessment of traumatic imagery in Israeli civilian patients with posttraumatic stress disorder. *American Journal of Psychiatry, 150,* 620–624.

Shalit, E. (1994). The relation between aggression and fear of annihilation in Israel. *Political Psychology, 15(3),* 415–434.

Shatan, C. F. (1973). The grief of soldiers: Vietnam combat veterans' self-help movement. *American Journal of Orthopsychiatry, 43,* 640–653.

Shaw, J. A. (1983). Comments on the individual psychology of combat exhaustion. *Military Medicine, 148,* 223–225.

Shaw, J. A., & Harris, J. J. (1994). Children of war and children at war: Child victims of terrorism in Mozambique. In R. J. Ursano, B. G. McCaughey, & C. S. Fullerton (Eds.), *Individual and community responses to trauma and disaster: The structure of human chaos* (pp. 287–305). Cambridge, England: Cambridge University Press.

Shay, J. (1991). Learning about combat stress from Homer's *Iliad. Journal of Traumatic Stress, 4,* 561–579.

Sherif, M. (1970). Group conflict and cooperation. In P. B. Smith (Ed.), *Group processes.* London: Penguin. (Original published in 1966)

Sichrovsky, P. (1988). *Born guilty.* London: I. B. Tauris.

Silber, E., Perry, S. E., & Bloch, D. A. (1957). Patterns of parent child interaction in a disaster. *Psychiatry, 21,* 159–167.

Silver, S. M., & Iacono, C. (1986). Symptom groups and family patterns of Vietnam veterans with post-traumatic stress disorders. In C. R. Figley (Ed.), *Trauma and its wake. Vol. II: Traumatic stress theory, research, and intervention* (pp. 78–96). New York: Brunner/Mazel.

Simpson, M. A. (1993). Traumatic stress and the bruising of the soul: The effects of torture and coercive interrogation. In J. Wilson & B. Raphael (Eds), *International handbook of traumatic stress syndromes* (pp. 667–684). New York: Plenum Press.

Siporin, M. (1976). Altruism, disaster, and crisis intervention. In H. Parad, H. L. P. Resnik, & L. G. Parad (Eds.), *Emergency and disaster management* (pp. 213–229). Bowie, MD: Charles Press.

Skinner, B. F. (1953). *Science and human behavior.* New York: Macmillan.

Smith, G. C. (1991). The brain and higher mental function. *Australian and New Zealand Journal of Psychiatry, 25,* 215–230.

Sobel, R. (1949). Anxiety-depressive reactions after prolonged combat experience—The "Old Sergeant Syndrome." In F. R. Hanson (Ed.), *Combat psychiatry: The bulletin of the US Army Medical Department, 9(*Suppl.),137–146.

Socarides, C. W. (1966). On vengeance: The desire to "get even." *Journal of the American Psychoanalytic Association, 35,* 98–107.

Socarides, C. (1977). *The world of emotions: Clinical studies of affects and their expression.* New York: International Universities Press.

Solnit, A., & Kris, M. (1967). Trauma and infantile experiences: A longitudinal perspective. In S. Furst (Ed.), *Psychic trauma* (pp. 175–224). New York: Basic Books.

Solomon, S. D. (1986). Mobilizing social support networks in times of disaster. In C. R. Figley (Ed.), *Trauma and its wake. Vol. II: Traumatic stress theory, research, and intervention* (pp. 232–263). New York: Brunner/Mazel.

Solomon, Z. (1989). Psychological sequelae of war: A three-year prospective study of Israeli combat stress reaction casualties. *Journal of Nervous and Mental Disease, 177*, 342–346.

Solomon, Z. (1993). *Combat stress reaction: The enduring toll of war.* New York: Plenum Press.

Solomon, Z. (1995). From denial to recognition: Attitudes toward Holocaust survivors from World War II to the present. *Journal of Traumatic Stress, 5*, 215–228.

Solomon, Z., Laor, N., & McFarlane, A. C. (1996). Acute posttraumatic reactions in soldiers and civilians. In B. A. Van der Kolk, A. C. McFarlane, & L. Weisath (Eds.), *Traumatic stress: The effects of overwhelming experience on mind, body, and society* (pp. 102–114). New York: Guilford.

Spiegel, H. X. (1944). Psychiatric observations in the Tunisian campaign. *American Journal of Orthopsychiatry, 14*, 381–385.

Spitz, R. A. (1965). *The first year of life: A psychoanalytic study of normal and deviant development of object relations.* New York: International Universities Press.

Staub, E. (1989). *The roots of evil.* Cambridge, England: Cambridge University Press.

Stearns, C. Z. (1993). Sadness. In M. Lewis & J. M. Haviland (Eds.), *Handbook of emotions* (pp. 547–561). New York: Guilford Press.

Stein, M. (1981). A biopsychosocial approach to immune function and medical disorders. *Psychiatric Clinics of North America, 1*, 203–221.

Steklis, H. D., & Kling, A. (1985). Topographically organized midbrain modulation of predatory and defensive aggression in the cat. *Brain Research, 336*, 308–312.

Steptoe, A. (1981). *Psychological factors in cardiovascular disorders.* London: Academic Press.

Stern, D. N. (1984). *The interpersonal world of the infant.* New York: Basic Books.

Stern, M. M. (1953). Trauma and symptom formation. *International Journal of Psychoanalysis, 34*, 202–217.

Stern, M. M. (1966, May). Fear of death and neurosis. Read at the annual meeting of the American Psychoanalytic Association, Atlantic City, NJ.

Sternberg, R. J. (Ed.). (1993). *Wisdom: Its nature, origins, and development.* New York: Cambridge University Press.

Stovkis, B. (1951). Observations of an Amsterdam psychiatrist during the Nazi occupation of 1940–1945. *Monatsschrift Für Psychiatrie und Neurologie (Berlin), 122*, 277–295.

Strecker, E. A. (1945). War psychiatry and its influence upon postwar psychiatry and upon civilization. *Journal of Nervous and Mental Disease, 101*, 401–13.

Stoudemire, A., & Hales, R. E. (1995). Psychological factors affecting medical conditions and DSM IV: An overview. In A. Stoudemire (Ed.). *Psychological factors affecting medical conditions* (pp. 1–17). Washington, DC: American Psychiatric Press.

Styron, W. (1979). *Sophie's choice.* London: Cape Press.

Sutker, P. B., Uddo, M., Brailey, K., Allain, A. N. & Errera, P. (1994). Psychological symptoms and psychiatric diagnoses in Operation Desert Storm troops serving graves registration duty. *Journal of Traumatic Stress, 7*, 159–172.

Swank, R. L. (1949). Combat exhaustion. *Journal of Nervous and Mental Disease, 109(6)*, 475–508.

Sweeney, D. R., Tinling, D. C., Schmale. A. H., & Rochester, N. Y. (1970). Differentiation of the "giving-up" affects: Helplessness and hopelessness. *Archives of General Psychiatry, 23*, 378–382.

Tas, J. (1951). Psychical disorders among inmates of concentration camps and repatriates. *Psychiatric Quarterly, 25*, 679–690.

Taylor, F. K. (1980). The concepts of disease. *Psychological Medicine, 10*, 419–424.

Taylor, G. J. (1987). *Psychosomatic medicine and contemporary psychoanalysis.* Madison, CT: International Universities Press.

Terr, L. C. (1983). Chowchilla revisited: The effects of psychic trauma four years after a school-bus kidnapping. *American Journal of Psychiatry, 140*, 1543–1550.

Terr, L. C. (1987). Childhood psychic trauma. In J. D. Noshpitz (Ed.), *Basic handbook of child psychiatry.* New York: Basic Books.

Terr, L. (1990). *Too scared to cry.* New York: Harper & Row.

Terr, L. C. (1991). Childhood traumas: An outline and overview. *American Journal of Psychiatry, 148(1),* 10–20.

Thrasher, F. M. (1927). *The gang.* Chicago: University of Chicago Press.

Threlkeld, M. E., & Thyer, B. A. (1992). Sexual and physical abuse histories among child and adolescent psychiatric outpatients. *Journal of Traumatic Stress, 5,* 491–496.

Thurlow, H. J. (1967). General susceptibility to illness: A selective review. *Canadian Medical Association Journal, 97,* 1397–1404.

Tiger, L., & Fox, R. (1971). *The imperial animal.* New York: Holt, Rinehart & Winston.

Tinnin, L. (1994). The double-mindedness of human memory. *ISTSS Stress Points, Fall, 3.*

Titchener, J. L., & Kapp, F. T. (1976). Family and character change at Buffalo Creek. *American Journal of Psychiatry, 133(3),* 295–299.

Trimble, M. R. (1985). Post-traumatic stress disorder: History of a concept. In C. Figley (Ed.), *Trauma and its wake: The study and treatment of post-traumatic stress disorder* (pp. 5–14). New York: Brunner/Mazel.

Trivers, R. L. (1971). The evolution of reciprocal altruism. *Quarterly Review of Biology, 46,* 35–57.

Troisi, A., D'Amato, F. R., Carnera, A., & Trinca, L. (1988). Maternal aggression by lactating group-living Japanese Macaque females. *Hormones and Behavior, 22,* 444–452.

Tuchman, B. (1983). *Practising history.* London: Papermac.

Tucker, R. C. (1986). The dictator and totalitarianism: Hitler and Stalin. In R. K. White (Ed.), *Psychology and the prevention of nuclear war* (pp. 307–321). New York: New York University Press.

Turner, S., & Gorst-Unsworth, C. (1990). Psychological sequelae of torture: A descriptive model. *British Journal of Psychiatry, 157,* 475–480.

Tyhurst, J. S. (1957). Psychological and social aspects of civilian disaster. *Canadian Medical Association Journal, 76,* 385–393.

Ursano, R. J., & McCarroll, J. E. (1994). Exposure to traumatic death: The nature of the stressor. In R. J. Ursano, B. G. McCaughey, & C. S. Fullerton (Eds.), *Individual and community responses to trauma and disaster: The structure of human chaos* (pp. 46–71). Cambridge, England: Cambridge University Press.

Ursin, H., Baade, E., & Levine, S. (Eds.). (1978). *Psychobiology of stress: A study of coping men.* New York: Academic Press.

Vachon, M. L. S. (1987). Unresolved grief in persons with cancer referred for psychotherapy. *Psychiatric Clinics of North America, 10,* 467–486.

Vaillant, G. E. (1984). The disadvantages of DSM-III outweigh its advantages (a debate on DSM-III). *American Journal of Psychiatry, 141,* 542–545.

Vaillant, G. E. (1992). *Ego mechanisms of defense: A guide for clinicians and researchers.* Washington, DC: American Psychiatric Press.

Vaillant, G. E. (1993). *The wisdom of the ego.* Cambridge, MA: Harvard University Press.

Valent, P. (1978). Issues with dying patients. *Medical Journal of Australia, 1,* 433–437.

Valent, P. (1979). Management of the dying patient. *Patient Management,3(3),* 7–9.

Valent, P. (1980). Death and the family. *Patient Management, 9(4),* 11–24.

Valent, P. (1982). Psychological attitudes and war. *Social Alternatives, 3,* 55–58.

Valent, P. (1984). The Ash Wednesday bushfires in Victoria. *Medical Journal of Australia, 141,* 291–300.

Valent, P. (1987). "Why War?" revisited. *Australian Journal of Psychotherapy, 6,* 48–73.

Valent, P. (1990). From shame to dignity. *Australian Journal of Psychotherapy, 9,* 36–46

Valent, P. (1992). *Stresses on staff of a general hospital closure and merger.* Unpublished manuscript.

Valent, P. (1993). *Psychosocial aspects of motor vehicle incidents.* Unpublished manuscript.

Valent, P. (1994). *Child survivors: Adults living with childhood trauma.* Melbourne, Victoria, Australia: Heinemann/Reed Books.

Valent, P. (1995a). Documented childhood trauma (Holocaust): Its sequelae and applications to other traumas. *Psychiatry, Psychology and Law, 2,* 81–89.

Valent, P. (1995b). Survival strategies: A framework for understanding secondary traumatic stress and coping in helpers. In C. R. Figley (Ed.), *Compassion fatigue: Secondary traumatic stress disorder in helpers* (pp. 21–50). New York: Brunner/Mazel.

Valent, P. (in press, a). *Trauma and fulfillment treatment: A wholist model.* Washington, DC: Taylor & Francis.

Valent, P. (in press, b). Child survivors: A review. In J. S. Kestenberg & C. Kahn (Eds.), *Children surviving persecution: An International Study of Trauma and Healing.* Westport: Praeger.

Van der Hart, O., & Horst, R. (1989). The dissociation theory of Pierre Janet. *Journal of Traumatic Stress, 2,* 397–412.

Van der Kolk, B. A. (1987). *Psychological trauma.* Washington, DC: American Psychiatric Press.

Van der Kolk, B. A. (1996a). The body keeps the score: Approaches to the psychobiology of posttraumatic stress disorder. In B. A. Van der Kolk, A. C. McFarlane, & L. Weisath (Eds.), *Traumatic stress: The effects of overwhelming experience on mind, body, and society* (pp. 214–241). New York: Guilford Press.

Van der Kolk, B. A. (1996b). The complexity of adaptation to trauma; self-regulation, stimulus discriminations, and characterological development. In B. A. Van der Kolk, A. C. McFarlane, & L. Weisath (Eds.), *Traumatic stress: The effects of overwhelming experience on mind, body, and society* (pp. 182–213). New York: Guilford Press.

Van der Kolk, B. A. (1996c). Trauma and memory. In B. A. Van der Kolk, A. C. McFarlane, & L. Weisath (Eds.), *Traumatic stress: The effects of overwhelming experience on mind, body, and society* (pp. 279–302). New York: Guilford Press.

Van der Kolk, B. A., Boyd, H., Krystal, J., & Greenberg, M. (1984). Post-traumatic stress disorder as a biologically based disorder: Implications of the animal model of inescapable shock. In B. A. van der Kolk (Ed.), *Post-traumatic stress disorder: Psychological and biological sequelae* (pp. 123–134). Washington, DC: American Psychiatric Press.

Van der Kolk, B. A., Brown, P., & van der Hart, O. (1989). Pierre Janet on post-traumatic stress. *Journal of Traumatic Stress, 2,* 365–378.

Van der Kolk, B. A., & Fisler, R. (1995). Dissociation and the fragmentary nature of traumatic memories: Overview and exploratory study. *Journal of Traumatic Stress, 8,* 505–526.

Van der Kolk, B. A., & Greenberg, M. S. (1987). The psychobiology of the trauma response: Hyperarousal, constriction, and addiction to traumatic reexposure. In B. A. Van der Kolk (Ed.), *Psychological trauma* (pp. 63–87). Washington, DC: American Psychiatric Press.

Van der Kolk, B. A., & McFarlane, A. C. (1996). The black hole of trauma. In B. A. Van der Kolk, A. C. McFarlane, & L. Weisath (Eds.), *Traumatic stress: The effects of overwhelming experience on mind, body, and society* (pp. 3–23). New York: Guilford Press.

Van der Kolk, B. A., McFarlane, A. C., & Weisath, L. (Eds.). (1996). *Traumatic stress: The effects of overwhelming experience on mind, body, and society.* New York: Guilford Press.

Van der Kolk, B. A., & Saporta, J. (1993). Biological response to psychic trauma. In J. Wilson & B. Raphael (Eds.), *International handbook of traumatic stress syndromes* (pp. 25–34). New York: Plenum Press.

Van der Kolk, B. A., Weisath, L., & van der Hart, O. (1996). History of trauma in psychiatry. In B. A. van der Kolk, a. C. McFarlane, & L. Weisath (Eds.), *Traumatic stress: The effects of overwhelming experience on mind, body, and society* (pp. 47–74).

Van Doornen, L. J. P., & van Blokland, R. W. (1989). The relation of Type A behavior and vital exhaustion with physiological reactions to real life stress. *Journal of Psychosomatic Research, 33,* 715–725.

Vargas, L. A., Loya, F., & Hodde-Vargas, J. (1989). Exploring the multidimensional aspects of grief reactions. *American Journal of Psychiatry, 146,* 1484–1488.

Veltfort, H. R., & Lee, G. E. (1943). The Cocoanut Grove fire: A study in scapegoating. *Journal of Abnormal and Social Psychology, 38,* 138–154.

Wallace, A. F. C. (1957). Mazeway disintegration: The individual's perception of socio-cultural disorganization. *Human Organization, 16*, 23–27.

Walsh, A. (1991). *Intellectual imbalance, love deprivation and violent delinquency.* Springfield, IL: Charles C Thomas.

Walzer, M. (1984). *Just and unjust wars.* Harmondsworth, England: Pelican.

Washburn, S. L., & Lancaster, C. S. (1977). The evolution of hunting. In R. B. Lee & I. DeVore (Eds.), *Man the hunter* (pp. 293–303). Chicago: Aldine.

Watson, P. (1980). *War on the mind.* Harmondsworth, England: Penguin.

Weiner, H. (1977). Summary and conclusions. In *Psychobiology and human disease* (pp. 640–641). New York: Elsevier North Holland.

Weiner, H. (1992). Specificity and specification: Two continuing problems in psychosomatic research. *Psychosomatic Medicine, 54*, 567–587.

Weiner, H., Thaler, M., Reiser, M. F., & Mirsky, I. A. (1959). Etiology of duodenal ulcer I: Relation of specific psychological characteristics to rate of gastric secretion (serum pepsinogen). *Psychosomatic Medicine, 19*, 1.

Weinstein, E. A. (1947). The function of interpersonal relations in the neurosis of combat. *Psychiatry, 10*, 307.

Weinstein, M. R. (1968). The illness process: Psychosocial hazards of disability programs. *Journal of American Medical Association, 204*, 117–121.

Weisaeth, L. (1985). Post-traumatic stress disorders after an industrial disaster: Point prevalences, etiological and prognostic factors. In P. Pichot, P. Berner, R. Wolf, & K. Thau (Eds.), *Psychiatry: The state of the art* (pp. 299–307). New York: Plenum.

Weisaeth, L. (1994). Psychological and psychiatric aspects of technological disasters. In R. J. Ursano, B. G. McCaughey, & C. S. Fullerton (Eds.), *Individual and community responses to trauma and disaster: The structure of human chaos.* Cambridge, England: Cambridge University Press.

Weisaeth, L., & Eitinger, L. (1993). Posttraumatic stress phenomena: Common themes across wars, disasters, and traumatic events. In J. Wilson & B. Raphael (Eds.), *International handbook of traumatic stress syndromes* (pp. 69–78). New York: Plenum.

Weiss, D. S., Marmar, C. S., Schlenger, W. E., Fairbank, J. A., Jordan, B. K., Hough, R. L., & Kulka, R. A. (1992). The prevalence of lifetime and partial post-traumatic stress disorder in Vietnam theater veterans. *Journal of Traumatic Stress, 5*, 365–376.

West, D. A., Kellner, R., & Moore-West, M. (1986). The effects of loneliness: A review of the literature. *Comprehensive Psychiatry, 27*, 351–363.

White, R. K. (1986). The role of fear. In R. K. White (Ed.), *Psychology and prevention of nuclear war* (pp. 240–249). New York: New York University Press.

Williams, L. M. (1995). Recovered memories of abuse in women with documented child sexual victimization histories. *Journal of Traumatic Stress, 8*, 649–674.

Wilson, E. O. (1975). *Sociobiology.* Cambridge, MA: Belknap Press of Harvard University Press.

Wilson, J. P., & Keane, T. M. (Eds.). (1996). *Assessing psychological trauma and PTSD* (pp. 5–30). New York: Guilford Press.

Wilson, J. P., & Lindy, J. D. (1994). Empathic strain and countertransference. In J. P. Wilson & J. D. Lindy (Eds.), *Countertransference in the treatment of PTSD.* New York: Guilford Press.

Winnicott, D. W. (1960a). The theory of the parent-infant relationship. *International Journal of Psychoanalysis, 41*, 585–595.

Winnicott, D. W. (1960b). Ego distortion in terms of true and false self. In J. S. Sutherland & M. M. R. Kahn (Eds.) (1965/1991), *The maturational processes and the facilitating environment: Studies in the theory of emotional development* (pp. 140–152). Madison, CT: International Universities Press.

Winnicott, D. W. (1963). From dependence towards independence in the development of the individual. In J. Sutherland & M. M. R. Khan (Eds.) (1965/1991), *D. W. Winnicott: The maturational processes and the facilitating environment: Studies in the theory of emotional development* (pp. 83–92). Madison, CT: International Universities Press.

Wolfenstein, M. (1977). *Disaster: A psychological essay.* New York: Arno Press.

Worthman, C. M., & Konner, M. J. (1987). Testosterone levels change with subsistence hunting effort in Kung San Men. *Psychoneuroendocrinology, 12,* 449–458.

Wright, Q. (1967). *A study of war.* Chicago: University of Chicago Press. (Original published in 1965)

Y Gasset, O. (1959). *On love: Aspects of a single theme.* London: Victor Gollancz.

Yager, J. (1975). Personal violence in infantry combat. *Archives of General Psychiatry, 32,* 257–261.

Yahr, P. (1983). Hormonal influences on shock-induced fighting. In B. B. Svare (Ed.), *Hormones and aggressive behavior* (pp. 145–175). New York: Plenum Press.

Yates, J. L., & Nasby, W. (1993). Dissociation, affect, and network models of memory: An integrative proposal. *Journal of Traumatic Stress, 6,* 305–326.

Yehuda, R., & McFarlane, A. C. (1995). Conflict between current knowledge about PTSD and its original conceptual basis. *American Journal of Psychiatry, 152,* 1705–1713.

Yehuda, R., Southwick, S. M., Mason, J. W., & Giller, F. M. (1990). Interactions of the hypothalamic-pituitary-adrenal axis and the catecholaminergic system of the stress disorder. In E. L. Giller (Ed.), *Biological assessment and treatment of PTSD* (pp. 115–134). Washington, DC: American Psychiatric Press.

Youniss, J. (1986). Development in reciprocity through friendship. In C. Zahn-Waxler, E. M. Cummings, & R. Iannotti (Eds.), *Altruism and aggression (biological and social origins).* (pp. 88–106). Cambridge, England: Cambridge University Press.

Yule, W., & Williams, R. M. (1990). Post-traumatic stress reactions in children. *Journal of Traumatic Stress, 3(2),* 279–295.

Zahn-Waxler, C., Cummings, E. M., & Iannotti, R. (1986). Introduction. In C. Zahn-Waxler, E. M. Cummings, & R. Iannotti (Eds.), *Altruism and aggression (biological and social origins).* (pp. 1–17). Cambridge, England: Cambridge University Press.

Zaidi, L. Y., & Foy, D. W. (1994). Childhood abuse experiences and combat-related PTSD. *Journal of Traumatic Stress, 7,* 33–42.

Zimbardo, P. (1972). Pathology of imprisonment. *Transaction, 9,* 4–8.

Name Index

Abramson, L. Y., 174
Adam, K. S., 35
Adamczak, K., 182
Alexander, F., 43, 137
Allain, A. N., 26
Allen, J. G., 136
Anderson, V., 130
Appel, J. W., 21, 22, 136
Appels, A., 147, 183
Ardrey, R., 89, 143, 144, 184
Arendt, H., 30, 166
Aristotle, 88, 91, 102, 162, 163
Asch, S. E., 165
Athens, L. H., 162, 163, 166, 168
Auerhahn, N. C., 75

Baade, E., 144
Bailey, S. L., 166
Baker, H. S., 192
Baker, M. N., 192
Baldessarini, R. J., 153
Balint, E., 190
Bar-On, D., 169
Barefoot, J. C., 164
Bartemeier, L. H., 22, 23
Bartrop, R. W., 59, 153
Batson, C. D., 127, 130
Battergay, R., 147
Bauer, M., 182
Baum, A., 52
Bayles, M. D., 90, 91
Bean, J., 135
Beaton, R. D., 129
Beck, A. T., 54
Becker, E., 3, 4, 158

Beebe, G. W., 21, 22, 31, 136
Behan, R. C., 35
Bemis, C., 155
Ben-David, A., 27
Benedict, R., 187
Bennet, G., 32
Bennett, A. E., 34
Benyakar, M., 69
Berah, E., 10, 33, 128
Bergland, R., 109
Bergman, A., 139
Bergman, M. S., 30
Bernard, Claude, 41, 55
Besch, N. F., 162
Best, C. L., 67
Bettelheim, B., 28, 155
Bey, D. R., 166
Bion, W. R., 82
Blanchard, D. C., 162, 181
Blanchard, R. J., 162, 181
Blank, A. S., 106
Bloch, D. A., 32
Bloch, H. S., 22
Boman, B., 25, 147
Booth, A., 180
Bostock, T., 139
Bourne, P. G., 22, 58, 127, 144
Bowlby, J., 44, 62, 67, 118, 134, 138, 139,
    152, 153, 154, 155, 156, 157
Boyd, H., 60
Bradley, A. J., 59
Brailey, K., 26
Brainerd, C. J., 84, 88, 90
Braun, B. G., 70, 107
Bremner, J. D., 57, 60, 74
Brende, J. O., 22, 162

Subject Index

Traffic accidents, 34–36
Trauma, 4. *See also* Defenses; Grief; Loss
    adaptation, 154–155, 159
    assertiveness, 145–146, 150
    attachment, 136–137, 140–141
    categorization of, 203
    competition, 182, 185–186. *See also*
        Defeat
    cooperation, 190
    description and definition, 68–70
    fight, 163–164, 168–169
    flight, 174, 177
    levels of destruction, 8
    long-term, 12
    love, 193–194
    parameters, 15
    rescue/caretaking, 131–132
    spiritual destruction, 87
    stress responses, 128
    survival strategies in, 120–121
    vulnerability and past, 67
Traumatic neurosis, 34
Traumatic situations
    competition, 183
    cooperation, 191
    escape, 175
    phases, 82
    variety of, 19, 45–46
Traumatic stress. *See also* Secondary
        traumatic stress
    appraisal, 54
    definition, 53
    depth axis, 48
    nonlinear concepts and, 109–110
    parameters axis, 47–48
    process axis, 47
    psychological defenses, 70
    social levels, 82, 89
    wholist view, 197–199
Traumatic syndrome, 23
Traumatology, ix–x. *See also* Symbols
    biopsychological approach to, 11–12,
        111
    defensive gaps and, 206
    descriptive experiential stream, 4–5
    dynamic stream, 106–107
    meaning and, 92–93
    morality and, 90
    trauma conceptualization, 4–5
    vs. religion, 3, 90
Triaxial framework, 15–17, 47–49
    illnesses and, 108–109

nonlinear concepts and, 109–110
    survival strategies in, 121, 201, 212
Trophotropic response, 58
Truth, 97–98. *See also* Fulfillment
Tyroxin, 58

Union, 134

Values, 93. *See also* Fulfillment
Vengeance, 162
Violence, 36, 161. *See also* Anger; Atrocities
    fight illnesses and, 165
    responses to, 37
    sympathetic nervous system and, 162
Vulnerability, 65–67
    definition, 67

War, 20–28. *See also* Combat; Defense; Fight
    civilian population traumatic sequelae
        from, 27
    sorcery and, 161
    traumatic sequelae for guerrillas children,
        26
    traumatic sequelae from Ancient Greek
        and Roman, 20
    traumatic sequelae from First World, 20–
        21
    traumatic sequelae from Israeli, 26
    traumatic sequelae from Second World,
        21–24
    traumatic sequelae from Vietnam, 24–25,
        169
Weeping, 152
Wholist view, ix–x, 1, 15. *See also* Triaxial
        framework
    clinical applications, 207–208, 213
    planning and education, 208
    traumatic stress, 197–199
Wisdom, 97–98, 194. *See also* Fulfillment
    flight and, 177
World, view of the, trauma and, 9, 37
Worthiness/unworthiness, 91–92. *See also*
        Fulfillment
    judgment of, 123

Xenophobia, 88
Xenophobic principle, 161

Yearning, 135